SWEET

DOUBLE LOVE
Collection

including
DOUBLE LOVE
SECRETS
PLAYING WITH FIRE

BANTAM BOOKS

TORONTO • NEW YORK • LONDON • SYDNEY • AUCKLAND

Visit the official Sweet Valley Web Site on the Internet at:
http://www.sweetvalley.com

SWEET VALLEY HIGH DOUBLE LOVE
COLLECTION
A BANTAM BOOK : 0 553 81280 7

Individual titles originally published in USA by Bantam Books
First published in Great Britain as individual titles in 1984
Collection first published in Great Britain

PRINTING HISTORY
Bantam Collection published 1999

including
DOUBLE LOVE
First published in Great Britain, 1984
Copyright © 1982 by Francine Pascal

SECRETS
First published in Great Britain, 1984
Copyright © 1983 by Francine Pascal

PLAYING WITH FIRE
First published in Great Britain, 1984
Copyright © 1983 by Francine Pascal

The trademarks "Sweet Valley" and "Sweet Valley High"
are owned by Francine Pascal and are used under license by
Bantam Books and Transworld Publishers Ltd.

Conceived by Francine Pascal

Produced by Daniel Weiss Associates, Inc,
33 West 17th Street, New York, NY 10011

All rights reserved.

Cover photo by Oliver Hunter
Cover photo of twins © 1994, 1995, 1996 Saban – All Rights Reserved.

Bantam Books are published by Transworld Publishers Ltd,
61–63 Uxbridge Road, Ealing, London W5 5SA,
in Australia by Transworld Publishers,
c/o Random House Australia Pty Ltd,
20 Alfred Street, Milsons Point, NSW 2061, Australia,
and in New Zealand by Transworld Publishers,
c/o Random House New Zealand,
18 Poland Road, Glenfield, Auckland, New Zealand.

Printed and bound in Great Britain by
Cox & Wyman Ltd, Reading, Berkshire.

SWEET VALLEY HIGH

DOUBLE LOVE

Written by
Kate William

Created by
FRANCINE PASCAL

BANTAM BOOKS
TORONTO • NEW YORK • LONDON • SYDNEY

DOUBLE
LOVE

Written by
Kate William

Created by
FRANCINE PASCAL

BANTAM BOOKS
TORONTO • NEW YORK • LONDON • SYDNEY • AUCKLAND

To Maria Guarnaschelli,
with thanks

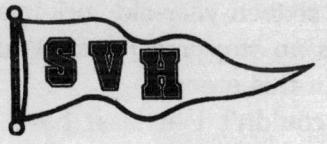

One

"Oh, Lizzie, do you believe how absolutely horrendous I look today!" Jessica Wakefield groaned as she stepped in front of her sister, Elizabeth, and stared at herself in the bedroom mirror. "I'm so gross! Just look at me. Everything is totally wrong. To begin with, I'm disgustingly fat. . . ." With that, she spun around to show off a stunning figure without an extra ounce visible anywhere.

She moaned again, this time holding out one perfectly shaped bronze leg. "Isn't that the grossest? I swear I must have the skinniest legs in America. And the bumpiest knees. What am I going to do? How can I possibly go to school looking like this today? Today of all days!"

Jessica, stared at herself in the full-length mirror and saw a picture of utter heartbreak and despair. But what was actually reflected in the glass was about the most adorable, most dazzling sixteen-year-old girl imaginable. Yet there was no stopping Jessica Wakefield when she was in this mood.

"Why couldn't I at least have had an oval face? It looks like someone stuck a pumpkin on top of my neck. And this hair—a dull yellow mess of split ends. I hate it!"

In a gesture of absolute hopelessness, she ran her hand under her silky blond hair, flipped it up, and watched as it drifted lightly back to her shoulders.

"Only thing duller are my eyes. Look at that color, Liz." She poked her face an inch from her sister's nose and fluttered long eyelashes over almond-shaped eyes the blue-green of the Caribbean. "They're so blah."

Without waiting for Elizabeth's response, Jessica reached again into her bag of sorrows. "I mean, there could be a telethon just for all the things that're wrong with me! I can't even look at myself another minute!" And with that she threw herself facedown on her sister's freshly made bed.

"Thanks a million," Elizabeth said in mock anger.

"I wasn't talking about you," came Jessica's pillow-muffled voice.

"Oh, no? All you said was that you're the

grossest-looking person in all of Sweet Valley. Your figure's terrible, your legs are chopsticks, your knees are bony, and on top of that, your face is all wrong. Right?"

"Right."

"And I just happen to be your identical twin sister. So what does that make me—Miss America?" Elizabeth asked, deciding to take a good look in the mirror. If Jessica were such a hopeless case, she might be in trouble, too. But the image she saw reflected in the mirror was hardly cause for alarm.

Both girls had the same shoulder-length, sun-streaked blond hair, the same sparkling blue-green eyes, the same perfect skin. Even the tiny dimple in Elizabeth's left cheek was duplicated in her younger sister's—younger by four minutes. Both girls were five feet six on the button and generously blessed with spectacular, all-American good looks. Both wore exactly the same size clothes, but they refused to dress alike, except for the exquisite identical lavalieres they wore on gold chains around their necks. The lavalieres had been presents from their parents on their sixteenth birthday.

The only way you could tell them apart was by the tiny beauty mark on Elizabeth's right shoulder. Their friends might notice that Elizabeth wore a watch and that Jessica did not. Time was never a problem for Jessica. She always felt that things didn't really start until she got there. And if she was late, let 'em wait. Otherwise, there was virtually no way to distinguish between the beautiful Wakefield twins. But beneath the skin, there was a world of difference. A wicked gleam of mischief lurked in the aquamarine depths of Jessica's eyes, while Elizabeth's reflected only sincerity.

When the phone in the hallway shrilled, Jessica leaped to answer it, assuming, of course, that it was for her.

"Jessica? Liz?" a boy's voice asked.

"Jessica, of course! And who's this?" she demanded.

"Oh, hi, Jessica. This is Todd. Todd Wilkins. Is Liz home?"

He wanted her sister! Jessica's eyes narrowed dangerously. One of the cutest boys at Sweet Valley High, and he was calling to talk to Elizabeth! Todd Wilkins was currently the basketball team's hottest star, and Jessica had been admiring him for some time now as she practiced her cheers in the gym alongside him. The idea that he would prefer Elizabeth to her infuriated Jessica, though she was extra careful to conceal this from him.

"Todd," she purred, "I should have known it was you just from your voice. I'm so glad you called. You know, I've been meaning to tell you—that was an absolutely fantastic drive shot

4

you made during practice today. I was really impressed."

"Uh, gee, Jessica—thanks." She could almost hear Todd blushing. "I didn't know you were watching."

"I *always* make it a point to watch the best players." *And the best-looking players*, she added silently. "You know, you could probably play professionally one of these days if you really wanted to, Todd." Jessica heaped on the flattery, hoping to distract him from the real purpose of his call.

But Todd hadn't forgotten. "That's really nice of you to say so, but it's probably too soon to tell." He paused. "Listen, Jessica, it's been nice talking to you, but is Liz around?"

Jessica frowned. "Uh, I think she's in the shower."

"I could wait," Todd said hopefully.

"Oh, you wouldn't want to do that. Liz stays in the shower practically *forever*."

"Maybe I should try calling back in a few minutes." His disappointment was evident.

"You could, but she probably won't be here. We've got to run, or we'll be late for school. This is the big day—they're announcing the Pi Beta pledges! Liz and I will just die if we don't get in!"

"I'm sure you won't have any trouble," said Todd. "But good luck anyway."

5

Jessica experienced a slight twinge of guilt about sidetracking Todd, but she quickly brushed it away, telling herself she really hadn't done any harm. It wasn't as if he were Elizabeth's boyfriend. She probably didn't even know he existed.

Jessica couldn't have been more mistaken. Just as she was hanging up, Elizabeth poked her head around the doorway. "Who was that?" she asked.

"Oh, just Todd Wilkins," Jessica replied, flashing her sister a brilliant smile to cover up the deception. "He called to wish me good luck with Pi Beta today. Wasn't that sweet of him?"

Elizabeth's heart sank, but she didn't let Jessica see her disappointment. She'd been hoping Todd would call her. The other day she'd caught him glancing at her in the cafeteria line. She'd turned around and there he was—tall, lean, his gorgeous brown eyes looking straight at her. She had quickly glanced down at her tray, a blush coloring her cheeks. Had Todd realized how much she liked him? He sat near her in Mr. Russo's science class, and though she'd never spoken to him, she'd always been aware of his compelling presence. In the cafeteria she had cast another glance over her shoulder. As their eyes met again, they both smiled. Elizabeth felt as if she'd been jolted by a thousand watts of electricity.

He was waiting for her after school that day. As she caught sight of him, leaning against the front railing, his sky-blue shirt open at the throat to reveal a glimpse of tanned, muscular chest, Elizabeth's pulse took off at a gallop. As he caught sight of her, a slow, shy smile spread across his features. He was nervous, too, she realized.

"Hey, Liz, I—I was wondering if you had today's chem assignment. I forgot to copy it down."

"Chemistry assignment?" Elizabeth couldn't tear her eyes off that blinding white smile. "Uh, sure, I think I have it somewhere. . . ."

Frantically, she began juggling books, searching for the assignment she'd scribbled hastily on a sheet of loose-leaf paper.

"Are you always this organized?" Todd teased, his coffee-colored eyes dancing.

"Only when it comes to chemistry." She laughed, thinking of the special chemistry between Todd and her and hoping he wouldn't notice how nervous he made her.

She walked away from Todd that day, feeling as if she were floating two feet off the pavement.

Now, discovering that Todd had preferred Jessica all along, Elizabeth felt as if she'd been grounded by a five-hundred-pound weight. Not wanting to reveal her true feelings about Todd, she quickly changed the subject.

7

"Speaking of Pi Beta," she said, "have you decided what you're going to wear today?"

At noon the Wakefield twins would find out if they had made Pi Beta Alpha, "the positively best sorority at Sweet Valley High," according to Jessica. That meant "the snobbiest" in Elizabeth's book.

"Wear?" squealed Jessica, her thoughts immediately switching from Todd back to the subject of her hideous appearance. "I have nothing, absolutely nothing to wear."

"This sounds like a job for my new tuxedo shirt," Elizabeth offered. She'd thought about wearing it herself, hoping to impress Todd when she saw him, but suddenly it didn't seem to matter.

"Nothing will help." Jessica moaned.

Elizabeth shrugged. "Well, it was just a thought." She began collecting the books she'd need for school.

"But it's a beginning," Jessica said quickly. "Could I wear the pants, too?"

"I think I've been had."

"And the little bow tie?"

"On one condition," Elizabeth said. "I want the whole outfit back, clean and hanging in my closet, by the weekend."

"On my honor."

Elizabeth groaned. "I'm doomed."

"Elizabeth Wakefield, you're the best!" Jes

sica headed for Elizabeth's closet. "At least now I won't have to look totally gross on the most important day of my life."

"Come on, Jess," Elizabeth argued. "Getting into Pi Beta isn't *that* big a deal. In fact, I'm beginning to wonder if I ever should have let you talk me into pledging."

"How can you say that?" Jessica shrieked. "You know how important a sorority is. Especially this one. All the top people are in it."

"You mean all the snootiest."

It was an echo of the argument they'd had two weeks earlier when Jessica had pleaded with her sister to pledge. Eventually Elizabeth had given in. Mostly because she and Jessica always did things together, and she didn't want anything as dumb as a sorority to come between them.

Jessica had assured Elizabeth that the pledge dares they'd be required to do would be nothing major. "Just a lot of silly fun!" she'd insisted.

Fun! Their first dare had been to order a pepperoni pizza from Guido's Pizza Palace, to be delivered during Mr. Russo's chemistry class.

"I'll die!" Elizabeth had protested. Just the thought of Mr. Russo's reaction petrified her. Bob Russo was the most brilliant—and most demanding—teacher at Sweet Valley. He was highly temperamental, with a biting sense of humor. You never knew when he would cut you down or stare you into a tiny, shrinking smudge for saying something stupid. Every kid at school was terrified of him. And now they were going to have a pizza . . .

"It'll be a scream," Jessica had said.

It had been a scream, all right. A delivery man wearing stereo headphones and a tomato-stained apron had walked right into the classroom carrying a humungous, steaming, smelly pepperoni pizza and stood there looking questioningly as Mr. Russo was writing a complicated formula on the blackboard.

"Yes?"

"Your pizza?" the delivery man had asked, and the class had gone into collective cardiac arrest. Somebody snorted, trying to stifle a laugh. Somebody else giggled. Elizabeth's face turned the color of the tomato stains on the delivery man's apron.

"Pardon me?" Mr. Russo asked innocently, still preoccupied with the lesson. That did it. The entire class cracked up and howled with laughter.

"One double pepperoni pizza for"—the delivery man examined his order form—"Elizabeth Wakefield."

Elizabeth's face was on fire. Everybody looked around at her in disbelief. Elizabeth Wakefield— the level-headed, serious twin—had flipped out!

Only Elizabeth knew who had really ordered the pizza—and given her name.

"Well, well," said Mr. Russo. "Elizabeth, is this by any chance a science project?" More laughter from the kids.

Elizabeth panicked. *What will I say?* Shooting a glance at Jessica, she knew instantly she was on her own. Her twin wore the angelic expression of a totally innocent bystander.

"Uh—yes, sir," Elizabeth stammered, groping for a way out. "Uh—see—we wondered how much heat the pizza would lose getting from the pizza parlor to here—and uh . . ."

Even Mr. Russo had to smile. He rummaged through a desk drawer and produced a thermometer. "I see," he said. "Well, then, let's take the pizza's temperature, before it undergoes a chemical change—commonly called digestion."

So they had gotten away with that pledge dare. They'd survived the other crazy pranks, too. Second on the list was delivering the singing telegram to Chrome Dome—Mr. Cooper, Sweet Valley High's somewhat stuffy principal. Finally, they'd grossed out the entire cafeteria by dyeing the mashed potatoes purple.

And now the big day had arrived. At noon they would find out if they were in Pi Beta. Elizabeth wasn't too excited about it, but Jessica had the date circled in red on her calendar. Nothing could spoil this day for her—except of course, not getting into the sorority, which wasn't a likely possibility.

For Elizabeth, the day was already spoiled. As she thought of Todd's phone call to Jessica, the tight feeling in her chest spread to a pressure behind her eyes. But she was determined not to let Jessica know how she felt about Todd. What was the point? It was obvious which sister Todd preferred. And why not? What girl could possibly compete with the dazzling Jessica Wakefield?

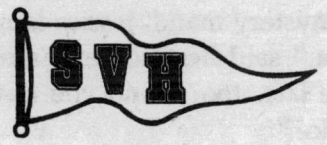

Two

Jessica was already at the breakfast table when Elizabeth sat down.

"Your father's going to be working late again tonight," Alice Wakefield told her daughters as she served french toast.

"What's up, Dad? A merger? A war between two giant conglomerates?" asked Jessica, bringing a smile to her father's face. Ned Wakefield was always a pushover for his lively daughters.

"Both—and then some," he said. "Big doings. There may be serious consequences for the Sweet Valley High football team. The playing field is becoming a battlefield."

"Really? What's going on?" Elizabeth asked.

"As a lawyer on the case, I can't tell you. It's too soon and too complicated," her father said. "Marianna and I are working on it. I will be late

13

again, though. Isn't that enough bad news for you?"

"OK, mystery man." Jessica laughed.

"Jessica," said her mother, "aren't you coming home late, too? Don't you have cheerleading practice?"

"Right, I won't be home till at least seven."

"And, Liz, isn't this a late afternoon for you at *The Oracle*?"

"Uh-huh. Looks like the whole Wakefield clan will be out doing things," Elizabeth said.

"Therefore . . ." said Alice Wakefield.

Elizabeth and Jessica knew what was coming.

"Therefore—you can drive the Fiat today," she said.

The twins squealed with delight. Only on rare occasions were they allowed to drive to school in the family's second car, a little red Spider convertible.

"Oh, wow," Jessica said, jumping up. "Am I going to be hot today! In my tuxedo shirt, driving my Fiat! Look out, Sweet Valley!"

"Jessica," her mother interrupted, "I'm sorry, honey, but Liz will have to drive."

"What?" Jessica's anguished wail filled the entire kitchen of the Wakefield's split-level home.

"Jessica, you know very well that you can't drive for three weeks. And you can stop looking at me that way. *You're* the one who had the acciden^

"That's not fair!" Jessica whined. "I'm not going to school to be humiliated like a kindergarten child! Oh, forget it, Mom, just forget it. I know Liz is your favorite, and I'm just an afterthought!"

"Come on, Jess, let's get going," Elizabeth said patiently. "You know you're not going to miss today for the world. What's Pi Beta Alpha going to do without *you*? Let's just go, or we'll be late for school."

"Accident!" Jessica muttered after they had climbed into the car and were driving through Sweet Valley, the little green jewel of a California town where they lived.

"It was just a tiny dent in the fender. She makes it sound like a six-car pileup on the L.A. freeway!"

"That *tiny dent* cost two hundred dollars to fix," Elizabeth said dryly, wishing her sister would stop complaining and let her enjoy the drive through the valley. As she did very often, Elizabeth thought how lucky she and Jessica were to live in Sweet Valley. Everything about it was terrific—the gently rolling hills, the quaint downtown area, and the fantastic white sand beach only fifteen minutes away. She and Jessica were even luckier now, with a new inground pool in the backyard.

15

"Don't you wish we lived up here on the hill like the Patmans and the Fowlers?"

"You can't be serious, Jess," Elizabeth admonished. But she knew perfectly well that her twin was totally serious about wanting to live on the hill where Sweet Valley's very rich lived in sprawling, imposing mansions. "Dad does all right," Elizabeth went on. "He certainly works hard enough. He's out late practically every night these days."

"Lizzie, I've been wondering about that. Does that seem funny?"

"What?"

"Dad out every night. And one night I called his office, and that new woman lawyer answered."

"You mean Ms. West?"

"Yes. But you heard what Dad called her this morning—*Marianna!*"

"Well, that's her name, silly," said Elizabeth, trying to sound more unconcerned than she really was. She had wondered about her father and Marianna, too.

"Well, I don't know, Liz. She sounded pretty seductive on the phone."

"Jessica, really! Sometimes I think you're wacko!"

"OK, OK, don't get so shook, Liz." Jessica glanced out at the spacious homes and heaved a great sigh. "Anyway, I'm not saying I don't

16

like our house, Liz. But having a lot of money, like Bruce Patman and Lila Fowler, can't be all bad."

"And what about what goes with it?" asked Elizabeth.

"You mean all those cars and servants?"

"C'mon, Jess, you know what I'm talking about. This crazy feud—the Patmans want every rock in Sweet Valley to stay exactly where it's been for fifty years, and the Fowlers want to build over everything in sight. Who needs that?"

Jessica changed the subject with her usual abruptness as the school came into view. "Oh, Liz, please stop and let me drive into the parking lot," she pleaded.

"Jess, you heard what Mom said."

Jessica sank into her seat. "You heard what Mom said," she mimicked nastily. "Sometimes I wonder how anybody so wimpy can be my sister."

Elizabeth slid the Fiat into an empty space in the student parking lot. "Come on, Jess, what difference does it make?"

"None, of course, Aunt Fanny!"

Elizabeth sighed. She knew that tone all too well. It meant a storm was brewing, one that could turn into Hurricane Jessica.

"I'm sure you'll be allowed to drive again soon," she said encouragingly.

But Jessica wasn't listening to a word. She

was out of the car in a flash, slamming the door so hard that Elizabeth winced. How did it always turn out this way? She just did what her mother said, and somehow she was always wrong. Even worse, she felt guilty.

"Jess, please!" Elizabeth said, scrambling out of the car and facing her stormy-eyed twin. Jessica just stood there smoldering, refusing to relent.

"Look, I'll talk to Mom for you," Elizabeth said. "I'll ask her to let you drive tomorrow."

"Tomorrow!" Jessica sneered. "You may be a tomorrow person. *I* am a today person. Don't do me any favors."

Jessica wasn't going to let up. She kept turning away, refusing to look at Elizabeth. Jessica could hold a grudge the way the Patmans held on to their money—forever!

Just as Elizabeth was deciding this was a lost cause, she saw Enid Rollins, her best friend, coming across the lawn, waving to her. Something was cooking with Enid. She had sounded excited when she called Elizabeth the night before and said she had something "vital" to tell her. Elizabeth was dying to find out, but Jessica was still pouting.

"Jess, I have to talk to Enid."

"How can you be best friends with somebody as blah as Eeny Rollins? I don't want you to go over there. Somebody might think it was *me* talking to her."

"Enid is a wonderful person. Why don't you like her?"

"Eeny is a nerd. And there's something weird about her."

Just then Jessica glanced over her shoulder. Apparently something she saw swept away her anger in a flash. She threw her arms around Elizabeth and gave her a swift, powerful hug, almost lifting her off the ground.

"I've decided to forgive you," she announced, beaming. "Go on, talk to Enid. I'll see you at noon."

Surprised, but not unaccustomed to Jessica's swift changes of mood, Elizabeth hugged her back and ran to catch up with Enid.

"So what's the big news?" Elizabeth asked as she fell in step with her friend.

"Shhhhhhhhh! Not so loud, Liz," Enid Rollins said, looking around and blushing, as though the entire student body were eavesdropping.

Elizabeth smiled. "Don't be silly. There's nobody near us."

When Enid didn't smile back, Elizabeth knew her friend had something serious to discuss. Elizabeth and Enid had become best friends when they had taken a creative writing class together the year before. Enid was a terrific person, Elizabeth thought, and absolutely *not* a nerd, no matter what Jessica said. With her shoulder-length brown hair and large green eyes, she was really pretty. And in her quiet way, she was very smart—and very funny. Jessica figured anyone who was quiet was dull, but Enid Rollins was anything but dull. There was something almost mysterious about her, as though she knew things that other people didn't, or had a secret she wanted to keep.

They were nearing the school door when Elizabeth saw handsome, spoiled Bruce Patman sliding his black Porsche into a parking spot. Enid tugged on her friend's arm.

"Let's sit a second," she said.

Elizabeth quickly sat down beside her on the grass, eager for the news. "Well?"

Enid blushed even redder than before. Then she smiled so radiantly that for a moment she became a brand-new person.

"Who is he?" Elizabeth asked.

"What?" Enid looked shocked.

"You heard me. Who is he?"

Enid shook her head in amazement. "How can you see into people like that, Liz? You could be a detective—or even a mystery writer."

Now it was Elizabeth's turn to blush. Enid knew her secret dream—to be a writer. Not just a reporter, the way she was on *The Oracle*, but a serious writer. Someday she wanted to write poems or plays or even novels. She was sharpening her skills, too, right now at the school newspaper. Elizabeth wrote the "Eyes and Ears" column for *The Oracle*, but no one knew who the writer of the column was—and Elizabeth couldn't even tell her best friend about it. Many times she ached to tell Enid or Jessica or *somebody*—but she didn't. Only Mr. Collins, the faculty adviser for the paper, knew.

It was a tradition at Sweet Valley that if the identity of the writer of the "Eyes and Ears" column was discovered before the end of the term, the students threw that person fully clothed into the swimming pool. Elizabeth Wakefield had no intention of being unmasked.

Now Elizabeth searched Enid's flushed face, wondering if Enid had figured out her big secret. But, no—Enid's mind was occupied with something entirely different.

"Guess who called me?" she finally blurted out.

"Who? Tell me!"

"Ronnie Edwards, the new guy in Miss Markey's class. I noticed him looking at me in the cafeteria the other day," Enid said dreamily.

"But he's so quiet. He never says a word!"

"You have to get to know him," Enid explained. "Some people need more time to open up, you know."

"Oh, yes, I know." Enid could have been describing herself, Elizabeth thought. It had taken

21

a long time to really get to know Enid, but it was worth it.

"So—what did he call about?"

"He asked me to the Phi Epsilon dance!"

"Oh, Enid, that's wonderful!"

"Isn't it great! I'm so happy!" Enid said. Then she asked quietly, "Who are you going with?"

"Well, I don't know."

"Don't worry. He'll ask you," Enid said.

"Who will?"

"You know."

That's why Enid Rollins was such a good friend. She knew exactly how to say something without really saying it. Enid was aware of Elizabeth's crush on Todd, but she was too nice to mention him by name when things were not settled yet.

Elizabeth was getting ready to dig for more news about Ronnie and Enid when Enid's eyes went wild and she pulled Elizabeth back.

"Look out! That maniac!" Enid screamed as she and Elizabeth tumbled over on the grass.

Elizabeth looked up in confusion, trying to figure out what was happening. She saw a red blur zip past them up the long school driveway. Then a little red car screeched to a rather spectacular stop next to Bruce Patman's black Porsche.

Jessica!

Elizabeth gave a quick look at the parking

spot where she had left the Fiat. She didn't see it. Then she shoved her hand into her pocket to feel the car keys. They were gone! And then she remembered Jessica's sudden hug—that was when she had filched the keys.

"I'll see you at noon, Enid," Elizabeth said angrily. "I've got to talk to my darling little sister!"

"OK. But don't tell anybody about—"

"Don't worry."

Elizabeth marched toward the black Porsche and the red Fiat. There sat tall, handsome, dark-haired Bruce Patman, lounging arrogantly behind the wheel of his flashy sports car. And there stood Jessica, acting as if absolutely nothing had happened.

This time I'm really going to let her have it, Elizabeth fumed to herself as she ran toward her sister. She was so angry that she didn't even notice somebody running alongside her.

"Hey, what's the hurry?" It was Todd Wilkins, and he was smiling. "I was hoping to talk to you."

Elizabeth was in total shock. There he was— Todd Wilkins—the man of her dreams, standing two inches away from her.

"Oh—uh, well," she stammered. "What about?" She could have kicked herself. Why did she turn into a complete idiot the minute Todd was near her?

23

"Said like an ace reporter." Todd laughed. "Right to the point. Lois Lane had better watch out for you."

They were both laughing now. Then Todd said, "I was wondering if—"

Just then the bell rang, and students started swarming toward the building.

Todd frowned. "We'll be late," he muttered. "Listen, will you be around after basketball practice?"

"Sure," Elizabeth said, her heart beating faster. "I have to stay late at *The Oracle*. How about under the clock—around five-fifteen?"

"I'll be there."

Elizabeth watched starry-eyed as Todd loped gracefully across the lawn. Suddenly she remembered Jessica! She whirled around and spotted the black Porsche and the red Fiat. Jessica was gone.

Between classes, the halls of Sweet Valley High resembled the battle scene from *Star Wars*, with bodies hurtling in all directions accompanied by collisions and dropped books. It was while Elizabeth was picking up hers that Jessica raced by, wearing a smile brighter than California sunshine in July.

"I have the most sensational news, Liz!"

Down on her hands and knees, Elizabeth

24

looked up. Why, she wondered, didn't Jessica ever get caught in such ungraceful situations? Because she was Jessica. If a book of hers ever fell, there was always a handy male eager to pick it up.

"What news, Jess?"

"You won't believe it."

"Is it about the dance?"

"You'll see." And she darted off, pausing to look back. "Lizzie, dear, do get up off the floor. I would positively die if anyone thought it was me grubbing around like that."

Bite your tongue, Elizabeth warned herself. *Don't say what you're thinking. Murder's still illegal in California!*

She gathered her books and stood up. It wasn't until she was halfway down the hall that she realized she'd been so angry at Jessica's remark that she had forgotten to ask for the car keys!

At noon, just as the president of Pi Beta Alpha was about to announce the list of new sorority members, Jessica leaned over to Elizabeth and whispered, "I think Todd's going to ask me to the Phi Epsilon dance."

Elizabeth felt as if a balloon had just burst inside her. Tears welled up in her eyes.

"Elizabeth Wakefield, congratulations!" the

president shouted. "Elizabeth, where are you? Come up here and join your sisters."

Heads turned to look at her. Everyone thought she was crying with happiness. Somehow she made herself stand up, but she couldn't make herself look at Jessica. She would never tell Jessica now how she felt about Todd. And she would never, *ever* stand in Jessica's way—but she couldn't look at her sister just then.

Jessica was tugging on her sleeve, trying to stop her as she was about to make her way to the front of the room.

"What about me?" Jessica hissed. "Why haven't they called *my* name?"

The president called out, "Cara Walker, congratulations!" Jessica applauded reluctantly for her friend.

Elizabeth stood beside Jessica's seat. She wouldn't go up there and accept membership until Jessica's name was called. After all, the only reason she had decided to pledge Pi Beta was so she and Jessica would be together.

Lila Fowler, another friend of Jessica's, was called. Even Enid Rollins got in, and she'd pledged Pi Beta mainly to keep Elizabeth company. Elizabeth applauded loudly for her best friend. But still Jessica's name was not called. Could it be that her sister might have been blackballed? Jessica, co-captain of the cheerleaders, beautiful, popular Jessica?

With a pleased smile, the president announced, "Last but absolutely not least— Jessica Wakefield, congratulations!"

Elizabeth and Jessica ran up to the front of the room. Even though her tears had dried, Elizabeth felt as if she were still sobbing on the inside.

Jessica was ecstatic. "There's so much I want to learn about Pi Beta Alpha," she was gushing to one of the senior girls. "For instance, just how many votes do you need to become president?"

For Elizabeth, the rest of the day was spent playing catch-up, but she never quite did. She was late getting to the newspaper office, late getting the column finished, and late going over it with Mr. Collins. Didn't it always happen that way when you had someplace special to go? she wondered. Todd was probably waiting for her under the clock right now. What did he want to talk about?

Please don't be angry with me for being late, she prayed silently. If only Todd wanted to ask her to the dance, it would be all right. She would forgive Jessica for everything—even for swiping the car keys.

Elizabeth ran down the last flight of stairs, tore through the lobby, and rushed toward the big Romanesque clock that was the pride of Sweet Valley High.

At first she didn't see Todd. But then, as she came outside, there he was—walking across the lawn to their little red Spider and climbing in beside Jessica!

Elizabeth's heart sank. She stood there, numb with shock, as the convertible backed up and spun merrily down the drive, carrying Jessica and Todd.

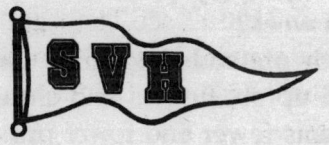

Three

"Hey, is anybody home?" The call brought Elizabeth to the top of the stairs.

"Steven!"

"You must be that ugly Wakefield twin I hear so much about. What's the matter? No hello for your older and infinitely wiser brother?"

Elizabeth hurtled down the stairs and into her brother's outstretched arms.

"Your repulsive face couldn't have shown up at a better time," she said with her first real laugh all day.

Disentangling himself from his sister's hug, Steven gave her a questioning look. "Yeah? What's up?"

"Oh, nothing," she lied hastily. "I just have these spells when I get totally weird—and actually start missing *you*."

29

"Sure you do. I'm repulsive but lovable. So tell me, how many princes did you turn into toads this week?"

Elizabeth pretended to think for a moment, then held up six fingers and shrugged. "Slow week. Seems fewer and fewer princes are passing through Sweet Valley these days. But I bet you have no trouble stopping clocks at State U. with that face of yours."

"You know it. When I get through with that place, no one will know what time it is."

Sister and brother stood smiling at each other, enjoying the special bond they shared. Elizabeth's blond beauty came from their mother, while Steven's dark good looks made him a younger version of Ned Wakefield. Slightly over six feet tall with beautiful brown eyes and a slim, athletic build, Steven had long been a target of crushes from Elizabeth and Jessica's girlfriends.

The two had started their "ugly" routine ages ago after spending a totally boring afternoon listening to a distant relative drone on and on about "how too, too adorable you children are. Just too, too!" They had invited Jessica to join in their game, but she was never bored when people discussed her beauty.

"Tell you what, little sister," Steven said now. "I'm starving. If you *insist* on fixing me something, I promise not to complain about your cooking."

"Insist! How do you know I don't have ten more important things to do?"

She couldn't resist the mock hangdog look on her brother's face. "OK, I insist, I insist! Let's go check the fridge for possibilities."

While Steven made himself comfortable at the round kitchen table, Elizabeth checked out the contents of the large, copper-colored refrigerator.

"How are things on the home front these days?" he asked.

"Oh, great, just great," Elizabeth mumbled, her back to him.

"What?"

Carrying cold cuts, mustard, pickles, and a carton of milk, she came over to the table. "Things are OK. The usual, I guess. School, homework. Stuff—you know."

Should she tell Steven about Todd? she asked herself. Or about Jessica? Or about Jessica *and* Todd, hating to link those two names even in her mind. No, she decided. It wouldn't be fair to put Steven in the middle.

"Stuff? You might not be much to look at, but I always thought you knew how to talk," Steven teased.

"One more crack out of you, Steven Wakefield, and I'll fix you a knuckle sandwich!"

"Peace!" he said, throwing up his arms in surrender. He grew serious as he watched Elizabeth fix him a huge sandwich.

"You know, Lizzie, big brothers are great listeners."

She smiled at his concern.

"Steve, things are fine. Just fine!" *Or they will be when I'm dead and can't think of Todd anymore,* she added to herself. "And now if you're through grilling me, big brother, how about telling me why you're home for the fourth weekend in a row. I thought sophisticated college men spent their weekends dating sophisticated college women."

"Well, you know, I, uh, like to see the family once in a while." Elizabeth could have sworn he was blushing.

"Sure you do, Steve. And we're really grateful for the fifteen minutes you spend with us every weekend. What I'm absolutely dying to know is where you spend the rest of the time."

"I see old friends. That kind of thing." Then he laughed. "You're getting to be a nosy brat, you know that?"

"OK," she relented. "I'll let you off the hook for now, but I'm not through with you yet. I sense a mystery here, and you know how I love a mystery."

"Nosy *and* weird—what a combination," he said, biting into his sandwich. "Tell me what's new with Jessica and the folks."

"Jess is fine." *Boy, is she ever,* Elizabeth thought. "And the folks are, too, I guess."

32

"You guess?" he asked between bites.

"They're so busy I hardly see them. Mom's always rushing off to meet a client. Her design business is really booming. And Dad—well, he's always out. He's working on a case with a new lawyer in the firm, somebody by the name of Marianna West. She used to be married to that big heart specialist, Gareth West."

"Dad and a divorcée? Hmmm." Steven lifted one eyebrow.

"For heaven's sake, Steve, you're as bad as Jessica. She said, and I quote, 'If I were married, I wouldn't let my husband spend so much time with a good-looking divorcée!' "

Steven nearly choked on his sandwich at Elizabeth's perfect imitation of their sister's voice.

"If I know Jess, she wouldn't let a husband of hers get any farther from her than the length of a two-foot leash," he said.

Just then the back door flew open, and Jessica whirled in, smiling as only she could when her day had been a perfect dream.

"Steve!" she squealed, dropping her books on the counter and rushing to hug her brother. "I didn't know you were coming this weekend!" She stepped back to get a better look at him.

"You're absolutely too gorgeous! Aren't we lucky, Lizzie?" she asked, turning to flash dazzling white teeth at her unsmiling sister. "We probably have the town's—maybe even the state's—handsomest brother!''

"What, that repulsive thing?" Elizabeth teased.

"What, this repulsive thing?" Steven added.

"Why in the world are you two still playing that ridiculous game? You wouldn't think it was funny if you really were gross-looking," Jessica said, shuddering at the thought of having anything other than an attractive family.

Elizabeth busied herself with cleaning up the table, tuning out Jessica and Steven for the moment. She wanted to ask Jessica where she and Todd had driven off to, but she just couldn't. *Maybe I'm afraid of the answer*, she thought. She felt tears starting to fill her eyes, but she willed herself not to cry. After all, she told herself, if Todd preferred Jessica—and that certainly was how it looked—she would not stand in the way. She'd do the decent thing. Die. Her unhappy thoughts were interrupted by Jessica's outraged cry.

"You didn't tell Steve about PBA? I simply don't understand how you could forget to tell him something so vital!"

"What about PBA?" Steven asked.

"We made it, Steve! We made it! Just today at lunch, Lizzie and I were accepted as full-fledged members of *the* most terrific sorority on campus!"

"No big deal," Elizabeth said.

"No big deal? Elizabeth, how can you say that?

How can you even think it? You've got to be seven hundred and thirty-seven kinds of idiots not to be excited about associating with the best girls at Sweet Valley High. What's wrong with you?"

"It's hard to get excited when your feet hurt," Elizabeth muttered.

"Your feet hurt? What in the world do your feet have to do with Pi Beta Alpha?" Jessica demanded.

"My feet always hurt when I have to walk all the way home from school," Elizabeth answered in an ominously quiet voice.

Sensing a crisis, Steven stood and said, "Hey, you two lovelies, I hate to eat and run, but I've got to go up and shower."

The twins ignored him. Their eyes were locked on one another.

"Look, I'll see you later," Steven said. "Take it easy on the guys this weekend. Broken hearts are not a lot of fun." He sighed, and there was a funny smile on his face.

Jessica turned suddenly toward Steven, grateful for an excuse to break away from Elizabeth's angry gaze. "Steve, I have the most terrific idea! If you're not busy this weekend, maybe you'd like me to arrange a date for you with Cara Walker," she said hopefully.

"Cara Walker?"

"You remember Cara, Steve—long dark hair,

35

terrific figure, fantastic tennis player. She's one of my best friends. She always thought you were soooo good-looking."

"Yeah, yeah, I remember. She's a cute kid, but a little young for me."

"Cara has become very mature, Steve. She's really ready to date a college man."

"Thanks, Jess, but no thanks. I have plans," he said, trying to edge out of the room.

"Plans? What kind of plans? Who is she?" Jessica shrieked.

" 'Who is she?' " Steven shrieked, mimicking Jessica.

"Well, you're coming home every weekend to see somebody," Jessica insisted. "Who is she? Somebody from college who lives in town?"

"Two nosy sisters are more than I need," Steven said, and there was an edge of anger in his voice. "See ya." He left the room quickly. They heard him go up the stairs and slam a door.

Jessica turned back to Elizabeth, who was brushing nonexistent crumbs from the butcher-block table.

"What's with him? Do you know who he's seeing?"

Elizabeth remained silent. She didn't trust herself to talk to her sister at this point.

Jessica fairly exploded. "*What* is going on? Steve won't talk. You won't talk. The air in here

36

is so cold I can practically see my breath! I might as well be in Siberia!"

Wouldn't that be wonderful? Elizabeth thought.

"Lizzie, talk to me, please," Jessica coaxed. "You're mad at me, but I don't know why. Please, Lizzie." Her eyes sparkled with unshed tears.

Elizabeth turned to face Jessica, determined to have it out with her. But she weakened when she looked into her sister's face. Maybe nothing had happened with Jessica and Todd. Maybe it was all innocent, she thought. *And maybe I'm a world-class marshmallow!*

"Jess, I didn't really appreciate having to walk home today."

Quick as lightning, Jessica wailed, "You didn't! I saw you get into a car with a bunch of the kids and zoom off without me! You should have told me you were going to do that. What would have happened if Mom saw me driving the car? Do you want to get me into trouble? I think it was sneaky and rotten of you to leave me like that when it was your responsibility to bring me home in the car!"

"Jess, I didn't leave without you—I got held up in *The Oracle* and didn't get out until late."

"Oh. In that case, I forgive you. And I'm sorry I suspected you of trying to get me into trouble. I must have been mistaken about you getting into that other car. Now, let's talk about

Steve. He's up to something, and I think you know what it is."

"Whoa, Jess. Let's back up a bit. Jess? Jess!"

Jessica, her head in the refrigerator, didn't answer. Finally she turned, holding a plastic bag full of green grapes. "I was sure we had grapes! Now, about Steve."

"No, Jess," said a determined Elizabeth. "Let's talk about what happened after school. *I* saw *you* drive off in our car with Todd Wilkins." *Please let there be a reasonable explanation*, she prayed.

"Oh, that! I was just helping Todd." Jessica sat at the table popping grapes into her mouth while Elizabeth's world crumbled around her.

"Helping him?" Helping herself *to* him was more like it.

"He had to pick up some decorations for the dance, so I offered him a ride into town. He's so sweet, Liz."

I know, I know. Elizabeth moaned inwardly. "Jess, did he say anything about meeting someone—or waiting for someone after school?"

Jessica rested her chin on one hand and thought for a moment. Putting her other hand behind her back, she crossed her fingers and finally answered, "I don't think so."

When it comes to being unforgettable, I have to be a minus ten, Elizabeth thought with disgust.

"Now can we talk about Steve?" Jessica said impatiently.

"What about him?"

"I don't believe you, Liz, I really don't. Our only brother is involved in a flaming love affair, and you don't care at all!"

"Steve? Flaming love affair?" Elizabeth shook her head in amazement. Was her sister trying to get off the subject of Todd, or did she know what she was talking about?

"It's totally obvious to anyone with half a brain that, *one*, Steve is involved with someone; *two*, that he hasn't said who it is; and *three*, that it must be someone we wouldn't like. And I'm going to find out what's going on!"

"Look, Sherlock," Elizabeth snapped, "has it ever occurred to you that, *one*, it's Steve's business; *two*, it's not our business; and *three*, you'd better butt out before Steve takes you apart?"

"You can do whatever you want, Elizabeth Wakefield, but it's just not in my nature to be cold and selfish when it comes to the happiness of a member of my family!" With an expression on her face that would make an angel envious, Jessica picked up her books and sailed out of the room.

In a rare display of temper, Elizabeth threw a sponge across the room, narrowly missing her mother, who stepped through the back door at that moment.

"Elizabeth, what in the world is going on here?"

"Oh! Mom. Nothing's going on. I was cleaning the table and the sponge just—just slipped out of my hand."

Alice Wakefield lowered the two grocery bags she was carrying onto the counter and gave her daughter a knowing look. "Something's wrong, honey, isn't it? Do you want to talk about it?" She walked over to Elizabeth and put her arm around her daughter's shoulder.

Elizabeth suddenly wished she were five years old again. Then she could cry and pour out all her troubles to her mother, who would make everything right. But that was then, and this was now.

Elizabeth shrugged off her mother's arm and walked over to pick up the sponge. "Mom, nothing is wrong!"

"Don't tell me nothing's wrong, Elizabeth. You're not acting like yourself at all. Now, talk to me, please. I have to meet a client, and I don't want to be late."

Count to ten, Elizabeth told herself. *Don't take your anger out on Mom.*

"Elizabeth, I'm waiting!"

And then she couldn't hold back her tears any longer. "Acting like myself—what's that,

Mom? Liz Wakefield is supposed to be good, sweet, kind, generous. . . ." The tears were streaming down her face. "Do you know what that adds up to, Mom? Boring, boring, boring! Sometimes I get hurt—sometimes I get angry. . . ."

"Honey, it's all right, I understand."

"Hey, is everybody in this family totally wacko?"

"Steve! I didn't know you were home."

"Hi, Mom. Bye, Mom." He dropped a kiss somewhere in the vicinity of his mother's forehead on his way to the door.

"Steve, I haven't had a chance to talk to you. Where are you going?"

"Out, Mom."

"Out? Out where? With whom?"

"Jeez! Is privacy a dirty word around here? The district attorney upstairs drove me up the wall with those kinds of questions. Fortunately, I was saved by the bell. The telephone bell. Sweet Jess is on the phone gushing all over some poor jerk named Todd. *Ciao*, you two!" Steven was out the door before Elizabeth or her mother could say another word.

Todd was on the phone with Jessica!

Elizabeth couldn't stand it one more minute. With tears streaming down her face, she threw the sponge in the sink and charged up to her room, leaving her mother openmouthed with surprise.

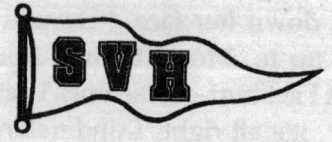

Four

Elizabeth's problems buzzed in her head like bees. Sitting in the *Oracle* office, she didn't know what to do first. She hadn't written a word for her "Eyes and Ears" column yet, and she still hadn't thought of a topic for her history paper. And then there was Steven—something was going on with him that wasn't quite right. It made her uneasy. And she couldn't get over an even more alarming suspicion about her father and Ms. West. She had seen Marianna recently, driving by with her father. She was a very beautiful woman. And she and her father had been so wrapped up in each other they hadn't even noticed Elizabeth. Even though she wanted to ignore it, Elizabeth smelled smoke. Did that mean there was fire?

She sighed. She didn't seem to have any answers lately. She looked down at her writing pad, which was absolutely blank except for the name Todd Wilkins scribbled across the top in large, dark letters. She knew it was hopeless to try to work when all she really wanted to do was lose herself in her special daydream. It was always the same funny little dream, but it made her feel so warm and good: They were sitting together, she and Todd, in the lunchroom at noon. It was jammed, and she was chattering on with Enid or some other friend when she became aware of Todd's hand affectionately caressing her hair. She turned to smile at him, and he pulled her close and kissed her gently on the forehead. That was it. Nothing more, but it was done right out there where everybody could see, as if it were the most natural thing in the world, Todd loving her. . . .

The daydream was like a favorite film Elizabeth played over and over again and never got tired of watching. That's what she was doing when Cara Walker burst noisily into the *Oracle* office, shattering the dream and bringing her back to her terrible reality.

"Liz," Cara gushed breathlessly, "I've got a great idea for an item."

"Good, Cara, what is it?"

"Well—do you know who writes the 'Eyes and Ears' column?"

"That's a secret, Cara. Nobody knows that except Mr. Collins."

"OK. Well, would you pass it on to him? The hottest new couple in the whole school is your very own sister Jessica—"

"Jessica?" Elizabeth asked, surprised.

"Yes! Now, I'm not a columnist," Cara gushed, "but the item could say something like—'The hottest new couple at Sweet Valley High is the co-captain of the cheerleaders and the captain of the basketball team!' "

"What?"

"See—they're both captains." Cara giggled. "That's why it's so neat!"

"Who told you about them?" Elizabeth asked, her heart thumping.

"It's all over school, Liz! Everybody's talking about it. They were driving around the other day in your mom's red convertible!"

"Oh."

"They were even seen up at Miller's Point," Cara continued. "And you know what goes on up there. Isn't it too much?" She sighed.

Elizabeth didn't even remember Cara running out. She felt totally destroyed. Todd and Jessica! Why did it have to be Jessica?

"Well, why not?" she heard herself saying aloud.

It was perfectly natural that Todd would like a terrific girl like her sister. Why shouldn't he?

Jessica was about the prettiest, most popular girl at Sweet Valley High.

And then a new, sinking realization shot through her heart like an arrow. Todd must have thought he was smiling at Jessica in the cafeteria the other day! She had built a fantasy, out of her own desires, about his feelings.

Well, at least that was clear now. Todd was interested in Jessica. Jessica knew it. And, as Cara had just said, the whole school knew it. Now at least she was sure what to write for the "Eyes and Ears" column. Elizabeth began typing it out, hardly noticing the tears that fell onto her typewriter keys.

No, she told herself sternly. *I won't be like this. I won't think about him anymore. Todd likes Jessica, and Jessica likes Todd, and that's that.*

She looked at what she had written:

"A certain tall, good-looking basketball player will be scoring high points off the court when he escorts a certain blond beauty who is co-captain of the cheerleading squad to the upcoming Phi Epsilon–Pi Beta Alpha dance."

Yes, Elizabeth told herself, *they're perfect for each other. I wish them the very best. I really do*, she insisted as she folded her head in her arms and sobbed.

"Elizabeth! What is it?"

She hadn't heard Mr. Collins walk in, yet

45

there he was, looking at her with concern, while tears slid down her face.

As usual, he knew what to do. Without another word he held out a crisp white handkerchief.

Elizabeth dabbed at her face, pulling herself together. She smiled weakly at the *Oracle's* good-looking adviser, and thanked him for his handkerchief. "If you don't need it back right away, I'll launder it for you tonight," she offered.

Mr. Collins smiled. "I think I can manage without it," he answered. Then he asked gently, "Need to talk?"

She did need to talk to someone, and there weren't many people she trusted and respected more than Mr. Collins. She told him about her feelings for Todd and how he seemed to be interested in Jessica. "I'm so down."

"I know how you must feel." Roger Collins sighed sympathetically, pushing back a stray lock of his strawberry-blond hair. "But I've always found hard work to be the best painkiller. Come on, let us see your column. It'll take your mind off other things."

Elizabeth handed him her "Eyes and Ears" column.

"OK, here's this week's scoop," she said. But before Mr. Collins had a chance to look at it, John Pfeifer, the sports editor of *The Oracle*, came in all worked up.

"Hey, Mr. Collins," he said, "I'm the biggest idiot in the world. I've got the sports pages all laid out, and I can't find the picture of Todd Wilkins."

At the mention of his name, Elizabeth grabbed her things and dashed from the office. She didn't run far enough, though, because all of a sudden there he was in the flesh in the corridor. And with Jessica!

"No, really, Todd," Jessica was saying, "don't laugh. It's not funny. Really. I really am one of the most unpopular girls in school. Everyone else has a date for the dance. Really, everyone. Every single girl I know. Everyone but me."

Elizabeth made an about-face and walked quickly the other way.

But Todd had seen her. "Hey, Liz. What's your rush?"

She didn't answer. She kept moving. She had to get away.

"My sister." Jessica sighed and took Todd's arm. "Always in a hurry. Always rushing off to meet some guy."

"Where's she off to today?" asked Todd. "I was going up to the *Oracle* office to apologize in person. Hey, Jess, you explained about the other day, didn't you?"

"Oh, Todd, Liz is always ten steps ahead of me. I never know if she hears a word I'm saying.

I wonder who the lucky guy is today—probably her date for the frat dance."

"For the what?" said Todd.

"The frat dance—you know, the one your fraternity is holding with my sorority. Are you going?"

"Gee, I don't know," Todd said. "Are you?"

"That's what I was telling you. Don't you remember? You thought it was so funny that Jessica Wakefield is really a poor, lonely, miserable thing."

"Yeah, now I remember," Todd said. "But— are you sure Liz has a date for the dance?"

If it had been anyone else, Jessica would have blown up by now. But Todd Wilkins was so cute. She controlled herself and tried again.

"Todd, I told you. I can't keep up with her, so—it looks like you and I are in the same boat. The only ones."

"Hmm," Todd said, really getting her message for the first time. "So, you don't have a date, and I don't have a date. . . ."

"Yes? And?" Jessica smiled coaxingly.

But suddenly Todd looked over his shoulder as though he were searching for someone down the hall. "Uh, Jess, listen, don't worry about the dance. I'm sure a million guys are dying to ask you. Don't get uptight about it. I'm not. There's still plenty of time. Anyway, I've got to go. See you around."

Todd was gone before Jessica could recover. *I don't believe that guy!* she screamed to herself. If she had been home, she probably would have kicked a pillow across the room, maybe even cursed a little. But here in school she couldn't exactly make a scene.

Jessica felt a tiny twinge of panic. Why was Todd ignoring her? Had something happened to the Wakefield magic? *Impossible!* she told herself. She was still the most fantastic girl in school.

So why didn't Todd know it? Tears of angry frustration filled her eyes. She decided she would walk home from school. Whenever she was out walking, she never failed to attract a good deal of attention from passing cars. *The more the better*, she thought, swinging her hips a little as she set off.

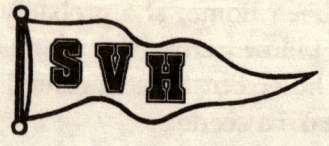

Five

"Pardon me, Heaven—which way to Mars?"

"What?" Jessica stared in astonishment at the boy leaning out the open window of the jacked-up Camaro.

She recognized him as Rick Andover, the most outrageous guy at Sweet Valley High—until he dropped out six months ago. Jessica found it hard to believe he was only seventeen. He looked older than most guys their age. He had the ice-cool handsómeness of a junior Clint Eastwood, and a hint of danger lurked in his sultry dark eyes. One elbow was hooked casually over the door. Jessica stared in fascination at the eagle emblem tattooed against the densely packed muscles of his forearm. Her stomach executed a slow somersault. She'd never been this close to Rick before.

50

"What are you staring at?" she finally asked, unnerved by the way his arrogant gaze raked over her.

One corner of his mouth turned up in a slow, sexy smile. "You," he answered. "I'm driving you home. That is, unless your mommy warned you never to take rides with strangers."

Jessica's eyes narrowed. Mr. Big-Shot Andover didn't know who he was talking to.

"I do as I please," she said, hesitating only a split second before she jumped into his car.

"I'm in for a lot of trouble." Rick grinned at her as they squealed away from the curb, shooting ahead of an elderly Pontiac, which had to slam on its brakes to keep from running into them.

"Why is that?" Jessica asked, a thrill that was half fear, half excitement racing up her backbone.

She'd heard a number of stories about Rick and the fast-lane life he led. He ran around with an older crowd and always had a lot of money in his pocket, even though it didn't look as if he had a job. He spent most of his time either working on his Camaro or cruising around in it—usually with a gorgeous girl at his side. Jessica squirmed with pleasure at having been selected as Rick's companion for that afternoon.

"Because *my* mother told *me* never to ride with strange young girls, that's why," said Rick.

"How do I know you won't try to take advantage of my innocence?"

Jessica giggled. She found Rick's sense of humor wickedly fascinating—like everything else about him.

"Don't worry," she replied, arching an eyebrow. "I'm fighting off the urge to attack you."

He shot her a look full of unmistakable meaning. "Just as long as you don't fight *too* hard. I'm not used to taking no for an answer."

Neither was Jessica, for that matter. At that moment she was reminded of Todd's indifference, which triggered a spurt of angry rebellion in her. She didn't resist as Rick's arm snaked around the back of the seat, his fingers squeezing her shoulder. She wished Todd could see her now. Maybe he would even be jealous.

"I'll pick you up at eight," Rick told her as they were cruising down Calico Drive, doing fifty in a thirty-five zone.

"What?"

He grinned. "Tomorrow, at eight. We've got a date, Heaven."

"But you never even *asked* me," she complained.

"I told you—I'm used to getting, not asking Are you saying no?" ne challenged as if the thought were unheard of.

"No." She frowned slightly, biting her lip. "It's just that I'm not sure my parents—"

"Mommy and Daddy wouldn't like the idea of their Little Red Riding Hood going out with the Big Bad Wolf?" he supplied, sneering. "What do *you* want?"

He was looking at her in a way that made her skin tingle. His heavy-lidded eyes held a hypnotic hint of the excitement to come if she decided to go out with him. Jessica found it irresistible.

"Did you say eight?"

"Yeah." He gave her shoulder a harder squeeze. "Don't be late. We've got some serious boogeying to do. And, hey, forget about the folks, they don't even have to know you're out with me."

"Where should I meet you?" she asked.

"Right here," he answered, jerking to a noisy stop just around the corner from her house. "This is where you live, isn't it?"

She stared at him. "H-how did you know?"

"You're Jessica Wakefield, right? I make it a habit to know where all the foxiest chicks in Sweet Valley live."

Jessica felt herself grow warm all over. It was good to know she wasn't invisible to *every* boy in town! Maybe Rick wasn't Todd, but he wasn't exactly a clown like Winston Egbert, either. In fact, Rick Andover might just turn out to be fun. . . .

Before she could get out of the car, Rick pulled her close, giving her a light, teasing kiss on the mouth that promised more than it delivered. He smelled sexy, but in a strange way—like leather and gasoline.

"Where are we going tomorrow?" she asked as she was climbing out.

He winked suggestively. "That's for me to know and you to find out." He gunned the engine, drowning any protests she might have had. "Catch you later, Heaven."

The Camaro shot away from the curb, swerved in front of a bus, and ducked back into traffic just in time to miss a red Fiat coming up Calico Drive. Jessica shuddered. It was her mother!

The Fiat pulled over, and Alice Wakefield waved at Jessica.

"Jessica, hi! Come on, I'll give you a lift."

Jessica climbed in, her pulse still racing from her encounter with Rick.

"Did you see the boy driving that silver Camaro?" her mother fumed. "He almost ran into me!"

"Uh, no, I didn't see," Jessica stammered.

"It was that wild Rick Andover, I'm sure of it," she said.

Jessica bit her lip and said nothing.

"That kid is headed straight for trouble!" Mrs.

Wakefield pronounced with unusual vehemence, her expression darkening.

Jessica was surprised to see her mother so uptight. She was usually pretty calm about things! Come to think of it, she'd been uncharacteristically tense for the past week or so. Could it have something to do with the fact that both she and Dad had been working so hard lately— and spending so little time with each other? But Dad had Marianna West to keep him company during those late nights at the office. Marianna West was beautiful, divorced, and, most of all, available.

Jessica's thoughts whirled in panicked confusion. Poor Mom! Did she suspect as well?

"You look pretty dressed up for someone who's just going over to the library to do some studying," remarked Elizabeth as she observed her sister's elaborate preparations in front of the mirror. Come to think of it, Jessica *had* seemed strangely secretive throughout dinner, Elizabeth thought, as if she had something up her sleeve.

Jessica finished applying her lipstick, then stood back to examine herself in the mirror. Finally she turned to Elizabeth and gave her a sly smile, her aquamarine eyes sparkling with mischief.

"The truth is, I'm *not* going to the library," she confessed in a low voice. "But if you tell Mom, I'll boil you in oil."

"Where *are* you going, Jess?"

"I have a date." Jessica went back to admiring her reflection. "Do you think the red blouse would look better with this skirt, or my new yellow T-shirt?"

"Jess, stop changing the subject!" Elizabeth practically screamed at her. "Who are you going out with?"

Borrowing Rick's phrase, she answered coyly, "That's for me to know and you to find out."

Elizabeth frowned. She had a sick suspicion who Jessica was going out with, but it didn't make sense. Why should she have to sneak to go out on a date with Todd? Knowing her sister, it was just one of the many detours Jessica took off the straight and narrow in order to spice up her life. She stared at Jessica, who was bubbling over with excitement, and her heart sank.

She was certain Jessica was going out with Todd.

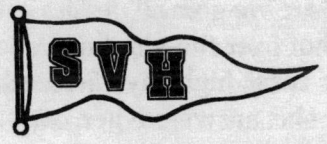

Six

"You're late," Rick said, gunning the engine impatiently as Jessica climbed in beside him. His dark eyes flickered over her. "But I can see it was worth the wait."

Jessica was glad she'd taken the trouble to curl her hair and put on her sexiest red blouse. She had even borrowed her sister's brand-new black sandal heels to go with her black silk-jersey skirt. She felt very grown-up, wedged beside Rick, with his arm clamped about her shoulders.

"Sorry, Rick," she breathed. "I had trouble getting away."

"Forget it. The night is young, and we've just begun, Heaven."

He pressed her even closer, turning his face briefly to nuzzle her hair. She caught the faint smell of cigarettes and liquor on his breath.

"Where are we going?" Jessica asked as Rick's Camaro shot over the winding valley road leading to the coast highway. Before he could say anything, she answered her own question: "I know—that's for you to know and me to find out, right?"

"Right. Hey, you're a fast learner. I can't wait to see what else you're good at."

Jessica shivered a little at his compliment. He talked the way he drove—fast and dangerously. For an instant she wondered if she would be able to keep him at bay, but she quickly dismissed the worry. She had yet to come up against a situation she couldn't handle.

Even so, nothing could squelch the nervous fluttering in her stomach as Rick's car spun to a stop in a shower of gravel in front of a seedy-looking beachfront roadhouse. A red, blinking neon sign advertised that it was Kelly's. Loud music spilled from the open doorway, punctuated by harsh bursts of laughter.

None of Jessica's friends had ever been inside Kelly's. It had the most notorious reputation of any bar in the whole valley. A mixture of alarm and excitement raced through Jessica's body. Boy, would she have something to talk about tomorrow!

Rick must have noticed how nervous she

looked, for he squeezed her shoulders in rough reassurance. "Take it easy, Heaven. You've just graduated into the real world. Think you can handle it?"

"Are you kidding?" she tossed back. "I can handle anything."

Once inside, she wasn't so sure. Kelly's was definitely out of her league. So was Rick Andover, she was beginning to think.

"That's my girl," he murmured against her ear, sliding his arm about her waist in a proprietary way as they passed through the bar area, heading for one of the dimly lit booths in back.

Jessica had never been so acutely aware of both her age and her appearance before. Several of the men stared at her, and one let forth a low wolf whistle. Her face was burning from anger and embarrassment, and her eyes watered from the cigarette smoke that wreathed the cramped room. As they slid into the cracked vinyl booth, she leaned over to tell Rick how uncomfortable she felt, but her words were drowned in a sudden burst of twangy country-western music from the jukebox.

Rick ordered a couple of boilermakers, something Jessica had never heard of before. She was relieved to see that it was only beer, until the waitress placed two shot glasses of whiskey beside their foaming mugs. She didn't even look at Jessica, much less ask for her I.D., despite the sign hanging over the bar: MINORS WILL NOT BE SERVED UNDER PENALTY OF LAW. With a growing sense of unease, Jessica sipped her beer while Rick tipped back his glass of whiskey as though it were water.

He laughed huskily. "Not exactly prom time, huh?" His hand found her knee under the table and gave it a squeeze.

Jessica winced but forced a smile anyway. "It's . . . it's fun," she agreed, lying through her gritted teeth.

"So are you." Rick's hand moved up an inch or two on her leg. "I knew the minute I laid eyes on you that you wouldn't let me down, little Jessica."

Jessica shifted her position, trying to maneuver herself out of his reach, but Rick only squeezed tighter. She giggled nervously in an attempt to cover up her unease.

"And *I* should have known you were the kind of guy who couldn't keep his hands to himself," she scolded lightly.

Rick's eyes narrowed. "All tease and no tickle, huh? Didn't your mommy tell you not to put anything in the window that you don't sell in the store?" His fingers groped higher, and she noticed he was beginning to slur his words "Well, I've seen the merchandise, baby, and I'm sold."

This time there was no pretense in the way

Jessica pulled away from Rick. Suddenly he didn't seem so fascinating anymore. Just dangerous. His eyes looked flat and black, like a snake's. His breath, as he leaned over to kiss her, reeked of alcohol.

"Rick, don't—" Jessica turned her head so that his lips found only her cheek, leaving a wet imprint, like the rings of moisture left on the table by their glasses.

"Whatsa matter?" he drawled. "You wanna go somewhere quieter? Listen, I know a place down the—"

"No!" Jessica cried in true alarm. "Rick, take me home. I—I told my parents I'd be back in an hour. I really can't stay."

He shrugged. "So call and tell 'em you'll be late. 'Less you're afraid of turning into a pumpkin." Rick laughed loudly at his own joke.

"Rick, *please*." She wasn't in the habit of begging, but she was getting desperate. A few more drinks and Rick would be in no condition to drive her home. Then she'd really be stuck.

"Forget it, baby." He gulped the last of his beer and finished off her untouched shot of whiskey. "I came here for a good time, and I'm not leaving."

"What about *me*?" she wailed, suddenly close to tears. "What am *I* supposed to do?"

Rick hooked a tattooed arm around her neck, dragging her into another one of his moist kisses.

"Do I have to spell it out for you? Relax, baby. You might even have a good time yourself."

Jessica slithered adroitly from his drunken clinch and stood up. "Sorry, Rick," she said, in command of herself once again, "but I'd have a better time with an octopus. Thanks for nothing. I think I'll just call a cab."

"Wait a minute," Rick hissed, grabbing her hand and jerking her back into the booth. "You're not going anywhere!"

Jessica let out a yelp as blunt fingers encircled her wrist. She struggled to free herself. A man sitting at a bar stool nearby swiveled around to see what was going on.

"He giving you trouble, miss?" the man asked.

"Yes," Jessica announced in a loud voice. "I have to go home, and he won't let me go!"

The man grinned. He was probably about her father's age, only rougher looking—in a funny kind of nice way. Like a cross between a teddy bear and *Jaws*.

"I'd be glad to give you a lift home if your boyfriend won't," he said.

"Thanks," Jessica said, "but he's not my boyfriend."

She had succeeded in wrenching away and was halfway to the door when Rick lunged after her, his black eyes spitting fire.

"Out of the way, lard bucket!" he growled at the man, who had stepped in front of him.

At that moment Jessica felt as if all the air in that smoky room had been sucked out. She could hardly breathe. As she watched in horror, Rick hunched forward, swinging his fist in a wide, drunken arc. The man easily blocked the punch. His own ham-sized fist exploded against Rick's jaw with an audible crack. Rick reeled backward, crashing into a table and knocking over several chairs. A trickle of blood oozed from one corner of his mouth.

Jessica stood frozen, unaware that any time had passed, until the howl of a siren brought her back to her senses with a sickening snap. The next thing she knew, there were two policemen barreling into the bar. One of them headed straight for Rick, who lay sprawled on the floor amid the cigarette butts, mumbling curses at everyone in sight.

"This time I'm pressing charges," the bartender was yelling. "His name's Andover, and this isn't the first time he's tried to bust up my place!"

The other policeman took Jessica aside. "Do your parents know you're here, young lady?" he demanded sternly.

"Oh, no, please, *please* don't tell them," she begged, tears pouring down her cheeks. She didn't have to turn on the waterworks—this time they were for real. "They would just *kill* me if they found out!"

"I doubt that," he answered, but his tone softened slightly. "Maybe it's best for your parents to find out. They might stop you from doing something even worse the next time. Now, why don't you give me your name?"

Panic swept through Jessica. Arrested! Taken home by the police from Kelly's! She'd be absolutely ruined—besides being grounded for five hundred years!

"Uh . . . Wakefield . . ." she managed to choke.

"Wakefield, huh?" The cop peered closely at her. "Sure, I know you. You're a friend of my niece, Emily Mayer. I've heard her mention Elizabeth Wakefield."

"Emily? Oh, sure!" Jessica ignored his mistake. "Emily's a terrific drummer, and the Droids are the hottest band in Sweet Valley," she babbled in relief.

The cop jotted something down in his notebook "OK, young lady," he said. "Let's get you home where you belong."

In the squad car Jessica began sobbing again with renewed desperation. She pulled out all the stops—every plea she could think of, from the trauma of being scarred for life to the fact that her father was a lawyer, and his reputation could be ruined. The cop said nothing until he'd pulled to a stop in front of her house.

Then he turned to her. "Listen," he said, giving her a long, hard look. "I'm going to let you off *this* time. No thanks to Niagara Falls, either. I just happen to believe in second chances."

"Oh, *thank* you, Officer!" Jessica leaped from the car like someone who had just been reprieved from death row. "I *swear* it'll never happen again!"

"It'd better not," he called after her as she bounded up the driveway. "Stay away from Rick Andover. I don't want to see you in the middle of any more brawls at Kelly's. And keep in mind, Elizabeth, I don't believe in third chances."

"Wait, I'm not—" She started to tell him she wasn't Elizabeth. Now that she was out of danger, she was suddenly stricken by a guilty conscience for letting him think she was her twin. But the squad car had already disappeared into the night.

Blinded by her overwhelming relief, Jessica hadn't seen the girl who walked past with a little black poodle on a leash. She probably wouldn't have noticed it was Caroline Pearce, her sorority sister and three-doors-down neighbor, even if she'd bumped into her. Jessica was so happy to have been let off the hook, she practically flew up the front steps to her house.

Caroline was heading home, too, straight for the white Princess phone in her bedroom, which served as the central switchboard for Sweet Valley High gossip. . . .

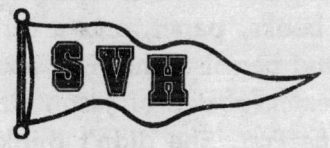

Seven

Elizabeth looked out her bedroom window to see what kind of day it was. No big surprise. The morning was bright and sunny, as it almost always was in Sweet Valley. *Why can't you get a cloudy day when you really need one?* she mused. *OK, Liz,* she told herself sternly. *Get your act together.* If Todd preferred Jessica, that's the way it was.

Elizabeth scanned the room. It was her haven, her sanctuary. She had decorated it herself. She had chosen the off-white carpeting, had painted the walls a soft cream, and had picked out the bed frame and matching dresser. She had also put up the two mirrors in the room, a small one over the dresser and a full-length one on the back of the door. One whole wall was a closet with louvered doors.

Instead of a desk, Elizabeth had decided on a large rectangular table. It held her typewriter, reference books, paper, and a ceramic holder for pens and pencils. And right above the table was a theater poster of Jason Robards in *A Touch of the Poet*. She didn't think she would ever be as good a writer as Eugene O'Neill, but it was a terrific-looking poster—and she *was*, after all, a writer.

Elizabeth looked longingly at the one curious piece of furniture in the room, a chaise longue she had found in a thrift shop and re-covered in a soft, pale velvet. Maybe she could just curl up there for the day, or maybe for the rest of her life. Then her eyes zeroed in on the digital clock-radio on her nightstand. *Oh, no*, she thought. *I'm not only miserable down to my toes, but I'm going to get an F in science if I miss Mr. Russo's test!*

She grabbed her knapsack and dashed out of the room, nearly knocking over Jessica, who was heading for the stairs.

"Liz!" Jessica yelped.

"Sorry, Jess. I just checked the time. We're going to be late! Are you ready for Russo's test?"

"Tests! Tests! Tests!" Jessica grumbled as the two went down the stairs. "Doesn't that man realize there are more important things to do at school besides take tests? Of course I'm not ready!"

Elizabeth headed for the front door. "I don't have time for breakfast. See you in school!"

"Wait, Liz, there's something I have to talk to you about. It's absolutely urgent!"

"No time, Jess. I promised Enid I'd meet her before first period. Later!" And she was gone before Jessica could tell her about the night before.

"Well, if meeting that wimpy Enid Rollins is more important than talking to her own sister . . ." Jessica muttered. Maybe nobody at school would find out about last night, she thought. "Yeah, fat chance. Maybe school will be canceled on account of a snowstorm."

Elizabeth spotted Enid sitting by herself. As she made her way across the broad green lawn, Elizabeth wondered what the latest "absolutely vital" matter was that Enid wanted to see her about. As she passed a group of boys, she noticed that they were staring at her. Before she could check to be sure she had all her clothes on, Bruce Patman stepped out of the group. He was smirking.

"Didn't know you had it in you, Wakefield. Really awesome."

"What?" Elizabeth stopped short and faced Bruce.

"You know, Wakefield, you know. And now I know."

"The only thing I know, *Patman*, is that you seem to be missing a few marbles," Elizabeth snapped. She turned her back on the group and walked over to Enid.

"Liz, I thought you'd never get here," Enid said, jumping to her feet.

"I just got waylaid by Mr. Wonderful," Elizabeth said, nodding in Bruce Patman's direction.

"You mean *the* gorgeous Bruce Patman?"

"Don't forget rich, Enid."

"Oh, yes. Gorgeous, rich, and let's not leave out—ta da!—star of the tennis team." Both girls started giggling. Most girls at Sweet Valley High would kill for a date with the son of the town's richest and oldest family, but not Elizabeth or Enid.

Suddenly getting serious, Enid asked, "What was Bruce saying to you?"

Elizabeth thought for a moment. "I'm not sure. He was totally weird. He said something about not knowing I had it in me, whatever *it* is."

"Oh." Enid looked down at her shoes.

"Oh? Do you know what he was talking about?"

"I'm not sure, but I think so. Liz, I want you

to know that you're my best friend. And I'll always be *your* best friend, no matter what."

"No matter what? Enid, what are you talking about?"

"I know something about making mistakes, Liz, and I meant it when I said we're friends. I don't want you to worry about losing my friendship. Ever."

Elizabeth stared openmouthed at her friend. What was the matter with everybody today?

"Enid, get to the point! Have I suddenly grown another head?"

"Liz, I know there are some things you think you can never tell anybody, but—oh, there's Ronnie waving at me. I have to talk to him before first bell." Enid seemed almost relieved to delay her conversation with her friend. "I'll talk to you later. Bye!"

Elizabeth stared in complete puzzlement as Enid hurried across the lawn toward Ronnie Edwards, who stood there frowning.

"Is something wrong, Ronnie?" Enid would die if Ronnie were mad at her. She felt her heart begin to race.

"Why were you talking to *her*?" he asked, still frowning.

"To Liz? She's my best friend!"

"Maybe you should be more careful about

71

choosing friends. Everybody's talking about that stunt she pulled last night."

"Everybody? Ronnie, that's not true. Besides, we haven't heard Liz's side yet."

"Enid, it's all over campus. Caroline Pearce saw the squad car bring Liz home. She went to Kelly's with Rick Andover and started a riot. You really want to be friends with someone like that?" Ronnie said accusingly.

"We're not sure about all that, Ronnie. It's just a lot of rumors. I can't believe she'd go out with Rick. She's my friend, and I'm going to stick by her, no matter what."

The sound of the bell cut off whatever Ronnie was going to say. But Enid knew he was angry.

What an absolutely unbelievable day, Elizabeth thought as she reached her front door. It was like being in the *Twilight Zone*. Everywhere she went, she got strange looks. Kids stopped talking as soon as she approached—in the lunchroom, in the library, in the halls. And what in the world was Enid trying to tell her?

Even Mr. Collins had insisted on being mysterious about some kind of problem with the school football field. She remembered her father mentioning the same thing the other morning at breakfast, but he wouldn't elaborate, either. It was spooky, and the day wasn't over yet.

As soon as she opened the door, Elizabeth heard angry voices coming from the kitchen.

"Steve, you were supposed to go back to school last night," Alice Wakefield said.

"Mom, don't get uptight. I didn't miss anything important today."

"That's not the point. You're being very secretive. Your father and I are concerned about you."

"I didn't know you and Dad had time for anything except work these days."

"Steve!"

"Sorry, Mom. I just don't like being hassled. Look, I've got to go. See you Friday."

Elizabeth entered the room just as Steven was opening the back door.

"Bye, Liz. Bye, Mom." He was gone.

Elizabeth and her mother exchanged confused looks.

"What's with Steve, Mom?"

"I was hoping you could tell me."

"I don't—"

The sharp ring of the phone interrupted Elizabeth.

"I'll get it, Mom! Hello?" She covered the mouthpiece with her hand. "It's for me. I'll take it on the upstairs extension. Hang it up for me, Mom."

"Sure. Then I've got to meet a client. Dad will be late, too. And there's a casserole in the

73

freezer for you and Jessica," she said, having to shout the last because Elizabeth was already upstairs. She was her usual organized self, but she sounded distracted, as if she had her own problems as well.

"Enid!" Elizabeth nearly shouted into the phone. "Talk to me! Tell me what's going on!"

Less than a minute later, a stunned Elizabeth was gasping for breath.

"I don't believe this! *I* was arrested, put on parole, and brought home in a squad car! Enid, that is the wildest, most idiotic, most— In Kelly's with Rick Andover? No wonder everybody—! They're lies, Enid, I would never . . . !"

When Elizabeth stopped to catch her breath, Enid filled her in on all the gruesome details.

"Caroline Pearce said she saw you, Liz. She said the policeman called you by name, that he has your name in his book, and that you're on parole! But, Liz, you and I are friends, no matter—"

"Stop saying that, Enid! There is no 'matter.' I don't know why Caroline would spread lies about me. For heaven's sake, I've never even spoken to Rick Andover!"

In a flash, though, Elizabeth realized that she did know someone who would speak to him— Jessica! But Caroline had heard the policeman say Elizabeth, not Jessica. She had to get to the bottom of this. There was only one person who

74

would have the answers, and that blond duplicate of herself should be home any minute.

"Enid, I don't know how in the world all this started, but I can't talk any more now," she said abruptly. "I'll call you back later. Bye!"

She hung up and went into her room. She paced from the window to the door, waiting for her sister to get home.

It was a nightmare. Please let it be a nightmare! But Elizabeth knew she was wide awake. Suddenly the most awful, totally terrible thought popped into her head. Todd! Todd Wilkins had heard this story! Maybe he even believed it! *I've got to tell him the truth*, she decided. But what *was* the truth?

The front door slammed, and a breathless Jessica ran upstairs, calling, "Liz! Liz, where are you?"

Jessica bolted into Elizabeth's room. The sisters stood facing one another, identical expressions on their lovely faces. Total panic.

"You've heard. I can tell you've heard, Lizzie!"

"Have I ever!"

"A thing like this could ruin the entire family, our futures!" She moaned. "What are we going to do?"

"Let's start with Rick Andover, Jess."

"Rick Andover? What's he got to do with anything?"

"He has everything to do with all the kids in

school thinking I have a police record and that I'm out on parole!" Elizabeth shouted, for once making no effort to control her temper.

"Oh, that." Jessica shrugged, flushing guiltily. "I can clear that little thing up in no time."

"Do it *now!*" Elizabeth said.

"*Later*, Liz! I'm talking about something *really* important. I found out this afternoon why Steve has been coming home every weekend. No wonder he's been so mysterious and obnoxious to everybody. He should be ashamed of himself! My whole life is going to go right down the tubes! How could he do this, Lizzie?" She began to cry.

"Stop babbling, Jess! And stop crying! Tell me what Steve has done."

"Our brother, a member of the Wakefield family, has been spending every weekend," Jessica got out between sobs, "with Betsy Martin!"

A stunned silence filled the room. Elizabeth plopped down onto her bed, all thoughts of her own troubles pushed aside. Steven was seeing Betsy Martin?

"Jess, are you sure? I can't believe it. Betsy's been doing drugs for years—she sleeps around—"

"And her father gets bombed out of his mind every night," Jessica said wildly.

A new worry occurred to Elizabeth. "Jess, what are Mom and Dad going to say when they find out?"

"Mom and Dad? Liz, what about the kids? I will be totally ruined forever when this gets around school! And you, too."

"*I'm* ruined already," Elizabeth cried. "Will you please tell me what this Rick Andover business is all about!"

"Later, Lizzie, please."

"No, I want to know *right now!*"

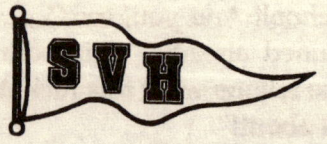

Eight

"Oh, Lizzie, it was so awful!" Jessica wailed, bursting into tears. "There was drinking and fighting, and Rick had his hands all over—"

"Rick!" Elizabeth cut in. "Did you say *Rick*? You mean you weren't with Todd?" Elizabeth was so relieved, she felt her anger deflate like a punctured balloon.

"I wish I *had* been with Todd," said Jessica. "He would never have taken me to that awful place! I'm telling you, it was all Rick's fault. He practically *dragged* me in there, for heaven's sake!"

"If it was all Rick's fault," Elizabeth asked, suspiciously, "then how come the police ended up with *my* name?" She wasn't letting Jessica worm her way out of it this time.

"It was a mix-up, Liz," Jessica cried. "You've

got to believe me! The cop was Emily's uncle, and he said he recognized you, and—"

"And you didn't correct him." Elizabeth's voice was hard.

"I tried to, Lizzie. Honest, I did. He—he wouldn't listen."

Jessica was sobbing uncontrollably now. Elizabeth felt torn between wanting to comfort her sister and wanting to murder her. Knowing she'd been with Rick instead of Todd made it easier for Elizabeth to forgive her.

"Stop crying, Jess," she commanded softly. "I know how scared you must have been. I guess I would've been, too. What I don't understand is how you could let people think *I* was arrested."

"That's so totally ridiculous," she said, grabbing a handful of tissues and mopping her face. "The cop just drove me home and gave me a warning. If I'd been arrested, Mom and Dad would've been called. I can't believe Caroline would spread a story like that about you!"

"I suppose this whole thing is Caroline's fault now, huh?"

"*Please* don't hate me," Jessica begged. "I'll clear your name, Liz. I promise. Even if it ruins me." She sneaked a look at her sister to see if she would demand such a sacrifice.

Elizabeth just thought for a moment.

"But you know, Liz, doing that just might

79

keep the gossip going on *forever*. You know how it is. Anyway, something will happen tomorrow, and everybody will forget about this," she said hopefully.

"Jessica, I don't care about the whole world. I just want my friends to know the truth."

Jessica sensed she was almost off the hook.

"Certainly you don't think your friends—your *real* friends—would think you were arrested. Don't tell me that your *very best* friend, wimpy Rollins, would turn on you?"

Jessica knew she shouldn't make a crack about Enid, but she couldn't resist. She didn't like Elizabeth being close friends with anyone but her.

Lost in thought, Elizabeth mumbled, "No, Enid is my friend. She'll stick." *But what about Todd?* she thought.

"Is there anyone else you want me to tell the truth to? Maybe Todd Wilkins? Are you and he kind of *buddies*?" Jessica asked, never taking her eyes off her sister's face.

Buddies? Buddies! The one boy in all the world whom Elizabeth loved, who made her heart beat faster and her breath catch in her throat. Buddies?

"Yeah, I guess that's what we are," she finally answered.

Knowing she had won the battle, Jessica gave Elizabeth a hug. "Don't worry about a thing,

Liz. Todd and I have gotten very close. I'll tell him the truth. I just know he's too terrific a guy to hold it against you. No way do I want him mad at you, Lizzie. Like, wouldn't it be impossible when he picks me up for dates for him not to say hello to you, at least?"

The picture of a smiling Todd picking up Jessica for dates, holding her hand—kissing her good night at the front door—made Elizabeth want to weep. She could only imagine in despair what Todd must think of her now. . . .

Ronnie and Enid had a date to spend what was left of the day at the beach, but when Ronnie knocked on Enid's door, Todd was standing beside him.

"You don't mind, do you, Enid?" Ronnie asked as they clattered down the deck steps. "Just look at Todd. He's a mess. I couldn't let a frat brother go moping around like that without doing something. So I asked him to come along with us today, OK?"

Enid took one look at Todd's sheepish, embarrassed expression and melted. She ruffled his hair, linked arms with the both of them, and said, "Come on, you gorgeous guys. Let's go!"

At first the job of cheering Todd up didn't appear to be very difficult. By the time they hit the blue-green water, he was actually laughing.

Immediately Enid and Ronnie announced, "It's water war time!" and splashed Todd from both sides. They all rode in on the waves like human surfboards. When they finally dragged themselves from the water, dripping and shivering, they were all in great spirits. That is, until Ronnie, sitting cross-legged on the small blanket Enid had brought along, said, "Hey, what do you think of Liz Wakefield and Rick Andover?"

Todd sat upright, scowling. "I heard the rumor," he muttered unhappily. He looked crushed.

Enid glared at Ronnie for being so stupid, but he didn't seem to get the message.

"That guy is such a beast. I can't believe her!" Ronnie added, not realizing he was rubbing salt in the wound.

"Now, wait a minute," Enid said. "We've all heard the same rumor and—"

"See?" Ronnie interrupted. "Even Liz's best friend—"

"No, no!" Enid protested. "We've just heard the rumor. But I know it's not true. I asked her about it."

Smiling sarcastically, Ronnie demanded, "And what did poor Liz do? Burst into tears?"

Enid didn't like Ronnie's attitude. "No, she didn't burst into tears. In fact, she seemed quite angry and confused that anybody would say such things about her. She flatly denied the rumor, Ronnie."

"And you believed her?" Ronnie asked, amazed.

"Of course I believed her!" Enid said hotly. "She wouldn't lie to me. She's my best friend!"

Sitting on the plaid blanket in the blazing sun, the three friends shared an awkward silence. Enid picked up handfuls of sand, letting the grains sift out from between her clenched fingers. "I know Liz better than just about anybody. And I can't imagine her with a guy like Rick— especially in a place like Kelly's."

"Well, sometimes a person is not what she *seems*," Ronnie said sharply.

Todd nodded in agreement. "Yeah, that's true. I mean, that's what I'm finding."

Enid couldn't believe her ears and told them so. "I know there's another explanation. I can't accept these rumors, especially after Liz has denied them."

Todd, a sad, faraway look in his brown eyes, said, "Maybe there's just so much a person can take. I mean, how long can you go on trusting someone, believing in someone?"

"If you're her friend," Enid said, "you should never stop."

Todd looked down at the sand.

Desperately, Enid turned to Ronnie. "Sometimes people make mistakes they're sorry for

83

later," she said slowly and from her heart. "Don't you think they should be forgiven?"

Ronnie thought for a moment, throwing a pebble over and over into the sand. Finally he shook his head. "Some things are unforgivable."

Enid was shaken by Ronnie's attitude. It was a side of him she hadn't known before—a cold, hard, unforgiving side—and it frightened her.

"How did you hear about Liz?" Todd asked Ronnie.

"I heard it from at least three people," Ronnie answered. "She was seen getting out of the police car. She was overheard promising never to go to Kelly's again—with Rick, especially."

"Well, I guess that's it, then," Todd said with bitter resignation. "There's no use arguing because it's a plain fact—Liz was there with Rick, and no amount of explaining can change that."

"Well, I don't believe she was there," Enid said, "but even if she was, the real question is, are you a true friend, and can you forgive her?" She was really asking Ronnie, pleading with Ronnie, but it was Todd who answered.

"I don't know. I really don't."

"Well, I *do* know," Ronnie said vehemently. "And if a girl I liked did something like that, I'd never speak to her again."

Though the day was still warm, Enid shivered and pulled on a shirt. She had made a decision. *He must never know about me. Never.* He must never know about the time she was arrested after that horrible accident. Lost in thought about herself, Enid forgot all about Elizabeth's problems.

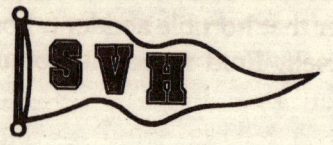

Nine

It was one of those mornings that made Elizabeth think her sister had been a bird in a former life. Jessica was chirping away nonstop at the breakfast table.

"Didn't I tell you, Miss Sourpuss, that it would all blow over?" Jessica burbled over her Rice Krispies. "Why, the entire school has totally forgotten about you and Rick."

"About who and who?"

"I mean about Rick and me. Nobody has said a word to me about it in days."

"How nice for you, Jess. They've talked to me about it. Practically *all* anybody talks about is me going to Kelly's and what I did with Rick."

"Who said that?"

"Actually, Jessica, you're right. Nobody talks

about it. They just *hint!* They talk to each other about it, but when I walk up, they stop. I'm a walking conversation stopper."

"I think you're just imagining things."

"No I'm not, Jessica. Enid filled me in. Everybody's talking about me and Rick, and they all believe it. On Wednesday there was a big message on the blackboard in the *Oracle* office when I walked in, too."

Jessica leaned forward. "What did it say?" she asked, as though it were some juicy gossip about somebody else.

"It said: 'Scoop! Big-shot editor Wakefield makes news! Why isn't it in the paper?' "

"That is vile," Jessica snapped. *"You're* not the editor! It isn't your decision to print such a story."

Elizabeth shook her head in dismay. "Jessica, sometimes I truly do wonder about you."

"Lizzie, I *promise* that anytime I hear anybody say anything about you, I'll set them straight."

Elizabeth stared forlornly out the window at the peaceful swimming pool. Wouldn't it be nice to sit out there all day and not have to face anyone at Sweet Valley High?

"Are there people you're worried about?" Jessica asked anxiously. "Because I'll tell them, if there are."

If only someone could convince Todd Wilkins

of the truth. Elizabeth felt tears forming behind her eyes. Enid had told her about their trip to the beach and how Todd had heard all the lurid details and believed them. How could he?

"No," said Elizabeth. "Anybody who would believe things about me without even finding out the truth isn't anybody I care about."

"You're not going to tell Mom and Dad on me?"

"Jessica, you know I'd never do something like that to you."

Jessica gazed at her wonderful sister, and a wave of love flooded through her. She grabbed Elizabeth and hugged her.

"You're so wonderful to me, Lizzie! Sometimes I think I don't deserve it!"

In Elizabeth's mood, that was all it took for the tears to flow. She wept, hugging Jessica as hard as she could. "Oh, Jessie, you're wonderful, too. You deserve everything. Everybody loves you, and they should."

"Lizzie—you're crying!"

"It's all right, Jessie. I'm just upset—about Steve and—things." And she hurried from the kitchen to fix her face. She would show none of this at school. Elizabeth Wakefield would hold her head high.

Actually, the gossip about the Kelly's Roadhouse fiasco did seem to be dying down. When Elizabeth got to school that day, the corridors were buzzing with a new and much more serious crisis—the Gladiators' football field. George Fowler—Lila Fowler's father—was throwing the school off the field, the rumor said. He was one of the richest men in Sweet Valley already, and he wanted to take over the football field to put up a factory. Now the big mystery of the football field made sense.

"George Fowler is stealing our football field," lanky, dark-haired Winston Egbert told Elizabeth breathlessly. For once, he didn't appear to be joking.

"No, you idiot," said Dana Larson, who was walking by. Dana was the lead singer for the Droids, Sweet Valley High's hottest rock band. "It's the Patmans. Bruce Patman's father has bought the land, and he's going to put in an amusement park."

"An amusement park?" said Winston, astounded. "Hey, that wouldn't be so bad!" He turned and dashed down the corridor. "Hey, did you hear? Bruce Patman's father is building a Disneyland on the football field."

Elizabeth, from her experience as a reporter for *The Oracle*, knew there was no sense believing the distorted rumors circulating through the halls. She headed for the newspaper office and Mr. Collins.

"Mr. Collins," she said, "what's going on? I've heard crazy rumors."

"They're not rumors, Elizabeth," said Mr. Collins, looking grim. "They're true enough."

Sweet Valley's two most powerful families, the Patmans and the Fowlers, were at each other's throats again, and the high school was caught in the middle. The Patman-Fowler feud—pitting the old, established Henry Wilson Patman and his canning industry money against George Fowler and his new money made through silicon chips—was going to be fought out on the Gladiators' football field.

"The school had leased the field from the city, but the lease ran out recently," said Mr. Collins. "Now George Fowler is trying to buy the land so he can put up a new factory."

"Right across from the school?" said Elizabeth, aghast.

"That's what he wants. The Fowlers judge everything by how they can make more money."

"But where would the Gladiators play football?"

"I don't think that interests George Fowler, Liz."

"But I heard the Patmans want the field, Mr. Collins."

"Oh, yes, they do. When they heard George Fowler was going to buy the land for a factory, they went into shock. They've gotten a court injunction to block the sale. They don't want a factory there."

"Well, good," said Elizabeth. "Then we support the Patmans."

"Wrong, Elizabeth. The Patmans don't want the Gladiators on the field either. They want to plant a formal English garden, the way it was in 1916 when it was part of the Vanderhorn estate."

"Who were the Vanderhorns?"

"The Vanderhorns were one of the original families in Sweet Valley."

"So?"

"Bruce Patman's mother was a Vanderhorn."

"My goodness," said Elizabeth. "What a mess."

"Yes. And I'm afraid it's all yours."

"Mine?" Elizabeth felt her pulse racing. She had never been given a story this big before.

"Yes. John is busy with the game against Palisades High. If we ever get to play it. So this one's all yours."

"You mean we might not be able to use the field for the Palisades game, Mr. Collins?"

"As of right now, Elizabeth, nobody can use the field for anything. The Fowlers have claimed it, and the Patmans' court injunction keeps everybody off the land until this is settled."

"But the team has to practice!"

"Not on their own field, Elizabeth. Have fun."

Court injunctions might keep school officials and even big shots like the Patmans and the

Fowlers off a disputed football field, but they were useless against the student body of Sweet Valley High. By lunchtime the rumors had totally engulfed the school. Kids were milling around in front on the steps and spilling over onto the lawn.

In the middle of the throng was Ken Matthews, the powerful blond captain of the Gladiators' football team. Next to him was Todd Wilkins and some of the other school jocks. All eyes were turned to them. Something had to be done.

"What are we going to do, Kenny?" somebody yelled. "They can't take our field."

"OK, calm down," Ken said, gazing out over the crowd. "Don't worry. Number one, the Gladiators have never lost anything without a fight!"

A roar of approval greeted this comment.

"And, number two," Todd added, "we need that field more than anyone else. They can build a factory or a garden anyplace!"

"Right on," somebody yelled.

"And it's ours!" Ken shouted.

Another roar from the assembled students.

Looking out the cafeteria window, Mrs. Waller, the school dietitian, saw the rally building in size. She put down her clipboard and hurried down the corridor to the gym.

"Coach!" Mrs. Waller called out.

Coach Schultz looked up from the play diagrams he was working on in preparation for the big game against the Palisades Pumas.

"What's the matter, Mrs. Waller?"

"Coach, I think we've got trouble. The football team is out in front of the school, and they're all worked up."

"My team?" said Coach Schultz, getting up quickly.

"Kenny Matthews is in the middle of it."

"What are we waiting for?"

And together, Coach Schultz and Mrs. Waller hurried upstairs toward the principal's office.

"Chrome Dome's going to have a fit," said Mrs. Waller.

"My boys won't do anything wrong," said Coach Schultz. "They're just high-spirited."

They swept into Mr. Cooper's office in time to hear the announcement on the school's intercom system.

"Coach Schultz, please report to the principal's office!"

"What are we going to do?" Jessica shouted, having pushed through the crowd to head up the cheerleaders.

"I'll tell you what we're going to do," Todd yelled. "We're going to stage a sit-in right on the football field!"

A cheer went up.

"If they want to build anything on this field, they're going to have to build it on top of us," Ken shouted to the crowd.

Another cheer went up, and the students began rushing across the great lawn toward the field.

"Come on!" Jessica yelled, piloting the cheerleaders.

"Follow me, Gladiators," Ken shouted.

And just like an army of Roman warriors, the student body cascaded across the campus, pouring out of the school, dropping everything, racing to take possession of the football field.

Inside his office Mr. Cooper watched in frustration.

"We've got to stop them!" he said.

But nobody could stop the rush of students now.

Elizabeth ran behind them, furiously taking notes on her steno pad about what was now the most exciting story ever to hit campus. And there was Todd, right in the middle of it all. By the time she got to the field, a group of angry kids had cornered Lila Fowler and Bruce Patman, the children of the two families involved.

"Hey, Fowler, what's with you?" Winston Egbert demanded of Lila. "Isn't your father rich enough already?"

"You leave my father out of this!" Lila screamed.

"A factory—how gross." Bruce Patman sneered. "That's all the Fowlers think of—grubby newcomers!"

"Listen to Mr. Two-Face," spat Winston.

"Yeah, your father wants some look-but-don't-touch *garden*," said Emily Mayer.

"Watch your face, Emily," Bruce said. "A garden would be an improvement over this mud shop. Besides, all the practice in the world won't help those lousy Gladiators!"

"You're a traitor, Patman!" somebody yelled.

"Where's your school spirit?" Jessica yelled at him.

"Aw, save it, Wakefield!"

"You and your family don't care about Sweet Valley High. You're a disgrace!" Jessica yelled.

"Hey, when it comes to having a disgrace in the family, Jessica Wakefield, just consider your dear sister, the pub crawler. And I do mean crawler!"

Elizabeth was taking notes when she heard it, and her face went bright red. Instantly she felt all eyes on her.

"You leave my sister out of this!" Jessica yelled.

"Why should we?" said Lila Fowler. "You're all treating Bruce and me like we're lepers! I thought you were a friend of mine, Jessica Wakefield."

"Lila, I am, but—"

"But, my backside," said Bruce. "And when it comes to a disgraceful family, Wakefield, how about your father and Marianna West—that trampy broad he's fooling around with."

"Now, just a minute," Elizabeth said, stepping forward. "Marianna West works for my father's law firm."

"Yeah? Where? On the couch, maybe?" Bruce sneered.

"You liar!"

Bruce laughed. "Sure! Your father spends all his time running around with a sexy woman, and you call that 'working for the firm.'"

"They're working together—to stop *you*," Elizabeth shouted.

"Yeah, yeah, yeah! Go put it in the paper!"

"Never mind that," Todd was saying, pushing his way to the front. "We're interested in saving the field. I think that's enough out of you," he told Bruce.

"OK," Ken shouted, climbing up onto the bleacher seats and addressing them all. "Are we giving up the field?"

"*No!*" came the roaring response.

"Are they putting up a factory?"

"*No!*"

"A garden?"

"*No!*"

96

"Come on, everybody," Jessica shouted. "The Gladiator cheer!"

She leaped down onto the track and led everybody in a Sweet Valley fight song.

Elizabeth frantically took notes, watching Todd from the corner of her eye.

This was the biggest story she had ever been given, but still Elizabeth kept hearing the hateful words Bruce Patman had flung out about her father and Marianna West.

Suddenly, as if seeing a missing puzzle piece falling into place, Elizabeth remembered the day the previous week when she'd accidentally walked into her parents' room while they were in the midst of an argument. Not an argument, really. They weren't shouting at each other or anything like that. It was more of a heated discussion. Her mother had seemed tense, and her father had worn an uncharacteristic frown.

She'd only caught the tail end of their conversation, but it had brought a sour taste to her mouth nevertheless.

"I never *said* my work was more important than yours," Ned Wakefield had argued in a voice straining to remain patient. "What I said was that it would be *nice* if we saw more of you. . . ."

It might have been just a minor complaint. Their mother had been working longer hours than usual lately, due to a special design project she was involved in. But the incident bothered Elizabeth because her parents almost never argued. The thought of anything coming between them struck her like a sudden blow. What if the argument was just the tip of an iceberg named Marianna West? *No*, Elizabeth told herself, *my imagination is running away with me again. It can't be true. It just can't.*

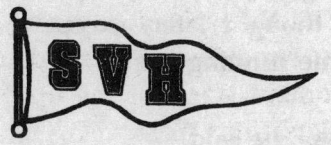

Ten

Elizabeth was almost finished taking notes and ready to head back to the *Oracle* office when it happened. There he was, suddenly, right in front of her, face to face, and there was no possibility of ignoring him.

"Hi, Todd."

"Liz," said Todd, his face lighting up. "Hey, isn't this something?"

"Yeah! I'm covering it for *The Oracle*."

"Wow, Liz, this is a big story. I always knew you'd be a great reporter."

"Really?"

"Sure."

Todd looked away then, as though remembering something, and fell silent.

"I was just heading back to school," Elizabeth said hopefully.

"Yeah? I'm going back, too."

They might have made up then and there, Elizabeth thought later, except that suddenly Jessica came running over.

"Todd!"

"Hi, Jess," he said.

"I want to talk to you. It's terribly important," she gushed.

"Oh—sure," Todd said.

Elizabeth walked away as quickly as she could. She thought she heard Todd call her, but she kept on going, across the campus to the *Oracle* office. It was the longest walk of her life.

Inside the office at last, Elizabeth sat at the typewriter and plunged into writing the story. It was like a doctor's prescription—it shut out all the pain and longing.

Write, she told herself. *Keep on writing. Forget everything else.*

Todd watched with a sense of loss as Elizabeth walked away. He'd had a precious moment when everything might have been set right, and he'd let it slip away.

Somebody was talking at him. It was Jessica Wakefield.

"Earth to Todd Wilkins," she was saying with a slight trace of irritation. He was such a hunk and just about the nicest guy at Sweet Valley High, but sometimes he seemed so dense!

"What did you say, Jessica?"

They were strolling along back toward the school again, and Jessica kept the pace leisurely. She wanted Todd to herself this time.

"Liz was sure in a hurry," he said.

"Yes," Jessica said slowly. "She's upset these days."

"I guess she would be," Todd said. "Living down a stunt like that isn't easy."

"That's what I wanted to talk to you about," Jessica began. "It's just terrible, what's happening. What kids are saying."

"But it's all true, Jessica! I'd give anything to find out it wasn't."

"Oh, Todd," Jessica whimpered, and she ran a few steps to a bench on the lawn and collapsed onto it. Todd was beside her in a minute.

"What's the matter, Jessica?"

Jessica was crying with abandon, holding her face in her hands and sobbing. Her shoulders shook. She wouldn't look at him.

"Hey—Jess!"

Todd sat beside her and pulled her close, holding her against him as she cried. "Come on, now. It can't be that bad."

"Oh, Todd! I just can't stand it, what people are saying about Elizabeth. I love her more than anything in the world. I can't let her be treated like this."

Jessica looked up into Todd's concerned face, into his wonderfully tender brown eyes, and her heart fluttered.

"Todd, it could have happened to anyone! It's not fair! Why, it could have happened to *me*."

"Come on, Jessica. It didn't just happen. She knew what she was doing."

Jessica took a deep breath. "Todd, I can't let this go on. Elizabeth is my sister. I love her! Todd—it wasn't Elizabeth at Kelly's."

"It wasn't?"

"No. Todd, it was me!"

"What?"

"Yes. Me. My sister is *not* going to be blamed for this thing. It's not fair."

Jessica was totally amazed at what happened next. Todd Wilkins stared deeply into her eyes for a long moment, then slowly shook his head as though in wonder.

"I've never heard anything so noble," he finally said.

"What?"

"You'd take the blame for your sister? Jessica, I don't think I've ever known how truly special you are until this moment."

"But, Todd—"

Todd pulled her close, holding her tightly in

102

his strong arms for what seemed an eternity. Then he gently kissed her. He didn't even hear the whistles and yells from the students who saw the whole thing, right in the center of the campus in the middle of the afternoon.

Jessica sat there, stunned. Never in her wildest dreams had she imagined that telling the truth could be so rewarding.

"Jessica, you're wonderful," Todd said.

"Todd, you're the greatest guy I've ever met, do you know that?"

"Listen! I'm taking you to the Phi Ep dance!"

"What?"

"That is, if you want to go with me."

"Want to? Oh, Todd!" And she was around his neck once more. "I want it more than anything in the world."

The first thing Elizabeth heard about as she left the *Oracle* office, was about the Big Love Scene between Todd and Jessica on the bench in the center of campus.

"Wow," Winston Egbert hooted, stopping Elizabeth as she came out of the school building. "The temperature went up about fifty degrees here a little while ago."

"What happened, Winston?"

"A certain beautiful cheerleader and a certain handsome basketball captain went into a clinch right out in front of the world, and the mercury soared!"

"Oh," said Elizabeth. Her heart ached.

"I thought Todd was going after you, but now I see it's Jessica. Boy, talk about showing your feelings in public."

"Why are you so surprised, Winston? You of all people. You've been in love with Jessica since fifth grade. She's fantastic, and you know it."

"Oh, I *know* she is, but so are you!"

"Oh, well . . ."

"Who are you going to the dance with?"

"Good question, Winston."

They walked down the steps. There, at the foot, Bruce Patman was gliding up to them in his black Porsche.

"Well, well, well," Bruce said to Elizabeth. "If it isn't Roadhouse Rhoda."

Elizabeth froze.

"Listen, I never thought you were such a fast number until now. But from what I hear, I've decided you're my type. I'd like to take you to the dance."

"Is that so?" Elizabeth snapped.

"Sure. I can't stand most of these wimpy girls. We can put in an appearance at the dance, then head for someplace where we can have some real fun."

All the pent-up fury suddenly burst from her.

All the anguish and the hurt and the pain caused by the snickering and whispering and innuendos spilled out.

"Bruce Patman, I'd rather stay home for the rest of my life than go anywhere with you! But, as a matter of fact, I have a date."

"Yeah? Who with?"

"Me!"

Elizabeth spun around.

There stood Winston Egbert, looking shocked at the sound of his own voice.

"You?" Bruce Patman laughed. "You, the joke of the school?"

"Yeah? Well, maybe I'm a joke, but you're an insult."

Bruce Patman started to climb out of the car, his face flushed and mean. "You stupid nothing, I'll fold you up and stuff you in the trash can!"

Elizabeth stepped between them. "Never mind, Bruce. It happens to be true. Win and I are going to the dance."

She linked her arm in Winston's and led him away, leaving Bruce Patman sitting in his car with his mouth open in astonishment.

"Listen, I'm sorry," Winston said when they were out of earshot from Bruce. "I just got so mad! I won't hold you to it."

'Wait a minute. What is this, Win? Are you standing me up?"

'Huh?"

"You asked me for a date, didn't you?"

"Well—I—aw, Liz, I just couldn't help it."

"Pick me up at seven-thirty, OK?"

Winston Egbert stared at the beautiful, popular, intelligent Elizabeth Wakefield and almost fainted.

"OK!" he said, astounded, then turned and raced madly across campus, screaming like a deranged chimpanzee.

For the first time in ages, Elizabeth laughed long and hard. Then she turned her steps toward home. She would have fun with Winston at the dance, she really would. It was difficult not to laugh when he was around.

She felt a lot better now and walked along jauntily. She even began whistling. It wasn't until she reached her own street that her steps faltered and she wondered if she was whistling for some reason other than happiness. Maybe, just maybe, it kept her from hearing her own painful thoughts.

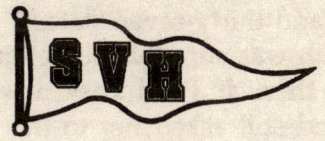

Eleven

Elizabeth dragged herself through the house and into the kitchen. She pulled a carton of milk out of the refrigerator and poured a glassful. As she drank, she chanted inwardly, *I am happy for Jess . . . I am happy for Jess. . . .But I'm so miserable I could die!*

Just then the front door slammed shut, and Elizabeth heard Jessica shout, "Lizzie! Lizzie! Oh, Lizzie, you're not going to believe this!"

Jessica burst into the room, and it was the Fourth of July, Christmas morning, and Mardi Gras all rolled into one ecstatic, beautiful, blond sixteen-year-old.

"I told him, Liz, I told him everything. I told him that it was me with Rick Andover at Kelly's—and he *still* invited me to the dance!"

"You told him, Jess? He knows it wasn't me?"

"I told him *everything*, and he forgave me! He has got to be the most wonderful boy in a hundred and thirty-seven states!"

Elizabeth was sure that something inside her died just then. If Todd knew it was Jessica at Kelly's and still asked her to the dance—well, she knew where that left her. Nowhere. She would go to the dance with Winston, have a wonderful time, get busy on her writing, and forget about Todd. *How in the world are you going to do that?* she asked herself.

"That's sensational, Jess. You're going to have a terrific time. I hear Todd is a great dancer."

"He's great at everything, I think!" Jessica was bubbling over. "Where's Mom? I can't wait to tell her all about this."

"She's going to be late. An appointment, I think."

"Again?" Jessica pouted. "That makes three nights in a row! I thought mothers were supposed to stay home and fix dinner once in a while!"

Elizabeth wondered how her sister could possibly descend from cloud nine with Todd Wilkins to the pits of depression so fast—and simply because she had to do a little thing like help fix dinner.

"Mom told us this morning that she was going to be late, Jess," Elizabeth said patiently, trying to hide her unhappiness and control her temper all at the same time.

"Well, it's not fair," Jessica complained, storming around the kitchen. "She has ruined my day, totally and absolutely!"

Elizabeth stared at her sister in amazement. Had Jessica flipped out? How could anyone ruin a day that included a dance invitation from Todd Wilkins? She imagined how she would feel if Todd had asked her. She would be so far off the ground she'd need a pilot's license. The thought of Todd's arms around her, the two of them dancing to slow, romantic music, made her knees so weak she had to clutch the counter with both hands to keep standing. Then she thought of how the evening would end—they'd be alone, totally alone . . . his arms would hold her close to him . . . his lips—

"Liz! You haven't heard a word I've said," Jessica accused.

"What?" said Elizabeth, reluctantly coming out of her daydream.

"My very own sister is turning into an airhead right before my eyes. I was *trying* to find out what time Mom will be home. *If* she's coming home at all. She's practically never home anymore. Of course, if you're too busy to talk to me, just say so, Elizabeth." Jessica was working herself up to the rage of the century.

Elizabeth turned toward her sister. One look at Jessica's unhappy face was all it took.

"Oh, Jess, I'm sorry," she said, giving her a

quick hug. "This hasn't been a world-class day for me. You have every right to be happy. I want you to know that I'm really pleased for you." *After all*, she thought with just a trace of bitterness, *somebody in this family should be happy*.

"Liz! Stop it, Lizzie! You're doing it again."

"I'm listening, I'm listening. I swear it! Why is it so important to know when Mom's going to get home?"

"I want to tell her about this sensational day. And I absolutely have to talk her into getting me that perfect—oh, Lizzie, you should see it— perfect dress at the mall." The sunshine was definitely back in Jessica's face and voice.

"Tell me all about it," Elizabeth said, then sighed, *"while* you're setting the table. Let me check out the freezer to see what I can toss into the microwave."

"Well, it's blue. It's slinky—"

"Don't forget the table, Jess."

Jessica glared at her sister's back for a moment but decided she'd better set the table if she expected Elizabeth to listen to her.

"Did I say blue—and slinky?" As Elizabeth nodded, Jessica continued. "It has a handkerchief hemline and—wait till you hear this, Lizzie— spaghetti straps and a neckline *so* low Todd will be panting."

"Sounds like a case of overkill to me, Jess, and as a man, I feel sorry for the intended victim."

Both girls spun around in surprise. Steven was standing just inside the archway between the kitchen and dining room.

"Steve!" they chorused.

"I'm starved. Is there enough of whatever that's going to be for one more?" he asked, gesturing at the frozen food package Elizabeth was opening.

"Sure," she said. "It's just the three of us for dinner tonight. But I thought you—I mean, aren't you going out tonight?"

"No," he answered flatly.

The twins exchanged worried looks.

"It's probably a good thing Mom and Dad aren't here," he said bitterly. "I'm definitely not up to a repeat of last weekend's third degree!"

"I'm sure they don't mean to grill you, Steve, they're just concerned and—"

"For Pete's sake, Liz, not you, too! Why can't *everyone* in this house mind their own business!"

"This family has got to be the biggest bummer in five hundred and thirty-seven cities!" Jessica exploded. "Boring! Boring! Boring!" She stomped around the room, with the full attention of her brother and sister. Then she whirled, pointing a finger at Elizabeth.

"You," she sputtered, "act like you're a candidate for the funny farm. All you do is mope, mope, mope! And *you!*" She suddenly shifted to Steven. "What a ray of sunshine you are!

And on top of everything else, I was humiliated in front of every single person in school because my very own father is having an affair with that—that *woman!*"

Steven's head snapped up, and he glared at Jessica. "What are you talking about?"

"Oh, Steve," she cried, "it's all over school, all over town. Dad has been with Marianna West almost every single night, and Mom acts like she doesn't care at all. They're headed for the divorce courts! What's going to happen to us?"

"Stop it, Jess," Elizabeth broke in. "Just because Bruce Patman shot off his mouth doesn't mean that any of it is true."

"Any of what?" Steven wanted to know. "Will one of you please tell me what's going on around here?"

"Well, Dad *has* been spending a lot of evenings with Ms. West," Elizabeth said, groping for the right words. "He says he's helping her with a case."

"He *says*," put in Jessica.

"But you two don't believe him?"

"No!" Jessica blurted out.

It took Elizabeth a few moments longer to speak. "I want to believe him, Steve, but things have been sort of strange around here lately, and—I just don't know."

"Does Mom seem worried or upset?" he asked.

112

"No, and that's the trouble!" Jessica raged. "How can she be so blind? Dad is so good-looking—at least for a man his age—and Mari-anna is kind of attractive, if you like the flashy type. Of course they're having an affair. What else are we supposed to think?"

"You could try believing Dad, for starters," Steve said angrily. He walked restlessly around the room. "Dad has never lied to us. If he says he's helping her with a case, that's what he's doing."

"Isn't that just like a man!" Jessica spat. "You always stick up for each other. You're just as bad as Dad. As a matter of fact, you're just like him. You *both* have bad taste in women!"

It would have taken a machete to slice through the tension in the room. Jessica and Steven sat glaring at each other.

Obviously trying to control his rage, Steven spoke in a low, cold voice. "You've got five seconds to explain that crack, Jessica!"

Jessica had spoken without thinking, not un-usual for her, and she was afraid of the consequences. She had never seen Steven so angry with her before. She had to say something, quickly.

"Steve, I meant—I mean, I didn't mean—how can you stand there glaring at me so hatefully? This was supposed to be my happy day, and now you're trying to ruin it!" Jessica buried her face in her arms, sobbing helplessly.

113

"You selfish little twerp," Steven said, glaring at Jessica.

Elizabeth jumped in quickly between them. "Steve, please, you don't understand," she pleaded.

"Don't you ever get tired of defending her?" Steve snapped.

"You don't understand what kind of a day it's been for Jess and me. You don't know what people said about Dad." Elizabeth was getting desperate. She had to make Steven see. "Steve, we know! We know about you and—her."

That stopped him. He looked at her for a long moment. "You know about me and *her*? What's that supposed to mean?" he demanded.

Elizabeth took a deep breath and plunged in. "Steve, we know everything. We weren't snooping around or trying to butt in, honest!"

"I'm sorry, too, Steve," Jessica added. "I shouldn't have blurted it like that. But you and Betsy Martin—it can't be. She's trash."

"*Betsy* Martin? What are you talking about? I'm in love with *Tricia* Martin."

"Tricia? You mean Betsy's sister?" Elizabeth asked, stunned.

"Yeah, Tricia." Saying her name conjured up memories for Steven. Lovely Tricia with her strawberry-blond hair, her sweet nature, everything he wanted in this world.

"That's wonderful, Steve," Elizabeth said.

114

"Tricia is a terrific girl—one of the best! I'm so happy for you!"

"She's still a Martin," Jessica reminded him.

"Not to worry, Jess. Nothing important is going to happen between the *respected* Wakefield family and the low-life Martins. Basically because I blew it. Oh, boy, did I blow it!"

Steven's unhappy story spilled out. As long as he and Tricia were alone together at Tricia's house, everything had been wonderful. But gradually Tricia had concluded that Steven didn't want to be seen in public with her, that he was ashamed to be associated with her family. That was why he never took her anywhere. "You're a snob, Steven Wakefield!" she had said.

"She's right, too," Steven said to the twins. "And now I've lost Tricia—forever."

As Elizabeth stared at her brother, she was filled with despair. She recalled the old saying about trouble coming in threes. She counted:

I've lost Todd.

Steve's lost Tricia.

Mom losing Dad would make it three.

Jessica, she noted coolly, was the only one who had managed to escape unscathed so far.

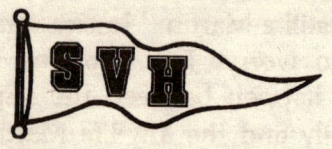

Twelve

"You're not serious. You absolutely cannot be going with Winston Egbert!" screeched Jessica as she stood in the middle of Elizabeth's room. "I can't believe my own sister dating that clown!"

It was the evening before the dance, but Jessica had been so preoccupied with her own plans for the big night that she hadn't heard about Elizabeth and Winston until an hour earlier at dinner.

"I don't understand why you're so upset about it, Jess," Elizabeth said as she sat on her bed, her history book in her lap. "Win's a nice guy. He's really funny. And even if he's not handsome, he doesn't have three heads, for heaven's sake!"

"But he's not romantic, Lizzie," Jessica pointed out.

"That suits me just fine. I can relax and have a good time without worrying about groping hands and fighting someone off at the front door." Elizabeth sighed, knowing Todd would never be so crude. A good-night kiss from him would be nothing short of heaven.

Jessica heard the sigh and saw the faraway look on her sister's face.

"Lizzie," she began in what she hoped was a casual tone, "are you going with Winston because you really want to, or because nobody else asked you?"

Elizabeth hesitated to tell her sister about Bruce Patman's invitation. She doubted that Jessica would see it her way. At the time it had made her furious, but now it seemed kind of funny. The look on his face had been priceless. Nobody, but *nobody*, turned Bruce Patman down for a date.

"Actually, Jess, someone else did ask me first. Bruce Patman."

"Bruce Patman!" Jessica squealed. "Liz Wakefield, how dare you sit there calmly and tell me Bruce asked you out as if it weren't important! You're incredible! No—you must be dead! No girl alive would turn Bruce down. He's handsome, Liz. He is sooooo rich. And he drives that awesome Porsche!" Jessica stood there, hands on hips, glaring down at her sister. Jessica would never say no to Bruce. She thought for a minute of how it would be to arrive at a dance with him. Once in a while it seemed to Jessica that Bruce was on the verge of asking her out, but it hadn't happened, *yet*.

"Are you saying you wish you were going to the dance with Bruce instead of Todd?" Elizabeth challenged.

"Of course not. Why in the world would you think that? Todd is terribly good-looking, and he's so sweet. I just wish he didn't drive that gross excuse for a car. Bruce's Porsche is so—so . . . I mean, it's a *Porsche*."

"Let's get off the subject of Bruce Patman, *please*." Elizabeth got up off the bed and walked over to her table, where she picked up some notes. "Right now I've got to study for tomorrow's history quiz."

"Yeah, OK, I'm going." Jessica hesitated at the door. "Just one thing, Liz."

Elizabeth looked up from the notes.

"Are you sure it's all right? You know, about Todd and me and the dance?" There was genuine concern in Jessica's blue-green eyes.

"Jess, I don't know what you're—"

"Please tell me the truth. Sometimes you get a funny faraway look when Todd's name is mentioned. I wondered if you sort of liked him. If it makes you unhappy, I won't go out with him, I swear! I'll stay home tomorrow." By this time, Jessica was on the other side of the table, clutching Elizabeth's hands. She really seemed concerned.

A flood of love for her sister washed over Elizabeth. She knew how important the dance was for Jessica. She couldn't, she *wouldn't* spoil it for her.

"Who's being an airhead now, Jess? We're both going to that dance, and we'll have a sensational time! The Wakefield sisters are going to be *so* terrific!"

"How terrific are we going to be, Liz?" asked Jessica, happy once again.

"Get out of here, you idiot," said Elizabeth, grabbing a small pillow and aiming it at Jessica.

As soon as Jessica left the room, the smile left Elizabeth's face. *Will it really be such a terrific night?* she asked herself, tears filling her eyes.

"Thanks, Jess. Thanks a bunch," Elizabeth called from the bathroom that adjoined the twins' rooms. She was wrapped in a towel.

"You're welcome, but for what?" Jessica shouted over the whir of the hair dryer.

"For leaving me the steamiest bathroom in the entire state and exactly thirty seconds of hot water!" Elizabeth hollered back.

"Oops," Jessica said, poking her head into the room. "I'm sorry. Would you believe I got carried away?"

"It wouldn't be the first time."

"What do you think?" Jessica gave her golden mane a toss. "I mean, be totally honest. Is my hair OK?"

"Ummm, let me look." She circled Jessica. Every hair was exactly where it should be—perfect.

"Sad, Jess. It's really sad."

"*What?*" screeched Jessica. "What are you saying?"

"I just thought, you know—poor Vidal Sassoon on the unemployment line because you're better than he is."

Elizabeth fell on the bed laughing. "Gotcha, Jess!" she shouted triumphantly.

"Hi, Mrs. Wakefield. I'm Todd Wilkins. I'm here to pick up Li—Jessica, I mean, for the dance."

"Come in, Todd. It's nice to meet you. Jess will be down in a minute." She ushered him into the large, airy living room.

The doorbell rang again.

"Excuse me, Todd, this seems to be a busy night."

Alice Wakefield brought Winston Egbert into the room. "You two know each other, I assume?"

"Sure. Hi, Winston."

"Hey, Todd! How about the two of us,

huh? Escorting the beautiful Wakefield sisters. Wow!"

Todd and Winston stood in the living room waiting for Elizabeth and Jessica. Gone were the school uniforms of jeans and T-shirts. Both wore neatly pressed cords, shirts and ties, and sport coats.

Elizabeth was the first to come down the stairs, and both Todd and Winston watched her descend. The white strapless dress was perfect with her tanned skin and blond hair. She kept the bright smile on her face even when she saw Todd. Why couldn't she and Winston have been gone before Todd arrived? she asked herself.

Winston nervously looked toward the stairs as if he were expecting someone else. Then he nearly threw himself at Elizabeth's feet. Spreading his arms wide and looking upward, he declared, "I've died. I've died and gone to heaven!" Getting up, he made a grand bow. "Princess Elizabeth, you are totally—totally—that's what you are, Liz Wakefield—totally!"

Elizabeth found herself laughing so hard she was nearly in tears. "Win Egbert, you are totally crazy! And if you make me cry and ruin my eye makeup, I'll kill you! So help me, I'll kill you!"

Alice Wakefield was smiling that particular smile every mother does when her child is happy.

Todd Wilkins, however, was not smiling. His

121

expression was a strange mixture of anger and sadness.

Jessica, out of sight but not out of earshot in the upstairs hall, was also not smiling. *How dare that idiot Win Egbert spoil my entrance?* she asked herself. He was acting like an airhead, and she would never speak to him again.

"My lady, our coach awaits!" Winston said as he opened the door with a flourish.

Elizabeth laughed. "I knew it. You're taking me to the dance in a pumpkin!"

Winston was still chuckling as he followed her outside. "Close," he said. "It's orange, and it doesn't go very fast."

They both dissolved into giggles as he led her over to the orange VW bug parked in the driveway.

Alice Wakefield was still laughing when the door closed. "Those two are really too much, aren't they, Todd?"

"Yeah, too much," he answered somewhat sourly.

Just then Jessica made her entrance. She looked nothing less than sensational. The blue dress with its delicate straps and full skirt showed off her slim body and gorgeous legs.

"Hello, Todd," she said softly, her mouth curved in a lovely smile.

"Hi, Jess," he answered. "You look nice— really very pretty."

Nice! she screamed silently. *Three hours of working on my nails, my hair, my makeup and I look "very pretty"? Whatever happened to gorgeous?*

"Thanks, Todd." *Maybe he's not good with words,* she thought. But she knew from the other day that he was good with kissing—and there certainly would be more kisses that evening!

The Droids were playing loudly, and the lights were bright as Jessica and Todd arrived at the dance.

"Oh, Todd, isn't it wonderful?" She wrapped her arm around his. "Look at the hearts!" she cried, pointing out the red and silver 3-D foil hearts with PBA on one side and PE on the other. "It's so romantic. A sweetheart dance!" She sighed.

"Yeah, it's nice, Jess," he answered, his eyes scanning the room.

Jessica wasn't sure how many more *nices* she could take. Something was going wrong with her evening, and it had better stop right now!

"Todd, look! There's Cara Walker. Let's go talk to her. And there's Lila Fowler. And poor Bruce Patman came stag tonight."

"*Poor* Bruce Patman?"

"Oh, I didn't mean *poor*," she bubbled. "It's just that he's one of the many guys who invited

Liz to the dance tonight. My sister is soooo popular, Todd."

"So I've heard, Jess, so I've heard." His voice tightened. "We're here to dance, right? Let's dance!"

The Droids were playing a hard, driving number as Todd pulled Jessica onto the dance floor. They were both great dancers, and they looked so terrific together that the other couples moved out of their way. Jessica danced around Todd, her dress flaring out as she twirled. Her beautiful tanned legs caught every boy's eyes. Then she and Todd really started getting into the music, in a very sexy way. As the number came to an end, the crowd erupted with applause, whistles, and cries for more. Jessica threw her arms around Todd and hugged him. She never noticed Todd staring across the room at a set of identical blue-green eyes.

"Hey, Liz, remember me? Your wonderful date-type person?" Winston said.

"Oh, Win!"

"Yeah, good old forgettable Win. How about a dance, Liz? Nobody's going to desert the floor when I do my thing, but I promise not to break all your toes."

"Let's go, Win," Elizabeth said, knowing she

couldn't spend the whole evening watching Jessica and Todd.

"We seem to be here with the wrong people, Liz," he said as they moved somewhat awkwardly around the floor. Contrary to Winston's promise, Elizabeth had to be very careful about her toes.

"Huh?"

"Well," he explained, "you're watching Todd, and he's practically got his eyes glued on you."

"Really, Win? You really think he's watching me?"

"Really, really, really, Liz. The only thing wrong is that your gorgeous sister is watching him, too. I wish she were watching me."

"Oh, Win. You're still loyal to Jessica, huh?"

"You'd better believe it," he said in a serious tone Elizabeth had never heard him use before. Then suddenly he made a hideous face that cracked her up. He was back to being the clown again.

"You want to know the sort of girl people fix me up with?" he asked. "It goes like this: 'Win, have I got a girl for you! What a personality!' That always means two hundred and fifty pounds and two-foot-five! I have to put her hamburger on the floor so she can reach it."

"But, Win," Elizabeth said, laughing, "looks aren't everything."

"Yeah, I know. I'm no prize package, either,

right?" He grinned affably. "Hey, Enid and Ronnie are waving at us. Let's go over and say hello, OK?"

As they made their way around the dancers, Elizabeth commented, "I don't think Ronnie has left her side all evening. He's certainly protective."

"Yeah. I think he was a Doberman in a former life," Winston cracked.

A set of brown eyes followed Elizabeth's every move, a fact that did not go unnoticed by Jessica, who was rapidly reaching the boiling point. Her evening was going right down the tubes, and it was all Todd's fault. She had done everything—and with Jessica, that was plenty—to keep his eyes on her. Except for that one sensational dance, he had hardly looked at her.

No guy—not even Todd Wilkins—could take Jessica Wakefield to a dance and treat her like a piece of furniture. He wasn't going to get away with it, she vowed.

Later that night Elizabeth sat on her bed and sighed with relief that the long evening was finally over. A bunch of the kids had gone out for pizza after the dance, but she had persuaded Winston to bring her home. She knew she couldn't bear seeing Todd and Jessica together one minute longer. What were they doing now? she wondered. Were they kissing? Were they . . . ? *Stop torturing yourself!*

At that very moment, Todd was saying good night to Jessica at the front door.

Nervously he shifted his weight from one foot to the other. "Jessica," he finally mumbled, "thanks. Thanks a lot. It's been a—a really great evening."

Not yet it hasn't, Jessica thought. *But it could still end up great.*

She placed her hands lightly on his shoulders and swayed close to him.

"Oh, Todd," she breathed, closing her eyes and raising her face for a kiss.

But the kiss, when it came, was nothing like what she'd expected. Jessica's heart went into a tailspin. A kiss on the cheek! Like he was her *brother*, for cripe's sake! She'd never been so humiliated in her entire life!

"Yeah, really great, Jess. See you at school."

And he was gone.

"You creep!" Jessica said aloud as she stood there by herself. "Todd Wilkins, I swear I'll get even with you if it's the last thing I ever do!"

Elizabeth reached out to turn off her light but stopped when she heard the front door close.

Jessica was home. *I suppose I'll have to listen to every dreamy detail.*

Jessica stuck her head into the room. "Can we talk for a minute, Liz?"

"Sure, Jess. Tell me all about it. I'll bet you had one fabulous time tonight!"

"Fabulous?"

"Well, of course. An evening with Todd. Good-looking, good dancer, super-nice guy. What more could you want?"

Jessica suddenly knew how she was going to get even with Todd. That "nice guy" image was about to be destroyed.

"Oh, Liz, it was so awful!" Jessica's eyes filled with tears.

"Awful? What are you talking about, Jess?"

"I thought he liked me, Lizzie," she said between sobs. "I thought he respected me and everything!"

"Jessie, what happened?"

"Oh, Liz, I can't. I can't tell you!" Jessica collapsed, covering her face with her hands. "I'm—I'm too ashamed."

Elizabeth put her arm around Jessica's shoulder. "It's all right, Jess. You can tell me anything, you know that."

"Maybe I should tell you." Jessica sniffled. "You really should be warned about him. You might go out with him sometime, and I'd just never forgive myself if I didn't tell you what the *real* Todd Wilkins is like."

"What did he do?"

"That rat tried just about everything. The horrible thing was that I could hardly make him stop. I had to beg him and beg him to please stop!"

"Oh, no." Elizabeth moaned, squeezing Jessica's shoulder in sympathy. "I can't believe it."

"I know. I couldn't believe it either. I even remember saying to him as I was fighting him off that I couldn't believe it."

"And what did he do *then*?" Elizabeth asked, flushed with anger.

"I don't remember. But, oh, Liz, it was awful. He just wouldn't stop. His hands! Oh, God, they were everywhere. And—"

"Don't tell me any more. I've heard enough."

Jessica wiped away the tears with the back of her hand. "Lizzie, you're not mad at me for telling you, are you?" she asked. "I just didn't want you ever to be in that kind of situation. I wanted to protect you, Lizzie."

"Of course I'm not mad, Jess. Not at *you*, anyway," Elizabeth exploded. "How dare Todd Wilkins treat you that way? How dare he! I'll kill him—absolutely kill him!" she raged.

No need, Liz, Jessica said to herself. *I just took care of that myself.*

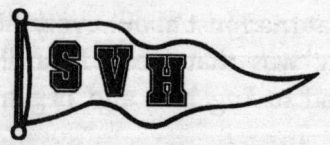

Thirteen

The knock on the door was soft but persistent.

"Steve?"

No answer. Ned Wakefield knocked again.

"I have to talk to you."

Mr. Wakefield turned the doorknob slowly. The room was in total darkness, although it was almost nine in the morning. He pulled up the shades and walked toward the bed, where his son was hidden under the blankets.

"Hey."

Steven didn't stir.

Ned Wakefield sat on the bed and poked the lump under the blankets. "I'm not going away, so you might as well come out."

The blanket fell away from his face, and Steven blinked at his father. There was a two-day beard on his face, and his eyes were bloodshot and swollen.

"You look terrible," said Mr. Wakefield.

Steven sat up on the side of the bed and held his face in his hands. "Why not? I feel terrible."

"Listen, Steve, I used to think my troubles would go away if I hid out long enough, too. But they won't."

"Thanks, Dr. Wakefield."

"You're welcome. Now, get up, shave, take a shower, and come on down. Let's talk."

"I thought you had an important case to work on."

"I have. Wakefield versus Wakefield. Up!"

Back downstairs, Alice Wakefield looked at her husband with concern. "Is he up?"

"He's coming down."

"Thank goodness."

They had known that Steven was depressed the last two weekends he had been home. This weekend was worse. Steven had been hiding in his bedroom for two days with no explanation. When he had not gone back to school Sunday night, Alice and Ned Wakefield had cornered the twins and demanded to know what was happening. It was like pulling teeth. Neither Elizabeth nor Jessica wanted to squeal on their older brother. But eventually the story about Tricia Martin had come out.

Steven looked much better when he came

downstairs. He sat down at the table, and his mother put orange juice in front of him, but he pushed it aside.

"Not hungry, Mom."

"Hmmm. This *must* be serious," his mother said lightly. She was rewarded with a glare that might have bored holes through a brick wall. "Sorry."

"Steve, let me tell you something," his father said. "Anything you're going through, *I* went through."

"Sure."

"Yeah—*sure*. And so did your mother."

"Mom?" That got his attention. "Aw, what do you mean. You two—"

"What?"

"Nothing."

"We never had a problem in our lives? Is that what you think?" said Mrs. Wakefield.

Steven picked up the glass of orange juice and sipped it. He felt uncomfortable talking about his mom and dad, especially now when there might be something going on with Marianna West.

"But never mind us," said his father. "What's all this about Tricia Martin?"

Steven sighed. "The twins told you? Oh, well. It doesn't matter anyway."

"Why'd you have to keep it a big secret?" Alice Wakefield asked. "Tricia's a lovely girl."

132

"Yeah, I know. But her family . . ."

Ned and Alice Wakefield exchanged glances. Tricia Martin's family was no bargain, and they knew it. Her father was the town drunk, and her sister Betsy had a horrible reputation. The mother had died of leukemia when the kids were little, which really had torn the family apart. It was all understandable, but that didn't make it any easier. And now Steven was mixed up with them. The question was, how seriously?

"Listen," Steven was saying, "this is really no big deal. Just forget it." He started to rise again, but his father's hand on his arm sat him back down.

"Steve, anything that's kept you hiding out for two days is important enough for me. How serious are you about Tricia?"

"Well, Dad, I think I'm in love with her. She's really terrific."

"And how does she feel about you?" Alice Wakefield asked.

Steven got up and paced around the kitchen. "She hates me! She'll never speak to me again. And it's all my fault. I don't deserve such a great girl."

The anguished tale then poured out of Steven Wakefield. He heaped abuse upon himself as he told them how he had pretended that her family's problems didn't matter. He loved her

133

"anyway," he had told her, and he was above that sort of thing.

"She saw right through me," Steven said bitterly. "She saw the truth—a truth I didn't even realize—that I was ashamed of her family. That I didn't consider her good enough for me but that I would accept her out of the goodness of my heart. What an idiot I was! Now it's all over. She never wants to see me again. And I don't blame her. I'm just miserable."

"Have you told Tricia what you just told us?" said his mother.

Steven stopped pacing. Slowly he sat down at the table. He poured some coffee and sipped it. He shook his head.

"I couldn't do that, Mom."

"Why?"

"It would be too—I'd sound like such a jerk."

"Is it the truth, Steven?"

"That I'm a jerk? Yes, it's true."

"No, no—that you didn't realize what you were doing."

"Yes," Steven said slowly. "That's true."

"Do you still love Tricia?"

"Oh, yes." Not a moment's hesitation.

"Then go and tell her exactly what you told us."

"It's the only thing you can do," Ned Wakefield urged.

Steven looked at the table for a moment, and

when he spoke, he couldn't face his parents. He asked quietly, "What do you think of my being involved with the Martins?"

"You're not involved with the Martins, Steven. You're involved with Tricia."

"You don't mind?"

Ned and Alice Wakefield glanced at each other.

"Steven, you can't judge a person by his or her family," said Mrs. Wakefield. "I won't pretend that the Martins don't make me uneasy. But if you love Tricia, then you've got to fight for her. She's *Tricia* Martin—not Betsy, not her father."

Steven was up on his feet again, pacing. "You're sure you approve of Tricia, Mom? Dad?"

"Steven, it's whether *you* approve of her," Ned Wakefield said. "Follow your own judgment—as well as your heart."

Steven searched his father's face anxiously and then his mother's, looking for a clue to the pain and suffering they might be undergoing. Was this long-lasting, seemingly warm and solid marriage on the verge of destruction? Steven wished he could tell, but it was impossible. Whatever their problems, they were united to help him. Steven felt love racing through him, and he suddenly grabbed his mother in a bear hug.

"Hey—"

"I love you, Mom!"

"I love you, too, Steve."

"You, too, Dad," he said, grabbing his father's hand.

And then Steven vaulted through the kitchen door, dashed out the front door, and was gone, on his way to Tricia Martin's house.

Steven drove up to the Martin's saggy-roofed ranch house, a neglected old place that badly needed a paint job and general cleanup. As he approached the door, he could hear Tricia coaxing her father into his room.

"Come on, Pop. Lie down and get some sleep. You'll feel a lot better," Tricia said.

Steven opened the door and entered quietly. Tricia was returning to the living room.

"Steve!" she gasped. "What are you doing here? I thought I'd made it clear—we have nothing more to say to one another."

"There is one more thing I have to say, Tricia," Steven said softly. "I'm sorry. I'm sorry I acted like such a jerk. You were right. I *was* being patronizing, but I was too stupid to realize it. Can you forgive me, Trish, for being a complete fool? I love you. I love you so much."

"Oh, Steve," Trish said. "I love you, too."

She was so beautiful and fragile at that moment, Steven thought, her brown eyes shining, her hair floating about her oval face in a red-gold cloud.

With tears streaming down their faces, Steven and Tricia shared a long, tender kiss.

"I'm sorry, sweetheart, I'm so sorry," Steven said softly, planting gentle kisses on her eyes, her nose, and her forehead.

"Tricia! Tricia, come here," a voice called from the other room.

"My father needs me, Steve. I have to go to him."

"Can we talk later? There's so much I want to tell you. How about a long conversation over clams and a shake at the Dairi Burger tonight?" Steven asked, holding her face in his hands.

Tricia beamed a radiant smile. "OK, see you around eight." She rushed into her father's room as a very happy and relieved Steven Wakefield let himself out the front door.

The evening had been beautiful, Steven mused as he drove home after dropping Tricia off. His thoughts swirled pleasantly around her lovely image. And then, as though to cap off the evening perfectly, he spotted his father's rust-brown LTD just ahead of him. It would be fun to follow his dad home and thank him for helping him with what had seemed a hopeless mess. Steven turned on some soft music and cruised quietly along, dreaming happy dreams. He wasn't ready for the turn his father suddenly made into a side street.

Without really thinking, Steven turned also and followed the car. Only then did he notice that there was someone else in the car with his father.

Marianna West!

Steven didn't know what to do. He certainly hadn't planned to spy on his father. But there he was, following his father and Marianna— and wondering what in heaven's name was going on. It was too late, he realized, for them to be coming home from work.

The LTD began to slow down.

Steven slowed down, too. He couldn't pass them now. He slid his car into the shadows of a hedge along the drive and parked there.

The LTD pulled into a driveway and stopped. Marianna West got out. So did Steven's father. They were laughing together about something as they walked toward Marianna's white-shuttered house.

"Oh, no." Steven moaned. He didn't *want* to believe it, but the evidence was too glaring to ignore.

He sat in the car for a long time, waiting for his father to come out. He listened to at least a dozen songs on the radio, without hearing any of the music, before he finally gave up and drove home. Everyone was asleep when he got there.

Steven paused outside his parents' bedroom door on his way upstairs. The lights were off, so he knew his mother wasn't sitting up worrying. *Poor Mom*, he thought, *if she only knew* . . .

Steven crawled into bed, but he didn't want to go to sleep. He wanted to be awake when his father arrived home—*if* he came home at all.

Fourteen

Elizabeth couldn't remember a time when life had been such a mess. Everything was in a shambles. Her father was chasing around after another woman, and her mother was blind to it. The money-grubbing Fowlers were grabbing the Sweet Valley High Gladiators' football field away from them just when they had a really terrific team. And who was trying to stop the Fowlers? The Patmans, who were just as bad—a formal English garden! The whole disgusting mess was now in the courts, which only threw her father and that woman lawyer, Marianna West, together even more.

And to top it off, Todd Wilkins had turned out to be practically as bad as Rick Andover. Elizabeth couldn't stop thinking about it, and every time she did, her stomach turned. How could Todd do such a thing! At the same time, she could never quite *picture* him doing it. She believed Jessica—after all, why would she lie about such a thing?—but the image simply refused to come.

Elizabeth had never been so miserable, but she supposed it didn't matter anymore. Jessica was through with Todd—and so was she. Furthermore, Todd was waltzing around Sweet Valley High as though nothing had happened. It was obvious he didn't even care!

And yet Elizabeth was astounded to notice that Todd was watching her. Every class they had together, she could feel his eyes on her.

When they passed in the corridors, when they bumped into each other in the cafeteria, Todd tried to engage her in conversation as though they were still friends.

"Hey, Liz," he said after history one morning, "how about getting something to eat after school?"

"I'm busy," she snapped, ignoring the hurt look on Todd's face.

In Mr. Russo's class he slipped her a note: "Meet me in front of the columns after school."

Elizabeth didn't bother to keep that appointment.

But he wouldn't stop pestering her. Every day Todd tried to corner her on the stairs or stop her in the hall. She brushed him off, but it only made her feel worse.

Even when Mr. Collins came over to her desk in the *Oracle* office and praised her for the story she had done on the football field crisis, she didn't feel much better.

"That was a really professional job," Mr. Collins said.

"Thanks."

"Want to talk about it?" he asked, leaning on the edge of the desk. He had a concerned expression on his face.

Elizabeth managed to smile. "I'm sorry, Mr. Collins. Things haven't exactly been going my way lately."

"Do you think you're up to covering the rest of the football field story for *The Oracle*?"

"Of course. What's next?"

"It's a court case now. You'll have to go down to the courthouse. Your father is handling it, I know, so you'll have to be careful to remain objective."

"I will, Mr. Collins, don't worry."

"Try not to jump to any conclusions. And don't prejudice the case. You can't be a fair reporter if you do. Remember, you have to have all the facts first."

"OK."

"What's her name—Ms. West—isn't she in on this, too?"

"Yes," Elizabeth said softly. *Oh, isn't she, though!*

"All right. Be in Superior Court at nine-thirty on Tuesday, and good luck."

The thought of having to watch her father and "that woman" working together in the courtroom only succeeded in making Elizabeth feel even more miserable. The telephone call the next night from Todd Wilkins did nothing to cheer her up, either.

"Liz?"

"Yes."

"It's Todd."

"What do you want!"

"Liz, something strange is going on."

"Nothing strange is going to go on between you and me, Todd Wilkins. So just get that straight."

"Would you mind making sense?" he said angrily.

"Why do you keep bothering us?"

"Us?"

"Jessica and me! Don't you realize we're not what you seem to think?"

"What are you talking about?"

"Oh, you know very well!"

"I do not!"

"Well, what do you want with me, Mr. Wilkins?"

"I've been trying to get you to meet me so I could tell you something, *Miss* Wakefield!"

"Oh?"

"I mean, well, I just wanted to tell you that I was wrong about something."

Elizabeth felt herself listening intently. If only he could explain things, she thought hopefully. If only there was a way to make things right. Even if he said he was sorry for what happened, that might help some.

"What is it, Todd?" she asked, her voice softening.

"Well, see, I just wanted to say that—well, people make mistakes. I know that. People do things without realizing it, and then they're sorry. And you can't hold it against them forever! It's not fair."

No, Elizabeth thought. That was true.

If Todd apologized for what he tried to do to Jessica, that wouldn't make it all right, exactly. But it would make her at least stop hating him some.

"I just want to apologize, Liz, for the way I've been acting."

"Well, Todd, it really did surprise me. You have no idea how shocked I was."

"Well, can you blame me, Liz? I've cooled down some now, but it took me a lot to be willing to forgive you."

Elizabeth's head spun wildly, trying to make sense of what he was saying.

"Forgive me?"

"But I do," he said hurriedly. "I forgive you on the condition that you promise not to see that creep again."

"What creep?"

"Aw, Liz, you know—Rick Andover."

"You still believe that?"

"Everybody *knows* it."

"Didn't Jessica talk to you?"

"Oh, sure. She's as loyal as the day is long, Liz. She tried to take the blame for you. It was really wonderful of her. But I want you to know it's all right. You made a mistake—it's over. I'm willing to forget about it."

"*You're* willing—?" Elizabeth felt she was going to explode. "Just forget it, Todd."

"Huh?"

"Don't do me any favors."

"Elizabeth, I'm trying to keep my cool. But this is getting to me."

"Isn't that too bad."

"Liz, listen. How about seeing me tonight? Maybe we can talk this out."

"See you tonight? You have nerve! After what you did! Todd, let's get this straight once and for all. I never want to speak to you again!"

Elizabeth slammed down the phone and cried for an hour. But at least it was finally, totally, absolutely finished. Forever!

Fifteen

The courthouse in downtown Sweet Valley was a fine, sprawling Colonial-style building. Elizabeth felt a little overwhelmed when she walked in and was directed to the press room.

"You mean reporters have their own room in the courthouse?" she asked the man in the information booth.

"Yes, young lady. Right down the hall, third door on the left."

Elizabeth walked hesitantly to the press room and peeked inside. There were large desks around the walls, most of them piled high with newspapers and stacks of official-looking court papers. A few reporters were there, too. *Maybe someday I'll work here*, Elizabeth thought.

Mr. Collins had told her to find Eric Garnet, a

146

reporter he knew who worked for *The Sweet Valley News*.

"Hello, Mr. Garnet," she said shyly.

"Ah, yes—the Barbara Walters of Sweet Valley High, I believe," Eric Garnet said and smiled.

Elizabeth smiled and blushed. "Not exactly."

"So, what can I do for you?"

"I'm here to cover the football field story."

"The what?"

Elizabeth felt her face reddening again. She checked her notebook. "Oh, I mean, Fowler versus the Board of Education."

He directed her to the second floor and wished her luck.

As she walked into the courtroom, Elizabeth noticed Coach Schultz and the principal, Mr. Cooper, sitting in the spectators section. Judge Robert Daly was already on the bench, wearing his black robes and looking stern and dignified.

There was George Fowler, sitting at a table with several lawyers in dark suits. He looked rather sinister and very determined. And at another table up near the judge's bench was her father and his assistant, Marianna West.

Elizabeth felt an icy stab of anger go through her at the sight of Marianna. Her father was being so attentive, leaning over with his head next to hers, whispering heaven knows what into her ear. If her mother saw that, she would die!

147

At a third table were Henry Wilson Patman and two more lawyers. Altogether, there were enough lawyers in the courtroom to sue everyone in the state of California.

"Are both sides ready for oral argument in this proceeding?" the judge asked, looking up from a stack of legal briefs he'd been reading.

"Ready, Your Honor," piped Marianna West before any of the others had spoken.

Elizabeth glared at Marianna West. That pushy creature didn't even let her father—a partner in the law firm—speak up; she jumped right in!

Elizabeth had little time to simmer about it, though, because one after another the lawyers started talking, throwing around long legal words that left her bewildered.

First, one of George Fowler's blue-suited lawyers got up and delivered a towering speech about how the Fowlers were entitled to the football field property because the lease held by the Sweet Valley Board of Education had lapsed and had not been renewed.

Then one of Henry Patman's lawyers got up and delivered an even more impassioned speech about how a factory would deface Sweet Valley with smoke and pollution, and insisted the public had an interest in the matter.

Elizabeth felt her spirits falling as she listened to both convincing-sounding arguments. Still, she thought, her father hadn't spoken yet. He was a wonderful lawyer. Maybe he could save the field for Sweet Valley High.

Elizabeth was stunned to see Marianna West rise to speak for the high school instead.

Marianna straightened the legal papers on the table in front of her, then began to speak. She addressed the courtroom in a clear, strong voice, arguing eloquently that the football field was "the heart" of Sweet Valley High as surely as the school building was its "mind."

Elizabeth scribbled frantically, trying to keep up with Marianna's powerful argument. She seemed to know everything about the matter, all right. Her father must have told her every detail.

Nevertheless, Elizabeth couldn't help admiring the ease with which Marianna had handled a difficult situation. She found herself writing in her notebook: "Ms. West was very impressive in marshaling the arguments for Sweet Valley High."

Elizabeth had begun to question her suspicions about Marianna West when the judge called a recess and the court retired to await his decision. She spotted her father in the corridor and rushed over to speak with him. She froze when she noticed that he had his arm slung around Marianna's shoulders. In front of everyone! What was going on?

When Ned Wakefield walked over and introduced the two of them, Elizabeth could scarcely find her voice. Fortunately, Marianna didn't notice. She was all smiles, bubbling over with her success in the courtroom. She greeted Elizabeth warmly.

"Ned told me what beautiful daughters he had," she said, "but I had no idea . . ."

Elizabeth blushed, overcome with confusion. Marianna was no phony. She was even someone Elizabeth felt she could like—a thought that made her feel traitorous toward her mother.

The bailiff stuck his head out the courtroom door and announced that the judge was back on the bench. They all filed back in and took their places. Elizabeth felt as if the entire room were holding its breath as they waited for him to announce his decision.

Amid a nearly unintelligible babble of legal jargon, the last part of what the judge was saying rang clear as a bell: "Petitions by George Fowler and Henry Patman are denied. The property shall be leased to the Sweet Valley Board of Education."

Coach Schultz, who was seated next to Chrome Dome Cooper, leaped to his feet and yelled, "Yea, Sweet Valley!"

Nobody heard the clerk calling for order in the ensuing din of cheers and excited conversation. Nobody noticed, except Elizabeth, as the Fowler and Patman entourages slunk out of the courtroom in sour-faced defeat.

Mr. Cooper and Coach Schultz drove Elizabeth back to the high school, where she was trailed down the corridors by Ken Matthews and the whole Gladiator football team.

"It's OK," she yelled. "We won!"

And then the entire backfield hoisted Elizabeth onto their shoulders and paraded her outside, down the steps, around the school, up the ramp, and through the cafeteria.

Afterward, as she wrote the story, kids kept dashing in to ask for more details.

"Did your father save us?"

"He was there, but Marianna West did the talking."

Mr. Collins read over her story and nodded approvingly. "Good, Elizabeth. Very objective."

Elizabeth sighed. She didn't feel very objective.

After school, walking home, Elizabeth sunk back into her blue mood. How could she be happy when her father was about to leave them for another woman?

When she walked in the house, her mother said, "Liz, honey, could you set the table with the good dishes and silverware? We're having guests."

"Really?"

"Yes, and I know you kids are tired of your father and me not being home for dinner. This one will be for all of us."

"That's great, Mom," Elizabeth said happily, giving her mother a hug and a kiss. "Who's coming for dinner?"

"Marianna West!" her mother said, smiling. "And—"

She didn't have a chance to say who the other guest was because Elizabeth interrupted. "Marianna West?"

"Yes! And your father has a very important announcement to make."

"An announcement about Marianna West?"

"Yes!"

Jessica hardly knew what hit her when Elizabeth dragged her into her bedroom and closed the door.

"What's the matter, Liz?"

"It's the end of the world, Jess! Marianna West is coming for dinner, and Dad's going to make an announcement. What do you think's going on?"

"I know!" cried Jessica, collapsing in tears on her bed. "They're going to announce they're getting a divorce! Oh, I could just die!"

"Oh, that's impossible. Dad would never make

152

that kind of announcement," Elizabeth said, but without much conviction.

"What difference does it make what he says?" sniffed Jessica. "He's in love with Marianna West, isn't he?"

"I don't know."

"Yes, you do."

The enormity of this treachery had hardly sunk in when they heard Steven come bounding up the stairs. Jessica threw open the door.

"Steve, I didn't know you were coming home tonight. Get in here! We've got a crisis! Dad's in love with Marianna West!"

"What?" said Steven, astonished.

"He's going to make an announcement at dinner," said Elizabeth. "We're not sure yet what it is, but under the circumstances, it's got to be terrible."

"Oh, no," he said, falling into a chair. "But I've invited Tricia Martin to dinner! That's why I came home tonight. We can't let her be in on this."

"This is the most horrible day in my entire existence!" Jessica raged, stomping out and heading for her room.

As the twins and Steven dressed for dinner that night, all were preparing for the worst.

Meanwhile, Alice Wakefield was busy preparing duck à l'orange, creamed asparagus, and

153

a chilled parfait. The twins heard her humming as she worked.

"I can't stand this!" Jessica muttered.

Looking thoroughly defeated, Steven came downstairs with Elizabeth and Jessica. He hadn't been able to reach Tricia to tell her not to come. She would discover that she was not the only one whose family was a mess.

Plans to confront their father and head off the crisis didn't succeed, either, because when they got downstairs Marianna was already there, looking positively radiant in an ice-blue suit. She was sipping a glass of white wine.

Not only that. Ned and Alice Wakefield were having drinks with her, and they were all laughing and smiling together.

Then Tricia Martin came in, looking shy and uncertain.

"Hello, Tricia," Mrs. Wakefield said warmly.

"Hi, Tricia," said Ned Wakefield.

They were all being so polite and civilized the twins thought they would throw up.

And then Mr. Wakefield raised his glass. "Listen, everybody," he said. "I was going to announce this at dinner, but I just can't wait."

Elizabeth held her breath. Jessica stared daggers at her father. Steven looked as though he were going to run from the room.

"I offer a toast to Marianna," said Ned Wakefield, "the newest partner in our law firm!"

Elizabeth stared at Jessica. Jessica stared at Elizabeth.

Marianna West looked first at Ned Wakefield and then at his wife. "What?"

Mr. Wakefield laughed. "They told me I could announce it tonight, Marianna. You're a full partner as of now. All those extra hours we put in were worth something, after all."

So that's what Dad had been doing—helping Ms. West gain the promotion he thought she deserved. Elizabeth blushed, ashamed of her unfounded suspicions, while Jessica looked simply incredulous.

"Oh, my goodness!" Marianna West blurted out. "Oh, Ned, you're terrific. I couldn't have done it without your support!" She threw herself into Ned Wakefield's arms and kissed him on the cheek. Then she kissed Alice Wakefield, too.

"Alice, you have the most wonderful husband in the world."

"I know," she said, smiling and taking Ned's arm.

"Now that we've all heard the good news," said Mr. Wakefield, "why don't we adjourn— and sit down for dinner."

Elizabeth linked arms with her sister and gave her brother and Tricia a brilliant smile, as they all practically skipped to the table

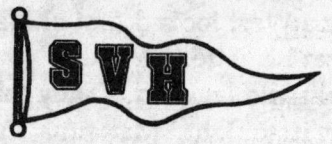

Sixteen

"I'll have a bacon cheeseburger and a root beer," Elizabeth said to the waitress before resuming her conversation with Enid. It was the next afternoon, and the girls had stopped in at the Dairi Burger after school.

"It was really something, Enid. You would have just died at the faces on Mr. Patman and Mr. Fowler! At least we don't have to worry about the football field anymore."

Suddenly Enid spotted something over Elizabeth's left shoulder.

"Let's go, Liz. I've got to get home!" Enid was on her feet, gathering up her books.

"What are you talking about, Enid? We haven't even gotten our food yet."

"I promised my mother I would clean up my room

"You did that over the weekend. I was with you, remember?"

"Oh, yeah. Well, I have to do something else. Now!"

"Stop being weird, Enid. What's the matter with you? You look like you've just seen a ghost."

Elizabeth turned in her chair and checked out the room. Then she saw Todd and Emily Mayer sitting in a booth near the front door.

"Oh." Elizabeth turned back to face Enid, her face white and her hands shaking.

"Nice try, Enid, but I would have seen them on the way out, anyway. Don't worry. It's no big deal."

Why should the sight of Todd with another girl shake me? Elizabeth wondered. *I hate him.*

"They're probably just talking about homework assignments," Enid suggested.

"I couldn't care less what they're talking about, Enid. Todd Wilkins means nothing to me!"

"Remember me, Liz? I'm your friend. You don't have to pretend with me."

"I'm not pretending. There is nothing at all between Todd and me." *There never has been anything—and there never will be anything*, she wanted to add.

Out of the corner of her eye, she sneaked another look at Todd and Emily and wondered why it hurt so much to see him smile at the small, dark-haired girl. In addition to being The Droids' drummer, Emily was a really nice person. *I wonder if she knows what she's letting herself in for,* Elizabeth thought bitterly.

The time seemed to drag as the waitress brought their food and Elizabeth and Enid ate, exchanging only a few words. Finally they could leave.

Elizabeth held her head high and wore her brightest smile as she and Enid approached the front of Dairi Burger.

"Hi, Emily. Hey, The Droids were terrific at the dance. You guys are really something else!"

"Thanks, Liz," said Emily.

"Hello, Liz."

"Hi, Todd. See you two around."

Elizabeth walked as fast as she could out the door, through the parking lot, and to the car. There was only one thought in her head: *don't let me cry, don't let me make a fool of myself!*

Seventeen

Of course Elizabeth had heard people say before that they didn't really feel the pain of being hurt until afterward, but she had never believed it before. The time she got her thumb stuck in the door and the time she hit her shin on the kitchen chair, there was no doubt about it. Both had hurt right away, and plenty. But Elizabeth didn't really feel the pain of losing Todd for several days after seeing him with Emily. And then she wished for that other kind of pain, the kind that came at once and went away almost as quickly. Because this pain sat in her heart as though it were a bird that had built its nest there and would never go away. She had known it was over, really. It had never even started. But seeing him with someone else—that made it final as nothing else could have.

She decided to go on other dates, too. She couldn't just think about Todd forever. She went skating with Ken Matthews one Friday night when the team went out together. It wasn't a real date, though. Just a celebration of getting the football field back. Still, Ken picked her up and brought her home, under the watchful eye of Jessica. It seemed Jessica thought Ken still had a girlfriend, and if she had known he didn't . . .

After that, Elizabeth told herself she was over Todd for good and she would absolutely stop thinking about him all the time. But she thought about practically nothing else.

One night after a sorority meeting at Caroline Pearce's house—at which Elizabeth totally ignored Caroline, still angry at her for spreading the rumors about Kelly's—they all trooped to the Dairi Burger for hamburgers, and there were Todd and all the Phi Eps. Elizabeth tried not to look at Todd, and she could tell he was doing the same. *Why is he acting this way?* she asked herself. It was over. He never called her anymore. They avoided each other in the halls. Still, Todd was being careful not to look at her, and she was being just as careful not to look at him.

After their burgers, they climbed into the Fiat convertible—Jessica was allowed to drive again—

and off they went with three of their friends in the car.

They dropped off Enid and Cara first. When they dropped off Lila Fowler, Elizabeth noticed that they were being followed.

"Oh, don't be silly," said Jessica.

"I tell you, there's a car on our tail, Jess."

They both noticed it after that. A sleek black sports car trailed them as they drove, and it was getting closer and closer.

"Oh, Liz," Jessica gasped. "I'm scared."

"Never mind. Just head straight for home."

But Jessica managed to stall the Fiat at the next red light, and then, in her anxiety, she couldn't get it started again. The pursuing car pulled over to the curb behind them. The driver got out, walked up, and leaned over the side to leer at them.

"Well, well, well. If it isn't Heaven and her sister, Heavenly."

Jessica exploded. "Rick Andover, you scared me to death! I didn't recognize you without your car."

"Aw, sorry," he said mockingly. "Mine's in the shop. I borrowed that little number. You like it? Or would you rather I took you for a ride in this one?"

"Jessie," Elizabeth whispered. "He's drunk."

"Now, is that nice?" Rick sneered. "I heard

you, Heavenly. And you're a smart girl. I *am* drunk, but not enough to matter. Look out!"

And before Jessica could stop him, Rick Andover pulled open the door and jumped into the driver's seat, squeezing her over next to Elizabeth.

"What are you doing?" Jessica raged. "You get out of this car!"

"Got to start it for you, Heaven," Rick slurred. "Can't let you sit here in the middle of Calico Drive."

"Well, start it and then get out," Elizabeth said.

As if on cue, the Spider's engine leaped to life. But Rick Andover did not get out. He floored the gas pedal, and the little red Fiat screeched down the drive as if it were in the Indianapolis 500.

"Stop!" Jessica screamed. "Stop this car!"

"You let us out!" Elizabeth shouted.

Rick Andover laughed drunkenly, stomping down harder on the gas pedal. The Fiat zoomed wildly, looping around toward the Dairi Burger on the bottom of the hill.

They careened past the Dairi Burger, and Elizabeth yelled out the window.

"Help! Somebody!"

Rick whipped the little car through the crowded parking lot of the Dairi Burger, swerving at the last second to miss a crowd of Sweet Valley kids coming out.

Elizabeth caught a fleeting glance of a face startled and pulling back with sudden fright. Todd Wilkins!

Again the Fiat screeched around the parking lot, scattering people with terrifying bursts of speed and last-minute sharp turns.

"Out of the way, you idiots!" Rick Andover yelled. "We're coming through!"

Rick zipped the little car backward, spun around, and tore out of the Dairi Burger lot, almost sideswiping one car and rear-ending another. The car plunged into the traffic and sped wildly off in the direction of the beach.

Looking back, the last thing Elizabeth saw was Todd Wilkins standing near the front door, looking after them in bewilderment.

But Todd's bewilderment vanished the instant he saw the terror on Elizabeth's face and turned to sheer fury at the sight of Rick Andover at the wheel. Within seconds, he had jumped into his Datsun and was speeding after them.

The red Fiat zipped in and out of traffic on the freeway, passing cars and trucks on the inside or the outside as the whim struck Rick.

Jessica's contorted face was wet with tears. "Make him stop," she begged Elizabeth.

"Rick, you stop this car, or I'll—" Elizabeth commanded.

Rick uttered a harsh bark of laughter. "Scream as loud as you like. Who's going to hear you?"

Elizabeth shot Jessica a terrified look. Rick was really crazy. He could wind up killing them!

"Oh, no!" Jessica wailed as he made a screeching turn down a familiar road. "He's taking us to Kelly's!"

"I'll show that creep," he was muttering. "Nobody shows Rick Andover the door if he knows what's good for him."

"They'll never believe we're not with him," Jessica hissed to her sister. "They'll really arrest us this time."

Rick's only response was to hit the gas pedal harder. He didn't notice that a battered old Datsun was slowly gaining on them. Finally, with a screaming skid, Rick spun the Fiat around the parking lot of Kelly's in a boiling cloud of dust and sand. He grabbed Jessica with one hand and Elizabeth with the other, yanking them out of the car. He cursed loudly as the Datsun jerked to a stop in front of him, blocking the entrance to the roadhouse.

"Hey, get that heap out of the way!" he yelled.

Todd Wilkins climbed from the Datsun, a tough look on his face, a look that meant business.

"Todd!" the twins screamed in unison.

"Get back in the car," Todd commanded them soberly as Rick released them to advance on this new menace. Rick's fists were knotted at his sides, and there was a murderous look in his eye.

"Who are you to give orders?" growled Rick. "Get out of my way before I teach you a lesson."

"The only one going anyplace is you, Rick," said Todd quietly. "Why don't you just go home and sleep it off, huh?"

Rick's fist caught Todd square on the jaw in a lightning punch that took him completely off guard. Todd jerked backward but didn't fall. Elizabeth gasped when she saw his nose was bleeding. But after that first stunned pause, Todd didn't miss a beat. He came to life in a fury of hard, short jabs to the middle that sent Rick jackknifing to his knees, clutching at his stomach and gasping for breath.

Todd turned to Elizabeth and Jessica. "Come on. I think he'll leave you alone now. It doesn't look as if he'll be bothering anyone for a while."

"Are you all right?" Elizabeth brought a trembling hand to Todd's face.

Todd smiled. "Sure—as long as nothing's broken. Are *you* OK?"

Elizabeth nodded.

"I thought he was going to kill you!" Jessica gushed. "Oh, Todd, you were wonderful! You practically saved our lives!" She glared in the direction of Rick and the roadhouse. "I never want to see this place again. It's even worse inside."

Todd gave her a funny look but said nothing.

"I could just kiss you!" Jessica squealed, rushing toward him.

She was intercepted as Elizabeth stepped in front of her. "Not this time, Jess. It's my turn." With that, she turned to kiss a surprised Todd squarely on the mouth.

It wasn't until the Fiat was back at the Wakefields' house and he was parked in front that Todd confronted Jessica.

"Hey, Jessica," he said. "What did you mean when you said you never wanted to see Kelly's Roadhouse *again*?"

"Well, I don't, Todd."

"But how do *you* know how rough it is in there?"

"I really am simply too worn out to go on with this," Jessica said suddenly, looking from Todd to Elizabeth. "Good night!"

And before either of them could say another word, Jessica had skipped into the house.

"Hey—"

"Todd, thank you so much. You saved our lives," Elizabeth said. "I didn't know what we were going to do."

"Liz, do you mean that—that other time—it really wasn't you?"

Elizabeth only looked at him.

166

"But—"

"Todd, didn't Jessica tell you it was her?"

"Well, yes. But—"

"But what?"

"That's really amazing. She said it was her, but—Liz, I'm so sorry. I should have known you wouldn't have—that you never could have. . . . How could I have been such an idiot?"

"You weren't alone, Todd. Everybody thought it was me—especially when *somebody* has a funny way of telling the truth." *Somebody who bears a striking resemblance to me,* she thought.

"I was such a fool," Todd was saying. "But you were so popular, with dates every night. I guess I thought anything was possible. You never would give me a look."

"What? Todd, who told you such insane things?"

"Jessica."

"Jessica?"

"Well, yes. She constantly told me how popular you were and that you had no time for me. Well, I could see it was true."

"I see. And that's why you decided to go after Jessica?"

"Go after Jessica? One date? And I tell you, I'm not quite sure how that even happened."

"Is that so? How's your memory on what happened at the *end* of that date when she had to beg you to stop—grabbing her?"

167

"When she had to do what? Who told you that?"

"Jessica!"

"Liz, I barely touched Jessica. I gave her a little peck on the cheek at the door—and I only did that 'cause she seemed to expect it!"

"What?"

"Yes! Liz, you're the only one I ever wanted. Not Jessica, not anybody."

Todd was moving closer to her.

"But what about Emily?"

"Emily Mayer? We have a history project together."

"You didn't touch Jessica?"

"No. You didn't go out with Rick?"

"Absolutely not!"

Todd shook his head in confusion. How could it all have happened? It was impossible.

Elizabeth smiled to herself, trying to picture the hilarious scene of Todd kissing Jessica on the cheek. Why, she must have been ready to burst into a million pieces!

Seeing her smile, Todd asked, "What's funny?"

"Nothing," Elizabeth said.

Whatever she was going to say next was lost forever because suddenly she was in Todd's arms, and they were locked in a long and searching kiss. Elizabeth felt her heart pounding and her ears ringing, and she found herself wishing the moment would last forever.

Todd's breath was warm against her ear. "There's never been anyone but you, Liz," he murmured.

"Only someone who *pretended* she was me." Elizabeth laughed softly, pulling Todd closer for another, longer kiss that was sweeter than anything she had imagined.

Eighteen

Elizabeth floated through the living room and up the stairs to her room. She headed straight for the mirror and smiled at what she saw reflected there.

Yes, that was most definitely the face of a person in love. What was even better, she thought, was that it was the face of a person who was loved in return.

She hurriedly got out of her clothes and slipped on her nightshirt. She could hardly wait to get to bed. Her dreams were bound to be terrific that night.

Wait, she reminded herself. There was one little thing that had to be done—immediately.

Elizabeth marched through the bathroom and into her sister's room.

"Jess," she said, "we have to talk."

Jessica was fussing with her new eye makeup.

"If I use this aqua liner, it makes my eyes look greener. What do you think?" Jessica asked, sticking her face right into Elizabeth's.

"I think it won't work."

"You like blue better?"

"Come on, Jess. You know what I'm talking about."

"Honestly, I don't," Jessica said, her eyes indeed looking almost pure green and very innocent. "If something's wrong, tell me."

"You bet I will."

"You know I'd do anything to help you, Lizzie," she said. "After all, you're the closest person in the whole world to me."

"Jessica."

"There's no one who means more."

"Todd told me everything."

"And you believe him over your own sister," she said, switching gears without missing a beat.

Elizabeth plowed on, paying no attention to the crushed look on Jessica's face. "He said he never tried to kiss you or anything else."

"Is that all?" She brightened. That was an easy one for a pro like Jessica.

"No. There's lots more."

"Like what?" Trouble again.

"Like your visit to Kelly's with Rick Andover."

"I've already explained that. Besides, it's ancient history. As for Todd trying to paw me,

171

well, it's true that he didn't, but I only told you he did for your own benefit."

"Oh, come on!"

"No, really, I thought I was helping you."

"Just how did it help me to think that the guy I liked was after my sister?"

"Lizzie, honey. I did it because I felt he was wrong for you. That you wouldn't be able to handle him."

"Jessie, *honey*. You're really full of it. You did it because you liked him yourself and you were trying to get rid of the competition."

Jessica, seeing that she was cornered, tried a different tack. "You're right," she confessed. "I guess I did like Todd a little. But, honestly, I didn't realize he was so important to you. Besides, it all turned out OK because he really does like you. He certainly showed it tonight. He's a terrific person, and I'm really happy for both of you."

"Jess, you were spying on us just now," Elizabeth accused.

"Come on, Liz. I said I was sorry. Can't we just forget it? After all, you make mistakes, too."

"What about Kelly's?"

"I've told you and *told* you about that. Jeez, Liz, I can't talk anymore. I've got to get to bed. My head is bursting. I must be coming down with something. Here, feel my forehead." She leaned over to her sister, her face pale with instant terminal illness.

Elizabeth ignored the extended forehead. Instead, she took Jessica by the shoulders and moved her back so that they were eye to eye. "Tell me one more time, Jessie."

"It was ages ago. Let's forget it."

"I mean it, Jessica."

Elizabeth was only four minutes older than Jessica, but in a pinch she could make those minutes really count. Like now. Elizabeth was in charge, and there was no way out for Jessica— who knew it. She burst into tears.

"How could you let everybody think I was at Kelly's?" she demanded of the sobbing Jessica. "How could you do such a horrendous thing to me?"

"I'm sorry, honestly, I swear I am. Forgive me." Jessica's pleading face was drenched in tears. "Even when it was happening, I knew it was a horrible thing to do."

"I never would have done such a thing to you."

"I know you wouldn't, and that's what makes it so awful. But I just couldn't help myself."

"Why not?"

"Because . . ." She started but couldn't go on. Her sobs turned everything into an unintelligible babble of how she was so ashamed of herself for being so selfish and awful and on and on. But Elizabeth was determined. She was not going to accept any apologies until Jessica made a full confession.

Finally Jessica, exhausting all her self-recriminations, saw that she had to tell Elizabeth the real reason.

"I knew if it got around school that I was in that bar with those terrible people, I'd be finished. It's a rule, an absolute rule, that you can't be on the cheering squad if you have any black marks against your name. I couldn't give that up, Liz. You know how much being co-captain of the cheerleaders means to me."

"What about me? Didn't you care if I got into trouble for something I didn't even do?"

"But you wouldn't have—and you didn't! You're not a cheerleader, and I knew they wouldn't kick you off the newspaper. Sure, some dumb kids gossiped about you, but so what? They do that, anyway. Still, I knew nothing really bad would happen to you, but it would have been the end of everything for me. I couldn't bear it. Besides, Liz, I know you would have helped if I asked you. Wouldn't you have?"

"I don't know."

"If you knew how much it meant to me?"

"I guess so."

"You know you would have." She sniffled. "But I couldn't ask you. It all happened too fast." Now the tears came again. "You know you're the most important person in the world to me. I'll die if you don't forgive me. Please, Lizzie."

This time the affection was sincere, and Elizabeth was won over.

"I can't ever stay angry with you," she said, and before she had a chance to say another word, Jessica threw her arms around her with such emotion that poor Elizabeth squealed.

Elizabeth hugged her back. No matter what happened between them, this mirror image, this other half of herself, would always be connected to her in some strange and powerful way. And that relationship would be different and separate from any other she would ever have in her life. Nothing could ever change that. Not for either of them.

Jessica's face was shining with pleasure and relief. She really couldn't bear to have her sister angry with her. Elizabeth knew that, and only wanted to see Jessica happy. And happy she was—for the moment.

But Elizabeth had a score to settle with Jessica, and she knew exactly how she was going to do it. She didn't intend to tell anyone but Todd— since he was a part of her fantastic plan.

Nineteen

Elizabeth checked herself in the mirror one last time. "Looking good, Liz," she told herself, twisting around to see if her tuxedo shirt was tucked in neatly at the back.

She was finally going to have a chance to wear her new outfit, and she couldn't have chosen a better time.

Now for the next step in her plan.

"Jess, are you almost ready?" she called. "Todd will be here to pick us up in a few minutes."

"I don't see why I have to ride to the rally with you and Todd," Jessica grumbled as she came into the room. "I could have driven the Spider."

"Not without the keys, and I guess Mom forgot to leave them." Elizabeth crossed her fingers behind her back.

"You and Todd will be crawling all over each other right in front of me!"

"I promise not to embarrass you, Jess. Maybe we'll do a little hand-holding." *Maybe a lot of hand-holding.*

Now for step three.

Elizabeth picked up the glass of water that was on her dresser, and somehow it spilled all over Jessica's white blouse and blue miniskirt.

"How could you be so clumsy?" *Look what you've done!*

"Oh, Jess, I'm sorry. I don't know how in the world I could have done such a thing. Let me help you dry it off."

"There isn't time! Now what am I going to wear? There isn't another clean outfit in my closet." Jessica moaned.

"Well, since it was my fault," Elizabeth said, guilt and a spark of something else radiating from her eyes, "it's up to me to solve your problem."

"How?"

"I just pressed my best jeans today and my blue button-down shirt that you've been dying to borrow."

Jessica was stunned. "You're serious? You'd let me borrow that outfit?"

"Yes, but just this once."

Jessica made a quick change, then stood admiring her image in the mirror.

"Look at us, Liz. Do you see something funny?"

"No. You look terrific."

"I don't mean that, silly. Look again. If I didn't know which of us was me, I would swear you were me and I was you."

It took all of Elizabeth's ample supply of self-control to keep from bursting into laughter. It was like taking candy from a baby.

"You know, you're right, Jess. You look just like me."

"What is that horrendous noise?"

"It's just Todd's car. He's having a little muffler trouble. Let's go. I don't want to keep him waiting."

The two girls dashed out to Todd. Jessica missed the conspiratorial wink Elizabeth and Todd exchanged because she was too busy complaining about being seen in such a gross car.

By the time they drove to school, parked the car, and walked over to where the crowd was gathered, Elizabeth was ready to put step four of her plan into action.

The Droids were entertaining the crowd before the football rally started, and Dana Larson was belting out a number in true Droid fashion.

"Excuse me a minute, you guys. I have to see Dana about an article on the Droids. I'm going to try and catch her at the end of this

178

number. Be right back." She hurried off into the crowd.

"I've got to go, too, Todd. I want to talk to Lila and Cara." She started off, but Todd grabbed her arm.

"Don't tell me you're deserting me, too, Jess. You can't leave me here all alone, friendless and unwanted," Todd teased with mock sadness. Then he gave Jessica his most charming grin.

"Oh, don't be silly, Todd. You know practically every single person here." She smiled up at him, the flirt in her unable to resist a good-looking guy's smile. She sighed. "You're a nut, Todd, but I'll stay until Liz gets back."

"Thanks, Jess. That will make Liz happy." *I'll say it'll make her happy*, he thought, smiling to himself.

Elizabeth made it over to the bandstand just as Dana finished her number and stepped down to the ground.

"Hey, Jess," Dana said, snapping her gum, "every time you wear that tuxedo outfit, you make the other fashion types around here look like they're wearing horse blankets."

"Thanks, Dana. It really is *me*, isn't it?" Elizabeth said, flashing a truly glorious Jessica Wakefield smile.

"Sure thing, Jess."

Elizabeth grinned to herself. It was working!

"Dana, I have the *most* sensational announcement for you to make about the 'Eyes and Ears' column."

It was a tradition that, every year, if the "Eyes and Ears" author was unmasked, the guilty party was thrown, fully clothed, into the school pool. Elizabeth couldn't remember any previous columnist escaping the students' playful punishment. Somebody always leaked the secret, at just about this point in the semester. Elizabeth suspected it was Mr. Collins and that her time was almost up. Well, this year, somebody else was going to spill the beans.

"I know who writes the column," Elizabeth said, imitating Jessica perfectly.

"Terrific, Jess. We have time for a little dunking before the rally starts. Who is it?"

"My sister. Liz is the author."

"And you're turning her in? What's the matter, you two have a fight?"

"No, no. It's just that sometimes she seems a little *too* good, you know? A little dunking won't hurt her."

"You're right. Besides, she's a good sport. Where is she?"

"Where else? Over there with Todd Wilkins, where she *always* is."

"OK! Let's tell the world the news." Dana jumped back onto the bandstand, grabbed the mike, and held up her hand for attention.

"Listen up, you guys! Have I got news for

you! What do we do to the writer of the 'Eyes and Ears' column?"

"Dunk him!" the crowd roared.

"Well, go get *her*. It's Liz Wakefield—and she's standing right over there with Todd Wilkins!"

Everyone turned to look. Jessica stood rooted to the ground. "Oh, no, Todd, they think I'm Liz. Help me, Todd. Stop them!"

Smiling broadly, Todd stepped away from her.

"Rules are rules, *Liz*. She's all yours, guys."

Two linebackers got to her first. One took her arms, the other her legs. They headed for the pool, followed by a laughing crowd.

"No! No! No! I'm not Liz, you jerks! I'm Jessica!"

One of the guys laughed. "Give me a break, Liz. I saw your sexy sister talking to Dana at the bandstand. I think she's the one who turned you in."

"One! Two! Three!" Jessica was thrown screaming into the middle of the pool.

Elizabeth made it down to Todd's side at the pool in time to see a sputtering, incensed, and very wet Jessica surface.

Elizabeth grinned down at her sister triumphantly. "You were right, Jessie. You certainly did look like me today."

"You planned this!" she shrieked. "You planned this whole rotten, mean, contemptible trick! I'll never forgive you, not if I live to be a hundred and thirty-seven years—"

"Bye, Jess." Elizabeth and Todd strolled off, arm in arm.

After the rally, Elizabeth and Todd finally said good night—a long good night filled with kisses and sweet words, and still more kisses.

Elizabeth watched Todd drive off, then went in, closed the door, and leaned against it, sighing happily.

The sharp ring of the doorbell announced Enid's arrival. Elizabeth had invited her friend to come over after dinner and spend the night. Elizabeth opened the door. There stood her friend, tears streaming down her face.

"Enid! What's wrong?"

"Liz, I don't know what to do. Something terrible has happened. I can't even tell you, it's so awful. But I know Ronnie is going to hate me, and I could just die! I'm afraid I'm going to lose everything."

SWEET VALLEY HIGH

SECRETS

Written by
Kate William

Created by
FRANCINE PASCAL

BANTAM BOOKS
TORONTO • NEW YORK • LONDON • SYDNEY • AUCKLAND

SECRETS

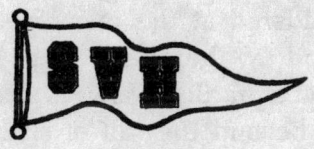

One

"My very own sister! How could she do such a hideous thing to me?" Jessica Wakefield fumed.

She shimmied into the dress she was wearing for her date with Tom McKay. Her best friend, Cara Walker, zipped her up, then stepped back and sighed. Jessica was, as usual, too gorgeous for words. Her sun-colored hair shimmered about tanned shoulders left bare by the silky Hawaiian print sun dress that perfectly complemented her blue-green eyes. A bewitching smile on her lovely oval face usually completed the picture of perfection. The only trouble was, she wasn't smiling right now

"Look at me," Jessica ranted. "I'm an absolute mess! I haven't been able to do a single thing with my hair since this afternoon." She tossed

1

her head in disgust, even though every golden strand seemed to be in place. "Can you imagine— being dunked with every stitch on? How positively humiliating!"

She shuddered at the memory. She'd been tricked—and by her very own twin sister, Elizabeth, who practically always shielded Jessica above and beyond the call of sisterly duty. It was almost too much to be believed. Jessica had been tossed, fully clothed, into the Sweet Valley High pool, the students' annual playful punishment for the author of the "Eyes and Ears" gossip column of the school paper. However, it was Elizabeth who was the columnist, but she'd engineered a mix-up in identity, a trick she'd picked up, no doubt, from Jessica herself.

Cara giggled. "I don't know. I thought you looked kind of cute. Even though you probably deserved to look like a drowned rat. You know, you really *did* have it coming after what you told me you pulled on Liz."

Jessica cut her dead with a glare. "You're lucky we're at your house instead of mine, or I'd really let you have it." Deep down, though, she knew she'd deserved it, too.

"Oh, come on, Jess, you know you really did look kind of sexy Like Bo Derek in that beach scene in *10*.'

A smile pulled at the corners of Jessica's mouth, and the harder she tried to keep a straight face, the worse it got. Finally she collapsed, laughing, onto Cara's bed.

"I did, didn't I? Even so, it *was* humiliating being set up like that." A thought occurred to her, and she clapped a hand over her mouth, sobering instantly. "Oh, Cara, I hope Bruce didn't see me. I'd die!"

She'd been in love with Bruce Patman since her freshman year. He was the most desirable guy in school. Besides being movie-star handsome, he was fabulously rich and drove a terrific black Porsche.

"Just keep thinking of how you'll feel when you're queen of the fall dance," Cara cajoled as she stood in front of the mirror, combing out her own shiny dark hair. "Bruce will be so blinded by your beauty he won't remember anything else"

Jessica wondered if even Cara knew just how badly she wanted that crown. The dance was two weeks away, and she could hardly wait. Bruce had been nominated for king, and it seemed a cinch he would win. None of the other nominees even came close. If she won, too, it would mean reigning at Bruce's side for many of the school-related activities during the semester. It would mean that, finally, Bruce would have to notice her—and, naturally, fall in love with her.

Winning that crown meant everything to her. And when Jessica Wakefield set out to get something, she let nothing and no one stand in her way. Usually it wasn't hard to get what she wanted. With her bewitching looks and beguiling ways, few people ever realized they'd been had by Jessica until it was too late.

Elizabeth Wakefield stared down at the shattered remains of the measuring cup her best friend, Enid Rollins, had just dropped.

"Oh, Liz, I'm sorry!" Enid cried, her eyes filling with tears. "I don't know what happened. It—it just slipped out of my hands!"

Elizabeth hugged her best friend, forgetting the fact that they were both covered in chocolate-chip cookie batter. Enid Rollins was spending the night at the Wakefields', and Elizabeth had initiated Project C.C. Cookie in the hope it would distract Enid from whatever it was she'd been so jumpy about all evening. Actually, Elizabeth had been noticing a nervous edge to Enid's behavior ever since she'd started going with Ronnie Edwards about two months earlier, but she hadn't wanted to pry. She figured Enid would tell her what was bothering her when she was ready. She didn't believe that being best friends with someone entitled her to pry into her friend's private business. But Enid had been in tears when she arrived, too upset even to talk, and things had gone downhill from there. This had gone too far.

"Forget the stupid cup," Elizabeth said. "What's *wrong*, Enid? You don't have to tell me if you don't want to, but just remember I'm your friend. I'm here to help if you need it."

Enid covered her face with her hands. Elizabeth noticed that they were trembling. "Oh, Liz, I'm so afraid!"

"Of *what?*"

"Of losing Ronnie. If he knew the truth about me, he'd hate me. Absolutely *despise* me!"

"How could he possibly hate you?" Elizabeth asked. "The only truth is that you're a fantastic person."

Enid shook her head. "You don't know, Liz. I've even been afraid to tell you. I didn't want you to hate me, either."

"I could never hate you, Enid."

"Maybe not, but I just know Ronnie would if he found out."

"OK, what's this terrible secret?" Elizabeth smiled in an attempt to lighten Enid's misery. "You're really a cat burglar, right? Straight-A student by day, jewel thief by night."

"Come on, Liz, it's not funny." Enid refused to be consoled. A tear trickled down one chocolate-smudged cheek.

"I'm sorry," Elizabeth said. "Really I am. It's just that I can't believe anything you did could be as terrible as all that."

Enid took a deep, shaky breath, then blurted, "Try a police record, then."

"You?" In spite of herself, Elizabeth couldn't help being shocked.

"Yeah, me. Oh, I know what you're thinking. Straight-as-an-arrow Enid. But I wasn't always so straight."

Enid haltingly poured out to her best friend the story that had burdened her for so long. Two years earlier, when her parents were getting divorced, she'd gone a little crazy. She was angry, hurt, upset. She'd drifted in with a bad crowd and gotten involved with a boy named George Warren. They'd gone from drinking to drugs—trying just about everything that came their way.

The situation came to a nightmarish climax the afternoon Enid and George went joyriding in George's GTO—stoned out of their minds—and struck a little boy who was playing near the road. For Enid the whole world stopped moving at that moment. She climbed out of the car as if in slow motion, her knees rubbery. Forever frozen in her memory was the sight of that tiny figure crumpled on the pavement, the horrifying sound of the scream of his mother as she came racing out of her house. Enid stood there as if paralyzed. A voice that didn't seem to be coming from her kept saying, over and over, "I'm sorry. I'm so sorry."

Luckily, the boy wasn't seriously injured. He'd suffered a broken arm and a mild concussion. Enid and George were arrested, but placed on six months' probation and signed into a drug counseling program at Juvenile Hall. Enid emerged from the experience a different person. She'd been shocked into seeing the roller-coaster ride of self-destruction she'd been on, and she'd set about putting her feet on solid ground. She was straight now, with grades to match. She hadn't seen George in two years, since his parents had sent him away to a strict private boarding school.

The whole time she'd been telling her story, Enid was staring down at the kitchen counter, unable to meet Elizabeth's gaze. Now she looked up into a pair of blue-green eyes shining with sympathy. Enid had always thought Elizabeth was pretty—though in a less flashy way than her identical twin sister Jessica—but it was a sparkle that went beyond her all-American good looks, the perfect white teeth, the spun-sunshine hair. Elizabeth was a person who *cared*. She was the first person in whom Enid had been able to confide her terrible secret. Somehow, deep down, she must have known that Elizabeth wouldn't condemn her.

"I'm glad you told me," Elizabeth said. "But it doesn't change a thing. You're still my best friend, and I *still* think you're a fantastic person. Even more fantastic than ever, now that I know what you've been through."

Enid was crying openly now, the tears pouring down her face. Part of it was the sheer relief of being able to unburden herself at last, but mostly she was still in agony over the fear of what would happen if the one person she *didn't* want to know should find out.

She forced a quavery smile. "Tell that to Ronnie. I'll bet he wouldn't think I was so terrific if he knew I'd been lying to him all this time."

"You haven't exactly lied to him," Elizabeth pointed out.

"I haven't exactly told the truth, either."

"Come on, Enid, it's not the most hideous secret in the world, no matter how bad it must have seemed at the time. Besides, it was two years ago—that's practically prehistoric by now."

"Easy for you to say. You don't have any skeletons in your closet."

"If I did, Jessica would've borrowed them." Elizabeth couldn't suppress a tiny smile, thinking of her twin's charming little habit of foraging in her closet whenever she ran out of her own things to wear.

"You wouldn't think it was so funny if you were in danger of losing Todd," Enid insisted.

"I know if it were me, I'd tell Todd. If Ronnie really loves you, he'll understand."

"Oh, Liz, you just don't know!"

Sighing, Enid sank down in the kitchen chair by the window that overlooked the patio. She stared mournfully out over the glassy surface of the lighted pool, shimmering sapphire against the backdrop of darkness. The exact blue of Ronnie's eyes, Enid noted.

"Ronnie's not like Todd," Enid explained. "He expects one hundred percent of my attention. If he knew about George . . ." She stopped, biting her lip.

"What about George? You said yourself you haven't seen him in a couple of years."

"It's true I haven't actually *seen* him. But"— she released a deep sigh—"we write to each other. It's not what you think. I mean, there's nothing going on between us. We're just friends. I started writing to George because he was so mixed-up and unhappy. I wanted him to know it didn't have to be that way forever."

"I think it's nice that you're helping George," Elizabeth said. "There's no reason Ronnie should be jealous over a few friendly letters."

Enid groaned. "You're talking about someone who turns green if I look sideways at another guy by accident. Last week he caught me going over a homework assignment with a guy in my history class. I thought he was going to blow a fuse!"

A tiny alarm went off inside Elizabeth. "But if you explained it just the way you did to me . . "

"He still wouldn't understand." Enid slumped forward against the table, burying her face in her arms. "I just know I'm going to lose him!"

Elizabeth laid a comforting hand on Enid's

shoulder. "Look at it this way. Nobody knows about these letters except you and me, right?"

"Right."

"So what's got you suddenly so afraid Ronnie will find out?"

"It's George," Enid explained. "In his last letter he said he's coming back to Sweet Valley for a visit in less than two weeks. He's come back before, but this time he wants to see me."

Up in Elizabeth's room Enid dug a sheaf of letters out of her overnight bag. "I brought them along, hoping I'd have the nerve to tell you," she said sheepishly, handing them over to Elizabeth.

Elizabeth read the one on top—George's most recent letter:

Dear Enid,

As you know, I've been keeping pretty busy with exams. They really sock it to us here, which I didn't like at first, but now I'm glad they do. I guess I've been pretty much of a goof-off all my life, so I've had a lot of catching up to do. Studying isn't exactly my idea of having a good time, but in a funny way it really kind of grows on you. I feel better about everything in general, as you know from my other letters. I used to be angry all the time, blaming my parents and everyone else for what was wrong with my life, but I think who I was really mad at was me. I don't want to sound weird or anything, but you helped me see that more than anyone, Enid. You'll never know how much your letters meant to me. I don't mind admitting to you that it was pretty depressing here at first. This is definitely *not* Disneyland. But I won't be here much longer—only until the end of the semester when I'll finally have enough credits to graduate—and the future is looking pretty good. I'm glad to hear things are going so well for you, too. Your last letter was definitely an upper (the only kind I go for these days). I'd really like to see you when I come home this time, but I'll understand if you'd rather not.

Love,
George

P.S. Thanks again for the brownies you sent on my birthday. They disappeared in about two seconds, but they were good while they lasted.

P.P.S. Say hi to my buddy Winston for me.

"I don't know what to do," Enid said when Elizabeth had put the letter down. "I don't want to stop being George's friend, but I *can't* see him. Ronnie would take it all wrong."

"I should think Ronnie would be glad to know how loyal you are to people you care about."

Enid shook her head with stubborn insistence. "It would be the ultimate end. He'd be furious. I'd lose him." She clutched at Elizabeth's arm. "Liz, you've got to promise me you won't tell anyone about the letters. Swear you won't!"

"Cross my heart, hope to die."

Solemnly Elizabeth placed her palm against the nearest thick book at hand, which just happened to be her dictionary. Being a writer, she was never very far from it. Of course, she didn't consider herself an Ernest Hemingway. Not yet, anyway. Right now most of the writing she did was for Sweet Valley High's *Oracle*, for which she was author of the "Eyes and Ears" column.

Elizabeth understood Enid's fear of having something like this leak out. Sweet Valley was still a small town, despite its rapidly growing silicon chip industry. And in small towns, as her father said, rumors had a tendency to multiply like mice in a cornfield.

In many ways Sweet Valley High was the biggest mousetrap of all—the cafeteria, the locker rooms, and the front lawn were favorite centers of communication on every subject from the color of someone's hair to scandals involving drugs and who was fooling around with whom. Most of the gossip was harmless, but occasionally a vicious rumor would spread like wildfire, burning innocent people in the process. Elizabeth recently had been on the receiving end of such a rumor herself, when her eternally two-faced twin was nearly arrested and let the police think she was Elizabeth. The cruel gossip had disturbed Elizabeth greatly, so she was in a better position than most to appreciate Enid's dilemma.

"I swear that if I ever tell about the letters, you can, uh—" Elizabeth grinned as inspiration struck. "You can bury me alive in chocolate-chip cookie batter!"

Enid moaned, holding her stomach. Both girls had eaten so many cookies they were sure they were going to gain at least fifty pounds apiece. But the joke had the desired effect of getting Enid to smile.

"Ugh!" Enid said. "I think I'll just take your word for it. I trust you, Liz, I really do. You're my very best friend."

"I should hope so." Elizabeth laughed, pretending to smother Enid with her pillow. "Who else would invite you to spend the night with the way you snore?"

"I don't snore!" Enid protested, leaping off the bed and dissolving into giggles as she beaned Elizabeth with her own pillow.

"Like a seven forty-seven at takeoff!" came Elizabeth's muffled shriek.

In all the commotion, neither girl noticed as one of George's letters fell to the carpet.

"I give—I give!" Elizabeth gasped at last.

"Come on, let's get into bed. We can tell ghost stories. I know a good one about these two teenage girls left all alone in this big creepy house. . . ."

"Elizabeth Wakefield!" Enid cried. "If you tell me one of your ghost stories, I'll never get any sleep. The last time I couldn't sleep for a week."

Elizabeth smelled a challenge—and rose to it. She flicked off the bedside lamp, plunging the room into shadowy darkness.

"It was a dark and stormy night. . . ." she intoned in her creakiest voice.

Enid settled back with a sigh of defeat, secretly glad to get her mind off the real-life fear that was pressing down on her. The thought of losing Ronnie was the worst nightmare she could imagine.

Two

Jessica stared restlessly out the window at the sloping green lawns of Sweet Valley High as Ms. Nora Dalton droned on and on, something to do with conjugating French verbs.

Bore, bored, boring, Jessica conjugated in her mind. It was such a gorgeous day, she wished she were at the beach instead, soaking up the rays in the bronze, wet-look, one-piece she'd bought the week before at Foxy Mama.

Out of the corner of her eye she caught Winston Egbert, seated across the aisle, gazing at her with a goofy, lovesick expression. Yech! Did he have to stare at her like that? Even so, she found herself shifting slightly to a more flattering pose.

"We're ready whenever you are, Jessica."

15

Jessica whipped about to find herself under the sudden scrutiny of Ms. Dalton, a tall, slender woman in her twenties, whose wide-set hazel eyes regarded her with a hint of knowing amusement.

"Sorry," Jessica said, "I didn't get the question."

"I was just wondering if you might like to let us in on the secret," Ms. Dalton said, her smile widening. She didn't smile often, but when she did, her normally pretty but serious face lit up to spectacular effect.

"Secret?" Jessica echoed, growing distinctly uncomfortable.

"*Oui.* The secret of how you expect to conjugate the verbs I've written on the board if you're not looking at it," she needled in a pleasant voice.

"Mental telepathy!" Winston piped, swooping to her rescue with clownish gallantry. "She's really Wonder Woman in disguise. Hey, Jess, show us how you leap tall buildings in a single bound."

"That's Superman, dummy," Ken Matthews said from the back of the classroom, where he sat with his long legs sprawled across the aisle. Ken also had a tendency to shoot off his mouth whenever the occasion arose. The difference between Ken and Winston was that Ken was tall, blond, gorgeous, and captain of the football team. "And you'll be out of here faster than a speeding bullet if you don't put a lid on it."

"Thank you, Ken," their teacher put in dryly.

"I think we can *all* settle down and get some work done now. Unless," she added, eyes sparkling, "any of you has X-ray vision and can see the answers I have hidden in my desk."

A ripple of laughter greeted this. Ken flashed her one of his thousand-watt grins. It was common knowledge that Ken was hopelessly in love with Ms. Dalton, who had been giving him extra tutoring after class to boost his near-failing grade. Even so, Jessica doubted that Ms. Dalton suspected that Ken had a crush on her.

Teachers could be so *dense* about some things, she thought. *She* was always the first to know it when a guy liked her—as well as the first to take advantage of it when it suited her. Even Winston might come in handy one of these days. The trouble was that right now the only one she really wanted was Bruce Patman, and she might as well live on the moon as far as he was concerned.

Jessica conjured up an image of Bruce—fabulously rich, popular, superstar-handsome Bruce of the ice-blue eyes and coal-black Porsche. If only he would ask her to the fall dance. . . .

Of course, there *was* a way, even if he didn't ask her. Jessica had been nominated for queen. Bruce Patman was up for king. She played out the scenario in her mind. There she would be, utterly ravishing, pretending to look shocked that her name had been chosen. She would glide demurely up to the stage, the merest hint

17

of a tear trembling on her lower lashes—not enough to smudge her eyeliner—as she bowed her head in humble acceptance of the crown.

Naturally, Bruce would be chosen king. He was easily the best-looking boy in school. He would smile at her and take her hand, and the two of them would drift onto the dance floor for a solo dance under the spotlight, as if they were the only two people in the world.

She simply *had* to win. It was her big chance to make Bruce fall in love with her. The dance was only two weeks away, and Jessica was desperate to find a way of winning the crown for sure. She would do anything, absolutely *anything*, to be queen. . . .

She was jolted from her daydream by the harsh jingle of the bell and the mad dash for the door.

Lila Fowler detached herself from the mob, falling in step with Jessica as she made her way toward the lockers, still caught up in the pink haze of her daydream.

"Don't you just *hate* her?" Lila hissed, a scowl twisting her pretty features.

"Who?" Jessica asked.

"Dalton. Who else? Didn't you care that she made a fool of you in front of the entire class?"

"Bite your tongue," Jessica returned blithely. "Nobody makes a fool of me. Least of all a cream puff like Ms. Dalton. Actually, she's not

18

so bad. I kind of like her, even if she *is* a teacher."

Ms. Dalton was one of the newer teachers at Sweet Valley High, so naturally there was a good deal of speculation about her. A lot of it had to do with her being young and pretty—a fact that wasn't lost on the male population of SVH, especially Mr. Roger Collins, faculty adviser for the school paper and resident "hunk" among the male teachers.

Jessica had learned that Ms. Dalton had recently begun dating Lila's divorced father, George Fowler. Anything to do with the Fowlers, one of the richest families in Sweet Valley, was news.

Lila enjoyed the attention, but what she didn't enjoy was the awful *thing* that was going on between her father and Nora Dalton. Jessica suspected that Lila was jealous. She was always vying for his attention, though it seemed as if he never had had enough time for her. Now that Ms. Dalton had entered the picture, he would have even less.

"I don't blame Daddy so much, even if he *is* being incredibly naive," Lila was saying. "After all, she practically threw herself at him. I'm positive she's only after his money."

Jessica wasn't normally in the habit of defending people, but even she thought Lila had gone overboard on the subject.

"Come on, Lila," she cajoled. "I just don't think Ms. Dalton is the man-eater type."

19

Lila shot her a look of disdain. "They're the worst kind, don't you see? The ones who don't *seem* the type. I mean, look at the way she keeps Ken Matthews dangling, for instance. It's positively disgusting!"

"Ken?" Jessica snorted. "I think you're just jealous because he'll be thinking of Ms. Dalton while he's at the dance with you."

"I am *not* jealous. Just because Ken's taking me to the dance doesn't make him the love of my life. Why should I care if he's got the hots for some other girl?"

"Girl? Lila, honey, Ms. Dalton is practically old enough to be his mother, for heaven's sake!"

"She's twenty-five," Lila replied haughtily. "I asked my father. That makes her exactly nine years older than us."

"It still doesn't explain why she'd be interested in Kenny. I mean, I know he'd probably jump off the Golden Gate Bridge if she asked him to, but—"

"Don't you see?" Lila broke in. She yanked her locker open savagely. "She's too subtle for anything *that* obvious. I'll bet there's a whole lot that we don't know about. I've seen the way she drapes herself across his desk when they're alone in the classroom."

"Really? I hadn't noticed." Jessica peered into the small mirror that was taped to the inside of the locker door as she concentrated on applying a fresh coat of Plum Passion gloss to her lips.

Actually, if Ms. Dalton was having an affair with Ken Matthews, it might even liven things up at school, she thought.

"I wish I could catch her *really* doing something with Ken," Lila muttered. "Then my father'd see what she's like under all that nicey-nice."

"Catch who?" Cara Walker strolled up beside them, her eyes alight with curiosity.

Cara was always looking for fresh gossip. It was one of the reasons she and Jessica were such good friends. Cara was content to let Hurricane Jessica make all the waves, while she followed in her wake, gathering up the debris of gossip that littered her path. With her sleek, dark good looks, Cara was pretty and popular in her own right, though certainly no match for the stunning Jessica—a crucial point in her favor, as far as Jessica was concerned.

"Ms. Dalton," Jessica drawled, forming her mouth into a sexy pout as she looked at herself in the mirror. "Lila's convinced she and Ken Matthews are having some kind of passionate affair."

"*What?*" Cara screeched. This was almost too good to be true. "I don't believe it!"

"Believe it," snapped Lila, slamming her locker shut with an ear-splitting clang.

"You mean, you've actually seen them—"

The rest of Cara's question was swallowed up as the second bell shattered the air. Jessica and

21

Cara both slammed their lockers shut, then locked them.

"Got to rush," said Lila. "I don't want to be late for choir. They're choosing soloists today for the Christmas program. "I'll just die if I don't get lead soprano!"

"Don't worry," Cara assured her. "I overheard Ms. Bellesario in the office telling old Chrome Dome that you were a sure thing."

Lila's brooding expression switched to a look of stunned happiness. First she hugged Cara, then Jessica, who squealed aloud in protest.

"Hey, watch it! You're going to smudge my masterpiece. I want to look absolutely perfect in case I happen to run into you-know-who."

Cara cast Jessica a knowing grin as she waved goodbye to Lila. "You-know-who's initials wouldn't happen to be B.P., by any chance, would they?"

"You've got it." Jessica giggled. "For Beautiful Person."

"Or maybe Black Porsche," Cara joked.

"You have to admit," said Jessica, "there *is* something wildly sexy about a man in a black Porsche—especially if he's six feet plus and has gorgeous blue eyes and is incredibly rich," she added.

Jessica sighed. She'd never wanted anything so badly in her entire life as she wanted to go to the dance with Bruce. It was a new feeling for her. She was used to getting what she wanted—

one way or another. And yet half the time Bruce acted as if he scarcely noticed she was alive, even though she'd done everything she could to get him to notice. Like the time she'd dropped half a ton of books right at his feet in study hall. Bruce had only grinned lazily and without lifting a single finger to help her pick anything up, commented, "Way to go, Wakefield."

This time she wasn't going to let him slide out of her grasp so easily. She had an idea. "Hey, Cara," she said, linking arms with her best friend as they strolled off toward class. "You sit next to Ronnie Edwards in history, don't you?"

"What of it? Got your eye on him, too? I don't blame you. He's not bad-looking."

"He's also head of the dance committee," Jessica put in quickly. "I was just wondering if you would feel him out for me. You know, next time you're talking to him, sort of casually try to influence him to get kids to vote for me."

"Sure thing," said Cara. "But frankly, Jess, I don't see what you're so worried about. I mean, look at the competition, will you? Enid Rollins, for instance. You're about a million times prettier."

Jessica's eyes narrowed at the mention of Enid's name. "Yeah, Enid's a nerd, all right, but she happens to be Ronnie's girlfriend, remember? He could get a lot of people to vote for her."

Cara shrugged. "Who knows? Maybe they'll break up before then."

"No way. Have you seen how they act around each other? You'd think they were joined at the hip!"

"Make that joined at the lip." Cara giggled.

But Jessica was too busy boiling to take notice. She had other reasons for disliking Enid, mainly the fact that lately she seemed to be taking up every spare minute of Elizabeth's time. Time Elizabeth could be spending with her adorable, fun-loving twin sister instead.

"Frankly," Jessica said, "I can't imagine what a cute guy like Ronnie sees in that little creep."

"Liz seems to like her pretty well, too," commented Cara, casting Jessica a sidelong glance.

"Liz!" Jessica snorted in disgust. "Listen, Cara, my sister has absolutely *no* taste when it comes to picking friends. It's positively embarrassing! I mean, what if someone thought it was *me* hanging out with Enid?"

As they turned the corner, Jessica caught sight of Bruce Patman in the crowded corridor. He was loping toward the staircase, looking impossibly gorgeous, as usual, in a pair of off-white cords and a heather-blue sweater that matched his eyes. Her knees went weak as warm Jell-O, and her heart thundered in her ears.

"I've got to go. I'll talk to you later," she tossed distractedly back at Cara, her eyes riveted on the glorious spectacle of Bruce climbing the stairs with the loose-limbed grace of a young lion.

Perfection, Jessica thought, feeling herself grow warm and prickly all over. Bruce was absolute perfection, from his toes to his carelessly tousled dark hair. He looked airbrushed, as if he'd just stepped from the pages of a magazine. Jessica stared after him, hopelessly mesmerized.

"Wait a minute," Cara protested, tugging at her arm. "You never did finish telling me about Ken and Ms. D—"

But Jessica had already forgotten about Ms. Dalton. She had Bruce in her sights, and like a bullet homing toward the target, she was dashing ahead to catch up with him

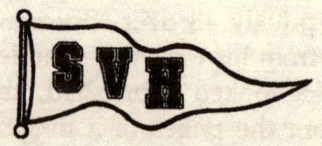

Three

"Well, well, if it isn't Little Bo-Peep," drawled Bruce as Jessica fell in step beside him. He raked her over with a flick of his heavy-lidded blue eyes. "Lost any sheep lately?"

Jessica laughed as if it were the funniest joke in the world. Bruce Patman could recite the Gettysburg Address in pig latin and have all the girls in school hanging on his every word.

"I don't know what you're talking about, Bruce," she parried, fluttering her lashes at him. "I'm practically the loneliest girl in the whole school. Would you believe I don't even have a date for the dance yet?"

"I'll bet Egbert would take you. I hear he's really got the hots for you."

Jessica made a disgusted noise. "He's the last

26

boy on earth I'd want to go with! I mean, honestly, he's like some kind of—of—cartoon!"

Bruce chuckled. "Sure, old Scooby-Doo. Winston's for you, though."

"Oh, he's nice enough, but—well, you *know* what I mean." Jessica rolled her eyes in an expression meant to communicate that Winston was utterly hopeless.

Bruce laughed. "Yeah, I think I do, Jessica."

She felt his gaze travel over her as if sizing her up to see if she was his type. Apparently she met his approval, for his mouth curled up in a slow smile that sent Jessica's pulse pounding out of control. *She* had always known she was Bruce's type. Was he finally getting around to figuring it out as well?

She ran the tip of her tongue over her lips, wondering what it would be like when Bruce got around to kissing her. When, not if. The word "if" simply wasn't part of Jessica's vocabulary.

They were at the top of the stairs, and Jessica cast about wildly for some excuse to keep him from leaving. And then inspiration struck. She reached up, checking to see if her necklace—one of a pair of matching gold lavalieres their parents had given the twins on their sixteenth birthday—was under her sweater. It was.

"Oh!" she gasped. "My necklace! It must have fallen off on the stairs just now. Bruce, you've got to help me find it. My parents would

27

absolutely murder me if I lost it. They practically went into debt for life to get it for me!"

Bruce cast an idle glance down the milling staircase. "I don't see it. But, listen, love, I'm sure it'll turn up. I've got to split. Catch you later." He was gone, leaving Jessica to gape after him in frustrated astonishment.

"Did I hear you say you lost your necklace?"

She turned to the voice behind her. There stood Winston Egbert, grinning foolishly and turning red to the tips of his ears.

She sighed. "Uh, yeah, but it's no big deal. I can look for it later."

"Gosh, Jessica, I don't mind helping you look," he gushed. "I'm good at finding things. My friends call me Sherlock Holmes. Once I even found a stamp my brother thought he'd lost out of his collection. You'd never guess in a million years where I found it. Sticking to the bottom of my shoe, that's where! I'll bet that's the last place in the world anyone else would've looked, huh?"

He advanced toward her just as Jessica was trying to step around him. "Ooops, sorry!" Winston blushed an even deeper shade of red. "I didn't mean to step on your toe. Are you OK?"

Jessica winced. Force of habit made her flash a dimpled smile anyway, in spite of her annoyance. "Thanks, Winston, but like I said, it's no big deal. I'm late for class."

"Sure, Jessica," he said, disappointment scrawled all over his face. "I guess I'll see you later, huh?"

The last sight she had as she rushed off down the corridor was of Winston Egbert down on his hands and knees, scouring the stairway for a nonexistent necklace.

Jessica arrived home from school in a black mood. Just when she'd come close to thinking Bruce might be interested in her, he'd done a complete turnabout, practically kicking her in the teeth. Now she was more hopelessly confused about him than ever. She simply *had* to find a way to get him. She remembered how his eyes had traveled over her—he certainly hadn't taken any shortcuts. Jessica warmed, just thinking about it. Maybe there really *was* a chance after all.

"Where's Liz?" she asked her mother, who was home from work early and was washing a head of lettuce.

"I think she's with Enid. Something about an art project. Posters for the dance, I believe."

Trim, tanned Alice Wakefield could easily have been mistaken for the twins' older sister. They shared the same beautiful all-American looks, down to the honey-colored hair that now swished softly about Alice Wakefield's shoulders as she bustled about the spacious, Spanish-tiled kitchen.

"Enid!" Jessica spat with exaggerated scorn. "Ugh! How can any sister of mine hang around with such a creepy little nerd?"

Mrs. Wakefield turned to give Jessica a gently reproving look. "I don't know how you can say that, Jess. Enid's a very nice girl. She and Liz seem to have a lot in common."

"Yeah, that's because she's turning herself into some kind of Liz-clone. It's positively revolting! She's always over here. Doesn't she have a home of her own?"

Alice Wakefield smiled as she patted the lettuce leaves dry. "Sounds like a slight case of the green-eyed monster to me."

"Me? Jealous of Enid Rollins?" Jessica made a gagging sound. "How could any mother say such a hideous thing to her own daughter?"

"Maybe because it's true," her mother suggested pleasantly.

"Mom!"

"Well, Liz *has* been spending a lot of time with Enid. You certainly don't see her as much as you used to."

"It's her business if she wants to associate with creeps, not mine. I mean, if *she* doesn't mind ruining her reputation by running around with that twerp, why should I care?"

"Good question. Honey, would you hand me the potato peeler out of the second drawer? That's it. Did I tell you Steve is coming home and bringing Tricia over for dinner tonight?"

Tricia Martin was her brother Steven's girl-friend. Although he lived in a dorm at the state university which was in a nearby town, he came home a lot, mostly because of Tricia. Most of the time Jessica was horrified that her very own brother was dating a girl from one of the worst families in town. But at the moment she was too preoccupied with thoughts of the social suicide Elizabeth was committing to give it half a second's notice.

"Liz can see who she wants," Jessica repeated. She scowled as she reached into the basket of cherry tomatoes on the sink and popped one into her mouth.

"Right."

"She can make friends with a one-eyed hippo-potamus for all I care."

"That's very open-minded of you. Don't eat all the tomatoes, Jess. Save a few for the salad."

"She can hang out with *ten* one-eyed hippos if that's what she wants to do. It's positively none of my business."

"I agree completely."

"If she'd rather be with Enid Rollins than me, why should it bother me? I have tons more friends than Liz does anyway. After all, I was the one who brought Enid home in the first place."

Jessica didn't like to admit it, but it was true. Enid had preferred Elizabeth's company to her own. To Jessica that was simply unforgivable.

She burst into tears. Darn Enid Rollins, she

31

thought. Darn Bruce Patman, too. She didn't need either of them. Everyone knew that she could get practically anyone to follow her simply by lifting her finger. Was it her fault that Enid and Bruce were blind to her charms?

Alice Wakefield laid a comforting hand on Jessica's shoulder. She was used to such tempests from her younger daughter (younger than Elizabeth by four minutes). From the time she was an infant, they had been as frequent, and usually as short-lived, as clouds passing in front of the sun.

"Don't worry, honey," she said. "No one could ever replace you as far as Liz is concerned."

"I should hope not!" Jessica stormed. "I'm the best friend Lizzie's got!"

"Then what are you getting so worked up about?"

"Nothing. Absolutely *nothing!*" She bit into another tomato and ended up squirting a red jet of juice and seeds down the front of her very favorite pink angora sweater.

"Ruined!" Jessica shrieked. "It's ruined for good!"

Mrs. Wakefield sighed as she handed her daughter the sponge. "Well, in that case, I suppose we could always have it for dinner, since that was the last tomato."

In a rage Jessica fled upstairs. She headed straight for Elizabeth's room and flung herself down on the bed. She preferred her sister's room to her own since it was always much neater. The Hershey Bar was what she called her room, due to its chocolate-colored walls. And it looked, in Elizabeth's immortal words, "like a cross between a mud-wrestling pit and the bargain table at K-Mart."

It wasn't fair, Jessica fumed. Elizabeth was going to the dance with Todd Wilkins. Even Enid had a date—with Ronnie Edwards, who was so blinded by love that as head of the dance committee, he'd probably swing a million votes her way. Ignoring the fact that she could have had her pick from any one of half a dozen boys if she'd wanted, Jessica refused to be consoled.

Then, out of the corner of one wet eye, she glimpsed a piece of paper sticking out from under the bed. It looked like a letter. Being naturally curious—and having absolutely zero scruples when it came to reading other people's mail—she snatched it up.

"Dear Enid," she read with a sudden, voracious interest. "Been so down lately. I can't seem to get my head on straight the way you have. I can't stop thinking about the past and trying to figure out how it all snowballed so quickly. It's like the time we took all those bennies, and before we knew it we were cooking along in the GTO doing eighty or ninety. . . ."

A smile crept slowly across Jessica's features as a plan shaped itself in her mind. She folded the letter, tucking it carefully into the back pocket of her jeans. She would have to put it back, of course, before Elizabeth discovered it was missing, but that was no problem.

Whistling under her breath, Jessica started back downstairs, heading for her father's den, where he kept a small Xerox machine for copying legal documents.

Four

"What is it with Ronnie and Enid?" Todd asked. "Are they having some kind of a fight?"

Todd and Elizabeth spoke in hushed tones while waiting for Ronnie and Enid to return to their seats with the popcorn. The two couples often double-dated, and the Valley Cinema was a favorite hangout. They'd always had a good time together in the past, but that night Elizabeth, too, noticed that something was off.

"Ronnie does seem to be acting strange," she admitted.

She didn't want him to know how truly worried she was for Enid, worried that somehow Ronnie might have found out her secret. She'd promised Enid she wouldn't tell, and that meant Todd, too, even though he was her boyfriend and she felt closer to him than anyone else.

Elizabeth looked over at Todd, more grateful than ever that he was hers—despite all the devious plots Jessica had cooked up in the beginning to keep them apart. Jessica had wanted him for herself, and Elizabeth could certainly see why. Todd was one of the best-looking boys at Sweet Valley High, besides being its hottest basketball star. He was tall and lean, with brown hair that curled down over his forehead and the kind of deep, coffee-colored eyes you could drown in. But the best thing about him was that he didn't give a darn whether he was popular or not. He was friendly with whomever he wanted to be friendly with, and he avoided people he considered snobs, no matter how popular they might be. In that way he and Elizabeth were alike. And she knew that she could tell him anything that was bothering her and he would have understood.

"Did you notice he didn't hold her hand during the movie?" Todd noted, giving Elizabeth's hand a reassuring squeeze. "Seemed kind of funny, since he's usually all over her."

She nodded. "Poor Enid. She really looked upset."

"I just hope Ronnie's not on one of his jealousy trips again. Remember the time he got mad at her for talking to that guy at Guido's?"

"All she was trying to do was make sure he didn't put anchovies on her pizza."

"It's crazy," Todd said, shaking his head. "If you love someone, you should trust him. Or her. Seems pretty dumb to get all worked up over nothing when you could be having a good time."

"Like us, you mean?" Elizabeth leaned close and brushed the side of his neck with her lips.

Todd kissed her softly in response.

She felt a tightening in her chest as she imagined what it would be like to lose Todd. Her heart went out to Enid, who had a thousand times more reason to worry.

"I hope Enid's all right," she said when she spotted Ronnie making his way down the aisle—alone. "Maybe I should go up and check."

She found Enid in the bathroom, dabbing at her eyes with a paper towel.

"Enid, what's wrong?" Elizabeth asked.

Enid shook her head. "I—I don't know. Ronnie's been acting like a different person all night. It's like he's a million miles away." Her eyes held a tortured expression. "Oh, Liz, do you think he knows?"

"Maybe it's something else," Elizabeth suggested not too hopefully. "A family problem. You mentioned his parents were divorced. . . ."

"Because his mother was fooling around with another man," Enid supplied bitterly.

"I'm sure it's not easy for him, living alone with just his father. Maybe they're not getting along. You really should talk to him, Enid. It might be something *he's* afraid to tell you."

"Yeah, like he wants to break up, only he's afraid I won't give him back his frat pin."

"Ronnie wouldn't do that. He loves you." But even as she said it, Elizabeth didn't feel very sure.

"To Ronnie, loving someone means absolute faithfulness," Enid said. "If he suspected for one second that I'd been writing to George, it would be the end. He'd never forgive me."

Anyone that inflexible didn't deserve someone as nice as Enid, Elizabeth thought.

"Don't worry," she said. "I'm the only one who knows about the letters. And even if he found out about the other stuff, it all happened way before you met him. He can't hold that against you, can he? It wouldn't be fair."

"Who ever said love was fair?" asked Enid, blowing loudly into a tissue.

She quickly fixed her makeup, then gave her shiny brown hair such a vigorous brushing that it flew up around her head in a crackle of electricity. She squared her shoulders as she gave her reflection a final inspection.

"Maybe I'm just imagining things," she said in a small voice. "Maybe Ronnie's just in a bad mood."

Elizabeth hoped she was right.

*　　*　　*

Riding home after they'd dropped off Elizabeth and Todd, Enid felt as if the gap between the bucket seats of Ronnie's Toyota had suddenly become the Continental Divide. She'd been hoping his silence was due to the fact that he felt uncomfortable about talking in front of Elizabeth and Todd, but he was acting just as distant now that they were gone.

"Where are we going?" she asked him when they passed the turnoff for her street.

"I thought we could park for a while," Ronnie replied in a neutral tone.

Glancing at his profile, silhouetted against the amber glow of a streetlight, Enid felt a surge of hope. He wanted to be with her after all! She longed to reach over and thread her fingers through the curly, reddish-brown hair at the nape of his neck, but she resisted the impulse. Even though it was clear he wanted to be with her, she still sensed something was wrong.

Ronnie found a place up on Miller's Point, a favorite Sweet Valley parking spot that overlooked the town. Already there were four or five other cars parked, and judging from the steaminess of their windows, they'd been there awhile.

Ronnie didn't waste any time. He lunged at Enid immediately after he switched off the engine, kissing her so roughly she was left gasping for breath.

"Hey, what's the big hurry?" She attempted

to make light of it, even though she was trembling when she'd finally managed to untangle herself from his crushing embrace.

Enid felt a growing sense of alarm. Ronnie had never acted like this before! Usually he was gentle, never pushing things beyond the limits she set. Tonight he was acting—uncontrollable. Something was terribly wrong.

"Sorry," he muttered. He sat back and began fiddling with the tape deck.

Loud, throbbing rock music filled the car. Usually, he chose something soft and romantic, but this evening he obviously wasn't in that sort of mood.

"Ronnie—what is it?" she blurted. "What's wrong?"

He drummed his fingers nervously against the steering wheel, unable to meet her eyes. "Uh, well, I didn't want to tell you, but it's about the dance. I, uh—"

Enid felt as if her heart were suspended in midair. "What about the dance?"

"I'm not sure I'll be able to make it. You see, I might have to work for my dad that night. He's going out of town, and he really needs someone to look after the store."

"Gee, Ronnie, that's too bad." Enid felt sick.

Ronnie's father owned a small all-night supermarket, but Enid knew he could have called upon any one of half a dozen people to replace him. Ronnie hadn't even bothered to come up with a halfway decent excuse for dumping her. A hot, pricking sensation behind her eyes warned that tears were dangerously close. She fought them. She was determined to hold her head up, not to let him see how much he was hurting her.

"Yeah, well, I'm sorry about it, Enid, but you know how it goes sometimes. Anyway, I'll let you know for sure one way or another in a couple of days."

He thinks he's letting me down easy, Enid thought. Easy? This was agony. She'd imagined this scene so many times, but now that it was actually happening, it didn't seem real. Enid shivered, suddenly feeling very cold and alone. She longed for the warmth of Ronnie's arms around her, even if he was acting strangely. She tried once again to make believe it was only her imagination. She wanted to put everything back the way it was, to pretend Ronnie loved her the same as always. In her desperation Enid felt herself begin to weaken as Ronnie's arms tightened around her again, his lips moving against hers with a hard, unrelenting pressure. But something inside her wouldn't let go. *No, this isn't the way!* She stiffened and pulled back.

"Ronnie—please. Can't we just sit here and talk for a while?" she pleaded.

"What about?" He sounded cold and defensive.

"Uh—" It was on the tip of her tongue to tell him right then and there, to blurt out everything

41

that had been building up since the first time she'd gone out with him. But somehow she just couldn't get the words unstuck from her throat. "I don't know. Just talk. Heard anything interesting around school lately?"

"You mean the latest about Ken Matthews and Ms. Dalton?"

"What about them?" she asked.

"I can't believe you haven't heard. It's all over school. They're having an affair."

"I don't believe it!" For a moment Enid forgot her own despair. "Ms. Dalton wouldn't do a thing like that!"

"How do you know?" Ronnie challenged. "People do crummy things all the time."

"I just can't believe she would—"

"Be interested in Ken?" he supplied, sneering. "I would. A lot of people are two-faced, especially when it comes to love."

Now it was Enid's turn to get angry. "Wait a minute. You don't know anything about it. Who told you all this, anyway? Did anyone actually see them together?"

The image of refined Ms. Dalton in the arms of some high school jock simply refused to come. Of course, Enid was prejudiced. Ms. Dalton happened to be her favorite teacher. Once when Enid had come to school practically in tears over a problem she was having with her mother, Ms. Dalton had taken her aside after class and comforted her. Ever since then, she'd found it easy to talk to her and had fallen into the habit of stopping by after school when something was bothering her. Ms. Dalton never seemed to mind, and always made time for her. The truth was, Enid didn't *want* to believe she was capable of anything so awful.

"Who cares?" Ronnie said carelessly. "It's probably true, anyway."

He pulled her against him. Even his face felt rough against her skin as he kissed her. When she tried to pull away, he only held on tighter.

Finally Enid managed to wrench free of his grasp. She twisted away from him, facing the window so he wouldn't see that she was crying. Hot tears dripped onto the hands she held tightly clenched in her lap, so tightly her fingernails dug into her palms.

"What's the matter?" Ronnie growled. "I don't rate up there with old Georgie-boy? You're not going to give me any of the same stuff you're giving him?"

Enid gasped as if she'd been punched in the stomach. "How—how do you know about George?"

"What difference does it make? The fact is, I *know*." His eyes narrowed with scorn. "I know a lot of things about you I didn't know before, Enid. I know, for instance, that you're not as pure as you'd like me to believe."

"Ronnie, don't . . ." Enid put her hands over

her face, unable to meet his eyes. He hated her. He really *hated* her.

He pried them away, forcing her to look at him. His fingers bit into her wrists, cutting off the circulation. "You've been deceiving me," he hissed, "I know all about it!"

"Ronnie, please, you don't understand! Let me explain!"

"Oh, I understand, all right. A lot of things. Like what an idiot I've been. All this time you were pretending to be in love with me, you were carrying on with someone else behind my back, writing him love letters. How could I have been so stupid!"

Enid felt as if her throat were being squeezed in a giant fist. She struggled against her sobs.

"Ronnie, please listen. George and I are only friends. It's true we used to date, but that was a long time ago. You've got to believe me!"

"Why *should* I believe you? You've been lying to me all along. Acting like Miss Goody Two-Shoes when the truth is you were hot and heavy with George and who knows who else."

Finally he'd gone too far. Giving a cry of anger, Enid yanked her wrists from his grasp. "OK, if that's what you want to think! It's obvious you don't even care what my side is! Why can't you *trust* me just a little?"

"Trust?" Ronnie sneered. "Isn't that kind of a funny word for you to use, Enid? Especially when all the time I was trusting you, you were

44

knifing me in the back. Forget it, baby. I'm taking you home."

Enid couldn't believe she was hearing Ronnie speak to her like this. It was as if he'd turned from Dr. Jekyll into Mr. Hyde. The nightmare she'd dreaded for so long was coming true, and it was even more awful than anything she could have imagined.

Ronnie drove her home in stony silence while she huddled in the seat beside him, desperately holding in her sobs. One thought scuttered through her mind like a rat in a maze, doubling the blow of betrayal she felt:

The letters. Liz must have told him about the letters.

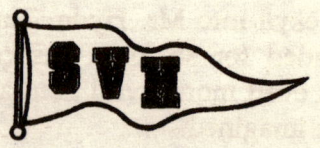

Five

Elizabeth had never seen her sister in such a good mood. Jessica was making her positively dizzy, flying around the room like a hyperactive bumblebee as she got ready to spend Saturday night out with Cara.

"What do you think?" Jessica held up her ribbed burgundy sweater dress. "With that new belt I bought at the mall last month?"

"You're certainly going to a lot of trouble fixing yourself up just to go somewhere with Cara," Elizabeth observed. "What's up?"

"That's for me to know—and you, big sister, to find out," Jessica replied, smiling mysteriously.

She hummed as she launched into the task of untangling her hair from the jumble of electric curlers that sprouted from her head. Elizabeth knew her game, though, and she wasn't going to play it.

She yawned. "Well, have fun—whatever it is."

Jessica stopped to glare at her sister's reflection in the mirror. "Aren't you even the tiniest bit curious about where we're going?"

"Not really." Elizabeth yawned again.

"You mean you're not even going to try to guess?" Jessica's lower lip edged out in a tiny pout.

"OK. Let me see . . . you've been invited to a White House reception and your fairy godmother is getting ready to turn a zucchini from Mom's garden into a jet."

Jessica threw a hairbrush at her sister, missing her by several inches. "Very funny." She was trying very hard not to laugh.

"OK." Elizabeth giggled. "I give up. Where *are* you going?"

"To a party at Lila's. You could've been invited, too, if you tried a little harder to be friends with Lila."

Elizabeth shrugged. "Why should I? I think she's a phony."

"No phonier than some of *your* friends," Jessica shot back. "I won't mention any names, but I think you know who I mean. Her first initial is E—and I'm not talking about E.T., either."

"No comment," said Elizabeth. It bothered

her that Jessica was so determined to dislike Enid, but she knew if her sister guessed what she was feeling, she'd never let up. "Anyway, I wouldn't go to Lila's party even if I was invited. Face it, Jess, the Fowlers are snobs. I guess it comes from getting rich practically overnight."

"I don't care if their money grows on trees," Jessica said. "The point is, they know *all* the right people. Everybody who's anybody will be at that party."

"You mean like Bruce Patman, Bruce Patman, and Bruce Patman?" Elizabeth couldn't resist teasing her.

"You can joke about it all you like," Jessica said. "As a matter of fact, he *is* going to be there, and I'm making sure he notices me. So what do you think? Is the sweater dress OK? You don't think it makes me look fat, do you?"

"Yes and no."

"*What?*" Jessica screeched as if she'd just been mortally wounded. She whirled to face her sister. "How dare you suggest I'm fat? We weigh exactly the same, for your information!"

"Cool it, Jess. I meant yes, the dress is fine, and no, it doesn't make you look fat."

"That's better." Jessica switched back to her usual ultra-charming self, flashing Elizabeth a brilliant smile.

She yanked the last curler from her hair, letting loose a mass of golden ringlets. Curly hair was the one thing Jessica regretted not having been blessed with.

Elizabeth went back to her room and to the book she was reading, but she couldn't seem to concentrate. She was thinking about Enid, worrying over the fact that she hadn't called. It had been a whole twenty-four hours since their double-date—a record for silence where Enid was concerned. Especially since she had to know that Elizabeth was dying to find out how her confrontation with Ronnie had come out. She'd tried calling Enid herself, but both times her mother had said that she was too busy to come to the phone.

Something strange was going on.

Elizabeth decided she would try calling once more, and if Enid wouldn't come to the phone, then she was going over there herself to see what was the matter. Had Ronnie broken up with Enid? she wondered anxiously. Was Enid angry with her for advising her to be truthful with him?

This time Enid answered the phone herself—though Elizabeth scarcely recognized her voice. She sounded so cold and distant.

"Are you OK, Enid?" Elizabeth asked. "You sound funny, like you have a cold or something."

"I'm all right."

"You don't *sound* all right. Aren't you going to tell me what happened last night?"

Enid laughed, but it was a dry, harsh sound. "I'm surprised you have to ask, Liz. I should think it would be pretty obvious to you."

"What are you talking about? Enid, hey, it's me, Liz. What's going on with you? Look, I'm sorry if I told you to level with Ronnie. Was he upset when you told him? Is that it?"

"*Upset?*" Enid choked. "Yeah, I'd say he was upset, all right. Only I wasn't the one who told him."

"So he knows about the police record. Big deal. He'll get over it in a day or two. After all, it happened such a long time ago. It has nothing to do with you and Ronnie now."

"He knows about the letters."

Elizabeth gasped. "How could he have found out? You and I were the only ones who knew!"

"That's right," Enid replied icily.

"Oh, Enid, you couldn't possibly think—"

"*What am I supposed to think?*" Enid was crying now. "*You* tell *me*."

"I—I don't know." Elizabeth was too stunned to think straight. "But, Enid, you've got to believe I never—"

"Why should I believe you? You're the only one who knew about those letters. *The only one.* I confided in you. It *had* to be you. Oh, Liz, how could you do this to me?"

"Enid, please—"

Before she could finish, Enid had slammed

50

the phone down. For a long time Elizabeth refused to believe what had just happened. She sat listening to the empty hum of the dial tone for several moments before slowly lowering the receiver.

"Who was that?" Jessica asked from behind her. "It sounded like you were having some kind of argument."

"Enid," Elizabeth replied, her eyes welling with tears. "It was Enid."

Jessica made a face. "What did *she* want? Wait a minute, don't tell me, let me guess—she couldn't walk from the living room into the kitchen without asking your opinion about it first, right?"

"Jessica, stop it!" Elizabeth snapped. "It's not funny. Enid was really upset. She and Ronnie have broken up—and she thinks it's all my fault."

In a burst, she confided in her sister about what had happened. Jessica rushed to her sister and threw her arms around her.

"It's so unfair! How could she accuse you of such a thing? There must have been some mistake. Enid probably let it slip out about the letters herself, and now she wants to blame someone else. I always knew she was just using you, Lizzie. I saw right through her from the very beginning. You're better off without her."

Elizabeth disentangled herself from her sister's

suffocating embrace. "I'm sure Enid didn't mean all those things she said. She was just upset about breaking up with Ronnie. It must have been pretty awful for her."

"What about you? Look what she's putting *you* through!"

"I'll survive. But I'm worried about Enid."

"For heaven's sake, Liz, are you trying to win the Nobel Peace Prize or something? Don't you ever fight back?"

"All I want to do is straighten out this whole mess. I just hope Enid will listen to me! I have a feeling if I called back right now, she'd only hang up on me again."

"So wait until you see her on Monday. Let her wait until then."

Elizabeth chewed her lip thoughtfully. "Maybe it would be better to wait. I don't think she's in the mood to listen to anybody right now. Poor Enid! I can't believe Ronnie would do this to her over a few crummy letters from a boy she's not even dating anymore."

"Don't you see? It's the principle of the thing. How could he ever trust her again, knowing how she'd covered up the truth? Honestly, Liz, I think it's better Ronnie *did* find out. Whoever told him about the letters was doing him a big favor."

"But *who*?" cried Elizabeth. "*Who* would have done such a hideous thing?"

She looked up to ask Jessica's opinion, but her twin was off again in a whirlwind of preparation for the party. Clearly, the subject was beginning to bore her.

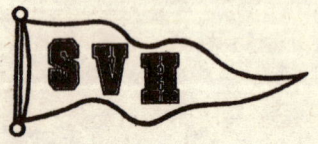

Six

Lila pressed a glass of red wine into Jessica's hand. "Try some," she said and giggled. "It's really good French stuff. I snitched a couple of bottles from my dad's wine cellar, but I'm sure he won't notice. He's got loads of it."

Jessica took a tentative sip. She felt very elegant, sitting there drinking wine at the Fowler mansion. Everything about Fowler Crest was elegant, from the magnificently landscaped grounds to the uniformed maid who had taken their coats when they had come in. It made Jessica's own comfortable split-level house seem like a shack in comparison.

"I can't believe your father lets you have parties like this when he's not here," she said to Lila.

A tiny frown creased Lila's forehead. "Well—I didn't exactly tell him I was having a party. I just said I was having a few friends over. What he doesn't know won't hurt him, right? Besides, it's his own fault for not spending more time at home. If he wasn't so busy running around with Ms. Dalton . . ." Her voice trailed off, and her frown darkened to a scowl.

"Speaking of Ms. D—" Cara began.

"Who *hasn't* been talking about her?" Jessica broke in impatiently. "Frankly, I'm sick of it. Can't anyone talk about anything else?" Jessica quickly grew bored with gossip that didn't directly concern her. It seemed that the girls of Pi Beta Alpha, the sorority that Jessica, Cara, and Lila belonged to, could talk of nothing else.

"Have you heard the news about Ronnie and Enid?" Cara whispered, catching sight of Ronnie standing over by the fireplace. Gossip was gossip, as far as she was concerned. It didn't much matter who the target was.

"Knowing you," Dana Larson put in as she glided up to the bar, "you probably found out about it before Enid did." She held out her empty glass to Lila. "Just Pepsi for me. Got to protect my pipes."

Dana was lead singer for The Droids, Sweet Valley High's answer to the Rolling Stones. They had a reputation for being pretty wild, but most of it was just conjecture. Not many outsiders knew what went on in the smoky confines of

Max Dellon's basement, where they held their practice sessions. As for Dana, she was fairly straight underneath the outrageous clothes she wore. Tonight she was decked out in tight black velvet jeans, a pair of sparkly pink leg warmers, and a purple satin blouse.

Cara nudged Jessica in the ribs. "Ronnie doesn't look too happy. Why don't you go over there and cheer him up?"

"No, thanks, I'm saving myself." She perched on a stool and crossed her legs, making sure her hemline was just far enough above her knee to make it interesting.

"If you mean Bruce, you can forget it," said Lila. "He's not coming."

"What?" Jessica nearly fell off her stool.

"He called at the last minute to tell me he was going to some bash at the college. You know Bruce, always hanging around with older women."

Jessica's heart plummeted into her shoes—Elizabeth's shoes, actually, which she'd borrowed. After all the trouble she'd gone to, Bruce didn't even have the decency to show up! She knew that if he'd just give her half a chance, she could have him wrapped around her little finger. The tricky part was getting him there in the first place. She could see it wasn't going to be easy, but Jessica didn't discourage easily, either. She was already halfway there—thanks to Enid's letter.

Jessica squelched a tiny twinge of guilt as she remembered how upset Elizabeth had been. After all, how was *she* to know Enid would blame her sister? Really, the whole thing was Enid's fault from start to finish. People who left letters lying around for anyone in the world to see were just begging for trouble.

"The girl he's taking to the dance is *nineteen*, for heaven's sake," Lila went on. "I can't believe anyone that *ancient* would want to hang out at a high school dance."

Jessica scarcely heard the rest of what Lila was saying. Her mind was stuck like a broken record on those first words: *The girl he's taking to the dance . . .*

She gulped down half her glass of wine, gasping as it burned a fiery path down her throat. Nevertheless, she refused to surrender. The battle was not lost yet. It just called for a little new strategy and a fresh round of ammunition.

"This isn't going to be just *any* high school dance," Dana said. "After all, when you've got the greatest band around . . ."

Jessica tuned out the conversation. With her eye on Ronnie, she slithered off her stool and made straight for her prey.

"Hey, heartbreaker," she drawled, linking her arm through Ronnie's. "Why don't you try cheering up? This is supposed to be a party. Aren't you having a good time?"

"Yeah," he snarled into his drink. "I'm having a ball."

"Well, you look like someone with a terminal case of the blahs. Come on, I know a terrific cure—let's dance."

"Thanks, Jessica, but I think I'll pass. I'm not really in the mood. Maybe later."

Jessica dropped her flirtatious pose and changed tactics. "Maybe you should have brought Enid," she suggested sweetly. "It's obvious you're miserable without her."

"Enid!" He looked as if she'd just injected him with poison. "No thanks, I'd be better off with Benedict Arnold."

Jessica cleverly jumped to Enid's defense.

"You shouldn't be so hard on her," she said. "After all, everyone makes mistakes. I suppose she's sorry, I'm sure there's no reason for you to hate her for life."

"Yeah, well, I happen to know Enid's not sorry at all. I even have written proof. Someone left a copy of a letter in my locker that some creep named George wrote to Enid."

Jessica pretended total innocence. "Liz did mention that George had been writing to Enid, but you know how those things are," she said. "When you're *involved* with someone the way Enid was with George, it's hard to break it off just like that."

"She's been writing to that jerk for two years!"

"Mmmm," Jessica conceded, taking a ladylike

58

sip of her wine. "That certainly does *seem* devoted. But just remember, appearances can be deceiving."

"Oh, I get the picture, all right," Ronnie said. "Look, Jessica, I appreciate what you're trying to do. It's nice of you to try to help Enid, but it's not going to work. It's over between us."

"What about the dance? Enid is up for queen."

"She should've thought of that before. It's her problem now, not mine. I'm sure she won't have any trouble conning some other poor jerk into taking her."

"What about you, though?" Jessica flashed him a smile oozing with sympathy.

He shrugged. "I'll probably just stay home. It's too late to get another date now."

"Well, what a coincidence!" she cried, clapping a hand over her mouth. "Would you believe I don't have a date, either?"

Several other boys had asked her, of course, but she'd turned them all down. She'd been saving herself for Bruce, and now it was too late—they all had other dates. And the dance was only a week away.

"Since *you* don't have a date and *I* don't have a date," she suggested, "why don't we go together?"

He looked at her as if she'd just suggested he carry her cross-country on his back. "I, uh, gosh, Jessica . . ."

"Just as friends, of course."

"It does make sense," he agreed then.

"Well, there's certainly no point in sitting home and getting even more depressed, is there?" she asked.

"I guess not." He looked slightly bewildered, like someone who'd been picked up by a tornado and dropped in a foreign land.

Jessica turned her most radiant smile on him. Sliding her hand down his arm, she laced her fingers through his. She led him over to the dance area, where several couples had gone into body lock.

"Oh, by the way, Ronnie," she cooed, "I'm allergic to gardenias, but I absolutely *adore* orchids. Just don't get me a pink one—I'll be wearing a red dress."

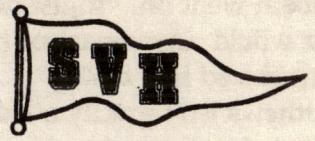

Seven

Elizabeth arrived at school Monday morning to find her problem with Enid overshadowed by an item of gossip that had taken off and, in the last week, spread rapidly.

Practically everyone at Sweet Valley High was buzzing about The Affair—the one supposedly going on between Ms. Dalton and Ken Matthews.

"I don't buy it for one minute," Elizabeth told Caroline Pearce, a member of Pi Beta Alpha sorority, after first period as they stood outside the French classroom.

They were waiting for Ms. Dalton to arrive and unlock the door. Elizabeth couldn't remember her ever having been late before. But then everything about Ms. Dalton had seemed not quite right this past week. In class she was nervous and distracted. Elizabeth had noticed dark circles under her eyes, as if she hadn't been sleeping well.

"I refuse to believe she's fooling around with Ken," Elizabeth went on. "It just doesn't make sense. Why would anyone as together as Ms. Dalton be interested in a *kid?*"

"Ken Matthews isn't exactly a kid," Caroline countered, primly tossing her impossibly neat red hair. Aside from Cara, she was probably the biggest gossip around—and the one person Jessica and Elizabeth could agree on disliking. "Besides, everyone knows she's tutoring him. The question is, *what* is she tutoring him in?"

"It's the law of human nature," put in Olivia Davidson, who worked with Elizabeth on the paper and was known for her liberal views on every subject from nuclear war to organic food. She was especially big these days on women's rights. "A woman doesn't reach her peak until she's in her thirties. Men are practically burned out by then. So it makes sense, really, when you think about it. Though I still can't imagine Ms. Dalton and Ken."

"What makes sense?" asked Lois Waller.

"For an older woman to be attracted to a younger man." Caroline filled her in.

"Maybe," said Elizabeth, "but I still don't think it's true in this case. Ms. Dalton is our teacher. She wouldn't do something as unprincipled as that, even if she wanted to."

"God, Liz, you are soooo naive," Caroline drawled. "Anyway, that's what makes it so perfect. It's so disgustingly tacky."

"I talked to someone in Ms. Dalton's first-period French class who told me Ms. Dalton seemed upset, like she was on the verge of tears or something."

"Maybe someone in her family just died," suggested Lois, a shaggy-haired girl with over-sized glasses which kept slipping down her nose as she talked.

"Or maybe someone's about to get fired," sneered Caroline. "My father plays golf with old Chrome Dome and says he's practically Billy Graham when it comes to stuff like teachers' morals."

"I'm with Liz," Olivia argued. "Ms. Dalton just doesn't seem like the type."

Guy Chesney, keyboard player for The Droids, skidded to a stop before them, whipping out a grubby pad and a pencil stub that looked as if it had been chewed by a pack of rats. His impish brown eyes were lit up with mischief. "I'm taking a poll," he said. "So far it's only one out of three in Ms. Dalton's favor. Goes to show, people always want to believe the worst. Me, I thrive on rumors."

"Has anyone bothered to ask Ms. Dalton whether it's true or not?" Elizabeth wondered.

"Why would she tell *us?*" Caroline replied,

looking horrified at the idea. "It's not exactly the kind of thing she'd want printed on the front page of *The Oracle*."

Guy laughed. "Sounds like a great idea to me. I'll bet it'd sell more copies than *Playboy*. Hey, maybe you could even staple in a fold-out of Ms. Dalton while you're at it."

All four girls eyed him with a drop-dead expression.

"OK, OK," he backed off. "It was just an idea. I mean, heck, any woman with a body like hers . . ." His voice trailed off when he saw he was only making it worse for himself.

At that moment the subject of their heated discussion arrived on the scene, putting an abrupt end to the conversation.

"*Bonjour*, class," Ms. Dalton greeted them as she unlocked the door.

She seemed more subdued than usual, and she was wearing a pair of very dark sunglasses—something Elizabeth had never seen her do before. A ripple of uneasiness edged its way up her spine. Suppose, just suppose, it *were* true. . . .

Ms. Dalton froze as she entered the classroom. Someone had scrawled on the blackboard in large block letters:

IF YOU DON'T KNOW WHAT A FRENCH KISS
IS,
ASK KEN MATTHEWS

Elizabeth gasped. She felt sick. But her reaction was nothing compared to Ms. Dalton's, who reeled back as if she'd been slapped, burst into tears, and rushed out into the corridor.

Elizabeth was still upset about what had happened in Ms. Dalton's classroom by the time she caught up with Enid at the end of third period, but she was determined to put a stop to this ridiculous business of not speaking to one another.

"It's no use avoiding me," said Elizabeth, blocking Enid's path as she attempted to brush past her. "Enid, we *have* to talk."

"I have nothing to say to you, Elizabeth Wakefield," Enid replied icily.

"Enid, you're my best friend. I would *never* betray you. You have to believe me. I swear I didn't tell anyone about those letters."

"The next thing you'll be telling me is that your room is bugged."

"Don't be ridiculous!" Elizabeth was starting to get a little angry herself. "Why can't you just trust me?"

"I *did* trust you, remember? Look where it got me. Thanks to you, my whole life is ruined!"

"Maybe if I talked to Ronnie . . ." Elizabeth began, desperate for any solution to heal this awful rift.

Enid's icy reserve cracked in a sudden flood

of fury. "Haven't you done enough talking?" she yelled. "Can't you just keep your big mouth shut?"

Elizabeth flinched, feeling the color drain from her face. With a choked cry, Enid whirled off in the opposite direction, her head down to hide the tears she couldn't stop from falling.

"Hi, Liz!" Cara called cheerily from her post by the water fountain, where the only thing she'd been drinking in was the sight of Elizabeth and Enid arguing.

By lunchtime it was all over school that Ronnie and Enid had broken up and that Elizabeth had something to do with it. Between Ms. Dalton and Enid, the gossip mongers of Sweet Valley High were in heaven.

"Don't worry," Jessica consoled her sister as they sat on the lawn eating their lunches. "You did everything you could. If Enid wants to be stubborn about it, you can't blame yourself."

"I just wish I didn't feel so helpless," Elizabeth said sadly, nibbling on a corn chip, even though she wasn't the least bit hungry.

"Maybe I should try talking to Enid myself," Jessica suggested sweetly.

"You? You don't even like her! Why should you?"

Jessica pretended to be hurt. "Jeez! Excuse me for breathing! I was only trying to help— you don't have to bite my head off. I just hate seeing you this way, Lizzie. And also, maybe because I'm the tiniest bit sorry for Enid. It really is awful the way Ronnie's been treating her."

"Would you really talk to Enid?" Elizabeth felt her initial skepticism begin to melt beneath the warmth of Jessica's generosity.

"Of course I will, if you want me to."

"Well, I suppose it couldn't hurt. Everything is so screwed up now, nothing and no one could possibly make it worse." *Not even you,* she added silently.

"Thanks for the vote of confidence."

"You know I didn't mean it that way, Jess," Elizabeth apologized, suddenly ashamed of the way she'd doubted her sister's motives. It was entirely possible that Jessica had undergone a change of heart where Enid was concerned.

Jessica hugged her twin, scattering Fritos across the grass as she did so. "I forgive you. Don't I always? Just leave it up to me, Lizzie. I promise I won't let you down."

"That shouldn't be too hard, since I've already hit bottom with Enid," Elizabeth replied glumly.

"Well, you know the old saying—when you're down, you have nowhere to go but up." Jessica smiled and took a huge bite out of her tuna sandwich.

Elizabeth hoped it was true, but she had her doubts. Jessica had a talent for proving comforting old clichés all wrong.

She opened her mouth to say something, but it was too late. Jessica had spotted Enid coming up from the parking lot and was after her like a streak of lightning.

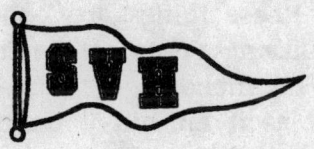

Eight

It was obvious Enid was in no mood for talking, but Jessica wasn't about to let a little thing like that stand in her way. She quickened her step as she fell in beside Enid, blocking her attempt to make a rapid getaway.

"I know how you feel," Jessica gushed sympathetically. "Well, actually, I've never been dumped by anyone, but I can *imagine* what it's like. You must feel awful!"

Enid's lips tightened. "I'm sure Liz filled you in on all the gory details. Why doesn't she just take out an ad in *The Sweet Valley News*?"

"Oh, come on, Enid, don't be that way. Why shouldn't Liz tell me? I *am* her sister. I'm closer to her than anyone in the whole world."

"That's pretty obvious."

"You shouldn't be so hard on her," Jessica cajoled. "I'm *sure* she never meant to hurt you. You know how these things are."

Enid stopped to look at her. "No, I don't know how these things are," she answered coldly. "Unlike *some* people, I'm not in the habit of stabbing my friends in the back."

"You act as if Liz did it on purpose, for heaven's sake! I'm positive she didn't mean to tell Ronnie. It probably just slipped out."

"Just slipped out? Is that what she told you?" Enid's eyes narrowed.

"Well, uh, not exactly, but I—"

"Oh, stop it!" Enid snapped. "Stop trying to defend her. Nothing can excuse what she did!"

"If only you knew how upset Liz is over this whole thing."

"What about me? *I'm* the one who lost her boyfriend, remember? Don't tell me about upset! Liz doesn't know the meaning of the word. She's still got Todd and I've got . . . nothing." Enid choked on the last word.

"I wouldn't exactly say that, Enid. You've still got George."

"That's right. I've still got George. After all, we outcasts have to stick together, right?"

"I wouldn't go so far as to call you an outcast, Enid," Jessica replied generously. "Sure you made some mistakes, but don't worry, people aren't going to believe *everything* Ronnie's been saying about you."

Enid seemed to fold up before Jessica's eyes. Like a dress slipping from its hanger, she slumped down on a bench.

"What has Ronnie been saying about me?" she asked in a hoarse whisper.

Jessica slid a consoling arm about her shoulders. "Believe me, you wouldn't want to know. I couldn't even *repeat* half of it."

"Oh!" Enid buried her face in her hands. "I could just die!"

"It can't be all that bad," Jessica told her. "Look at the bright side. Now you don't have to hide in the closet anymore. It must be a relief not to wonder what people are whispering about you all the time."

"Yeah, now I *know* what they're whispering about me." Enid rose slowly, painfully, to her feet. "Thanks, Jessica, I know you're only trying to help, but you can tell Liz to forget it. If I live to be a hundred and ninety-nine, I'll never forgive her for this!"

"I think you're making a mistake, Enid," Jessica replied lightly.

Enid's mouth twisted in a bitter smile. "Yeah, well, it wouldn't be the first time."

This time Jessica made no attempt to stop her as she rushed off. Elizabeth was better off without Enid for a friend, she thought. Who knew what kind of trouble Elizabeth might get into if she hung around Enid long enough? In

71

the long run, Jessica told herself, she was doing everyone a big favor.

Including herself.

And why not? Didn't she deserve to be happy as much as anyone?

A smile tugged at the corners of her mouth. Since Enid was no longer with Ronnie, she couldn't possibly get enough votes on her own to be chosen queen. Now that Enid was out of the running, Jessica could almost feel the delicious weight of the crown on her head.

"Watch out, Bruce Patman," she murmured under her breath. "Here I come!"

"Why would Ronnie Edwards be calling you?" Elizabeth asked later that evening as Jessica returned from a huddled conversation on the upstairs extension.

Elizabeth looked up from the paper on Shakespeare's *Julius Caesar* she was working on, then went back to it.

"*O, pardon me, thou bleeding piece of Enid,*" she unconsciously copied. She scratched out Enid's name and corrected it to "earth."

"I, uh, well—you might as well know." Jessica flopped down on the bed beside her. "I'm going to the dance with Ronnie."

"You're what?" Elizabeth's pen clattered to the floor.

"It wasn't easy convincing him. He was pretty angry. But I finally managed."

"Jessica, what on earth are you talking about? How can you even *think* of doing such a thing? It would absolutely kill Enid!"

Jessica's expression turned sulky. "Don't you see? I'm doing it *for* Enid. I felt so bad about botching things up with her this afternoon. So I decided to talk to Ronnie."

"What did he say?"

"He was still pretty upset, like I said. I could see it was going to be really hard to get those two back together."

"But you decided to do it, right?"

"What else could I do? He absolutely wasn't going to budge on his own, even after I told him how sorry Enid was and all."

"He's the one who should be sorry," Elizabeth muttered.

"So I figured the only way was for him to see Enid at the dance. If we could arrange to set them up for at least one dance, I'm sure everything will work itself out."

"True love conquers all?" Elizabeth remained skeptical. She was even more skeptical about why Jessica was doing all this, but she decided not to ask. "I'm not so sure it's the best idea in the world. Maybe we should just let them work it out on their own. Besides, I doubt if Enid is going to the dance now that Ronnie broke their date."

"In that case, you'll just have to find a way of talking her into it. I wouldn't want anyone to think I was going with Ronnie for my own selfish purposes." She looked positively horrified at the thought.

Elizabeth relented at the sincerity in her sister's tone. "I'm sorry, Jess," she said. "I know you're just trying to help."

"I'm doing it for *you*, Lizzie!" cried Jessica, giving Elizabeth's hand a warm squeeze.

"How does all this benefit me?"

"I just thought that if Enid and Ronnie got back together, then Enid wouldn't be so mad at you anymore."

"Ah, the mists are clearing."

"You don't need to get sarcastic—even though I know you're still furious at me for blowing it with Enid today."

"She took one look at me in gym class today and burst into tears," Elizabeth said miserably. "I felt like an ax murderer or something. Jess, what did you *say* to her?"

"Nothing much, really. Actually, it was Enid who did most of the talking. She said some *awful* things about you, Liz!"

"She did?" Elizabeth's heart sank.

"I could hardly believe my ears! You know, I think she's always been jealous of you, Lizzie. She was probably just waiting around for an excuse like this to pounce on you."

74

"I know Enid is angry with me, but somehow that just doesn't sound like her."

"Well, you *asked* me."

"I'm sorry I did, in that case."

"Hmphhh!" Jessica tossed her head in disdain. "That's the last time I ever try to do you a favor."

She leaped from the bed in a huff that lasted about thirty seconds—the time it took for her to plow through Elizabeth's closet.

"I *might* forgive you, if you'll loan me your beaded bag for the dance," she said.

"No way. I'm planning on using it myself."

"But you'll be wearing your green dress. It'll go so much better with mine. You can borrow Mom's gold purse. I'm sure she won't mind lending it to you. I mean, think of what a sacrifice I'm making by going at all. The least you could do is appreciate it."

Elizabeth sighed. "I guess the gold purse *would* look better with green."

Jessica blew her sister a hasty kiss as she dashed out of the room. "I've got to call Cara and see what she's going to wear."

Elizabeth was left to wonder why, if Jessica was doing her such a big favor, *she* was the one making all the sacrifices.

Nine

The next day Elizabeth broke down and confided in Mr. Collins. Besides being the faculty adviser for *The Oracle*, Roger Collins had become a sort of unofficial "Dear Abby" to the kids who worked with him. Of course, he resembled anyone *but* Abby—more like a taller Robert Redford, Elizabeth thought, with his crinkly blue eyes and ruggedly handsome features. Sometimes it was hard to keep her mind on what she was saying when she talked to him.

"Mmm, sounds like you've got a bit of a mystery on your hands," he said. "Seems to me the first step you have to take is figuring out why someone would want to tell Ronnie about those letters."

"Motivation, right?" Elizabeth's writer's mind

clicked into gear. "The trouble is, nobody else knew about those letters besides me."

"That's what Enid thinks. But somebody else must have known. What about this boy she was exchanging these letters with? Does he have any friends here at school?"

Elizabeth thought for a moment. "I suppose he could have told Winston Egbert." She knew they'd been friends from the age of about five, though Winston had kept far away from the trouble George had gotten himself into.

"It's a possibility. But even if Winston did know, I can't think of why he would have told Ronnie."

Mr. Collins smiled. "I'm sure he wouldn't have said anything to be malicious, but sometimes people tell secrets just to get attention."

Winston did have a tendency to be a blabbermouth, Elizabeth thought, but he would have had to go out of his way to tell Ronnie, someone he wasn't even friends with, about the letters. Still, she had to admit it was the best possibility so far.

"I suppose I could ask him," she said.

"That's using your head." Mr. Collins winked at her as if she'd thought it up all on her own. "I'm sure it'll turn out one way or another, Liz. Enid's hurting right now, and when people are hurt, they want someone to lash out at. Often it's someone they love."

"Why is that?"

"Because the people we love, who love us, are the ones who will forgive us later on when it all blows over."

Elizabeth looked at him, a slow smile flickering across her features. "How did you get to be so smart, Mr. Collins?"

He shrugged. "Remember, I've been around a few more years than you."

"Yes, Grandpa," she teased.

"Not *that* long." He laughed. "I've got a way to go yet before they put me out to pasture. Besides, how would all you goof-offs get along without me to crack the whip over you?"

"We'd probably turn this paper into *The National Enquirer*," Olivia interjected as she sailed past, bearing an armload of letters she'd collected from the box outside their office. "Honestly, you should *see* some of this garbage!"

Mr. Collins's expression darkened as he examined a few of the letters she'd dumped on his desk. "*This*," he said, jabbing his finger at an offending note, "is what I call malicious gossip. The worst kind, since it's totally unfounded. I spoke with Nora Dalton this morning in the teachers' lounge, and I can tell you she's pretty upset about all this talk. She's actually made herself sick over it. In fact, she looked so bad, I talked her into going home and getting some rest."

"I heard she even got some obscene phone calls at her apartment," Olivia said. "Gosh, I

78

don't know what I'd do if it were me. How does she stand it?"

"The best way she knows how—by not giving it more credence than it deserves. I think we should all do the same." With one swoop, he swept the letters into the trash can.

Everyone suspected that Mr. Collins had a special interest in the pretty Ms. Dalton, so he had double the reason to be disturbed over what was happening. At least *he* trusted her, though, Elizabeth thought.

"I wonder how Kenny's taking it," she mused aloud.

"Nobody seems to know," Olivia answered. "He's been absent the past couple of days. There's a nasty rumor that he got mononucleosis from k—"

"That's enough!" In a rare show of temper, Mr. Collins slammed a book down on his desk. "Haven't you two got anything better to do than talk about this thing?"

Elizabeth blushed. Mr. Collins was right—the best way to deal with gossip was just to ignore it. But that was easier said than done when you were on the receiving end. Her heart went out to both Ms. Dalton and Enid. She knew only too well what it was like having conversations end abruptly when you walked into a room, having people look at you as if you'd just sprouted another head or something. People had treated her like that when Jessica had been picked up at an off-limits bar during a wild brawl—and had let the police believe she was Elizabeth. The next day everyone at school was smirking behind her back. Elizabeth would never forget what a miserable time that had been.

She went back to the "Eyes and Ears" column she was working on. News about the upcoming dance. A story about Winston Egbert and his wrong turn down a one-way street during drivers' ed. Thinking of Winston, her mind flashed to the last line from George's letter:

P.P.S. Say hi to my buddy Winston.

Was Winston really such a good buddy? Elizabeth was determined to find out.

"Sure, Liz, I knew George had been writing to Enid." Winston sat hunched on the bleachers, watching basketball practice. "But I never thought it was any big deal. You know, like he and Enid were—were—uh—"

"I get the message, Win. You knew that Enid and George were just friends, right? That Enid was only trying to help George?"

"Yeah, that's it." He relaxed. Underneath all his clowning, Winston was really very shy.

She took a deep breath. "Win, did you by any chance tell Ronnie Edwards about the letters?"

Winston shot her a startled look, "Why would I do a thing like that? I hardly even know Ronnie.

80

What's he got to do with it, anyway?" He turned his attention back to the court. "Hey, check out that drive shot. Way to go, Wilkins!" he bellowed down to Todd, who flashed him a grin and blew Elizabeth a kiss. Even with his shirt stuck to his chest in sweaty patches, Todd looked beautiful to Elizabeth.

"The thing is," she pressed on, "*someone* told Ronnie about the letters, and Enid thinks it was me."

"Gosh, Liz, that's awful!"

She sighed. "Tell me about it."

"What're you going to do?"

"What I'm trying to do is find out who's responsible."

"You don't really think it was me, do you?"

"I didn't think you'd do it to be mean, Win. I just thought maybe you'd let it slip out by accident or something."

"Nope. I promised George I wouldn't. He figured Enid wouldn't want anyone to know. I mean, she's so straight now and everything. Anyway, George is a good guy. He's really changed. I can't wait to see him when he gets back."

"It sounds like he really cares about Enid."

"Sure he does. What're friends for? Anyhow, in my book a friend isn't someone who blabs a secret all over the place. I know everyone thinks I have a big mouth, but I know how to keep it shut when it counts."

Elizabeth looked at Winston with new respect. She realized she was seeing a side of him that few people were lucky enough to glimpse. It was too bad Jessica didn't see him as the sensitive, honorable person he was, instead of just a nerd who had a crush on her. In Elizabeth's opinion Winston was far superior to that stuck-up Bruce Patman, who roared around in that flashy car of his and acted generally obnoxious.

"I believe you, Win," she said, leaning over to plant a kiss on his cheek.

"Hey, watch it, Egbert!" Todd yelled good-naturedly from his position under the basket. "That's my girl!"

Elizabeth couldn't help thinking that if Winston got any redder, they'd have to paint a white line in front of him and use him as a stop sign.

Ten

Todd reached across the table at the Dairi Burger to lace his fingers through Elizabeth's.

"Hey," he said, "you don't look too happy for someone who's going to the dance tonight with the most fantastic guy on the West Coast."

She forced a weak smile. "Burt Reynolds is taking me to the dance?"

Todd laughed. "That's what I like about you, Liz. Even when you're down, you can always smile."

"That's me, all right—smiling on the outside, crying on the inside." Her smile wilted even as she spoke. "Oh, Todd, what am I going to do? I've tried everything, and Enid still won't speak to me."

The day before, she'd gone over to Enid's

house after school, hoping to catch her alone so that Enid wouldn't be able to run away from her. But she hadn't even gotten past the front door. Enid's mother explained that Enid wasn't feeling well and didn't want any visitors. Visitors! Since when had she been just a visitor? She had turned away in tears, so blinded by her hurt that she nearly collided with Enid's little brother as he came barreling up the front drive on his bicycle.

"You've done what you could," said Todd. "If she doesn't want to believe you're innocent, there's not much you can do."

"Something's wrong, Todd. This just isn't like Enid. She's never stayed mad at me for this long before. If I didn't know better, I'd swear someone was feeding her lies about me. But who would want to do a terrible thing like that?"

Todd shrugged as he stuffed a french fry into his mouth. "Anyone who's really your friend wouldn't believe a bunch of lies—not for long, anyway. If Enid really cares about you, she'll come around."

Elizabeth sighed. "I just hope you're right, Todd. Jess says I'm better off without her, but I really miss her."

"I wouldn't exactly call your sister the world's foremost expert on friendship," said Todd. "Look at what she almost did to us."

He was referring to the way in which Jessica

had manipulated him into thinking Elizabeth didn't care for him, and vice versa. Among other things, Jessica had led him to believe her sister was too busy dating other boys to bother with him. She'd told Elizabeth a story about Todd attacking her, when all he'd done was reluctantly kiss her on the cheek. Todd trusted Jessica about as far as he could throw her.

Elizabeth defended her twin. "Jessica means well. It really is nice of her to want to help Enid."

"I'm not so sure," Todd warned. "Anyway, you should go by your own instincts about Enid, not listen to Jessica."

"I'm not sure I can trust them anymore. This whole thing has gotten me so mixed up I can hardly see straight."

"As long as you can see your way straight to going to the dance with me tonight, you're in good shape. Just forget about all this for one night and have a good time, OK?"

"I wish it were that easy. I wish I didn't feel so guilty about having a good time when I know Enid will be sitting home feeling miserable. I mean, I know it's not my fault or anything, but I feel bad anyway."

"I know what you mean," he said. "It's like the time when I was a little kid and my brother got sick on Halloween, and he had to stay in bed while I went trick-or-treating. Somehow it just wasn't the same. Part of me felt like I should have stayed home, too." He grinned. "It worked out for him, though, because I ended up giving him most of my candy."

"I'm glad you understand, Todd." She squeezed his hand. "I hope I don't act too depressed tonight."

"Goes to show how well you know my tastes," he said, brown eyes flashing. "I happen to love depressed blondes."

"Thanks a lot!"

Elizabeth blew a straw wrapper at him, starting a war that quickly escalated and ended up with Todd the victor—thirteen wrappers to her eight.

Out in the parking lot he slid his arms around her, dropping a kiss on her upturned mouth. He tasted salty-sweet, a combination of french fries and vanilla milkshake. Todd's kisses were one of the things Elizabeth loved best about him. They were like Todd himself—firm, but so gentle. . . .

She wished she could stay this way, wrapped in his arms forever.

"Mom says that if we don't get our rooms clean, we're not going to the dance!" Jessica attacked Elizabeth with the news as she walked in through the door. "Can you believe it? It's positively *medieval*. I feel like Cinderella!"

Elizabeth shrugged. "So what's the big deal?

86

We've got plenty of time before we have to start getting ready."

"Easy for you to say. Your room is already so disgustingly neat. It'll take me a hundred and thirty-seven years to clean up *mine*," she wailed. "It's so unfair. Who cares what my room looks like? Nobody ever goes in it except me."

"And that's hardly ever," said Elizabeth. "You spend most of your time in my room, making a mess of it, too. Honestly, Jess, a person is entitled to a little privacy, you know."

"Mmmm," Jessica murmured, shooting her sister an oddly sheepish look.

She'd been acting strangely secretive these past few days, Elizabeth thought, wondering what she was up to. With Jessica, you never knew.

While Jessica disappeared into the Hershey Bar, Elizabeth set about straightening the few items that were out of place in her room. Mostly that meant books and papers. She was always scribbling something or other, and consequently there were notebooks and typewritten pages strewn about the floor. As she stooped to pick up some paper, she caught sight of a piece of pale blue stationery barely visible under the bed

One of George's letters!

She realized it must have been there all along and felt a sick, plummeting sensation in her stomach. Anyone could have come along and seen it.

No, not just *anyone*.

Only one person in this house besides their mother would have gone into her room.

Jessica.

Suddenly it was all horribly clear. She was certain her sister had read the letter and told Ronnie about it. That would explain the strange mood Jessica had been in for the last week. Elizabeth knew her twin well enough to have a pretty good idea why she'd told, too. Nothing or nobody was going to stand in the way of Jessica getting crowned queen. Including Enid.

Trembling with rage, she folded the letter and tucked it away in a drawer. She was so furious with Jessica at this moment that she could have strangled her.

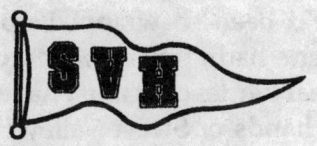

Eleven

"Enid!" Surprise was stamped on Nora Dalton's pale features as she opened the door to her apartment to find Enid standing there. "What on earth are you doing here?"

"I—I hope you don't mind, Ms. Dalton," Enid said haltingly, "but I really had to talk to you, and since you haven't been at school . . ." She let her voice trail off as she took in the unfamiliar sight of Ms. Dalton wearing a bathrobe in the middle of the afternoon.

"Of course I don't mind. It's just . . ." She touched her straight black hair as if wondering if she'd remembered to comb it. "I wasn't expecting company. You'll have to forgive me if I look a mess. I haven't been very well these last couple of days."

"I, uh, heard you were sick. I'm really sorry if I'm bothering you."

Enid reddened, suddenly feeling terribly awkward. She'd been so wrapped up in her own problem, she hadn't given much consideration to the ordeal her teacher must have been suffering at the hands of Sweet Valley High's gossip hounds.

"You're not bothering me, Enid. Come in. I'm glad you came." Nora Dalton looked thinner and paler than the last time Enid had seen her. There were faint purplish smudges under her eyes.

They sat on the couch in the slanting late-afternoon sunlight while Enid poured out her story. Talking to her mother had been difficult ever since the divorce—Mom had enough problems of her own without being dumped on by her kids, Enid figured. But she'd always felt free to confide in Ms. Dalton, sort of like an older sister. The three days she had been absent seemed like the longest days of Enid's life.

"I'm probably the last person who should be advising you about this," Ms. Dalton said quietly when Enid had finished. "But I certainly know how you feel. It's not easy being convicted without a trial, is it?"

"The worst part is knowing it was your best friend who put your head in the noose."

Ms. Dalton shook her head slowly. "I still can't believe Liz would do such a thing."

90

"Who else could it be?"

"I don't know, but there has to be another explanation. Why would Liz want to hurt you? She's your best friend."

"Maybe it's like Jessica said. It just slipped out. But she *knew* how important it was to me that no one find out. That's what really hurts. It's like my feelings didn't matter to her at all."

"What does Liz have to say about all this?" Ms. Dalton asked, her hazel eyes filled with sympathy.

"She denies it, of course."

"Have you considered the possibility that maybe she's telling the truth?"

Enid stared at the carpet. "I—I guess I've been too busy being mad to really listen to Liz."

"You should listen, you know. No one should be condemned before all the testimony is in. If you don't trust Liz, aren't you doing the same thing to her that Ronnie did to you?"

"I never thought about it that way," Enid said sheepishly.

"Talk to Liz. I'm sure she'll understand. She knows how upset you've been. Sometimes people don't think things through when they're hurting."

Enid got the feeling Ms. Dalton knew all too well what she was going through. The latest rumor around school was that Lila's father had broken off with her.

"I doubt if Liz is still speaking to me," Enid said. "I haven't exactly been overly friendly to her lately."

"I don't think it's ever too late to say you're sorry in a situation like this, Enid."

Impulsively Enid threw her arms around her teacher. "You know something? I suddenly feel about a hundred pounds lighter. Even if I don't have a date for the dance," she ended on a glum note.

"Why not go alone then?" Ms. Dalton suggested. "Just because you don't have a date, that's no reason to stay home. Plenty of kids go without dates. Just hold your head up, that's what counts. You might even surprise yourself and have a good time."

"Do you really think I should?"

"Of course I do! I'd go with you myself, if it weren't for—" She broke off, clearly uncomfortable about discussing her own problem with Enid.

"Oh, Ms. Dalton," Enid cried, "it's so unfair! I hate what everyone's been saying about you!"

"Enid," she said, her voice catching a little, "I probably shouldn't be telling you this, but I've been thinking quite seriously about resigning. I've spoken to Mr Cooper about it, and he—"

"No!" Enid leaped to her feet in a blaze of indignation. "You can't. You can't just quit!

What about all that stuff you just told me? How can you expect me to hold my head up if you won't do the same?"

Ms. Dalton was staring at her with a dazed expression. "You don't understand, Enid. It's not the same thing."

"Why isn't it? We've both been accused of something we didn't do. What's the difference?"

All the tears Enid had been holding back now streamed down her cheeks. She got up and grabbed her jacket, suddenly feeling as if Ms. Dalton had abandoned her.

"Running away is running away—no matter what excuses you make!" Enid cried as she stumbled blindly toward the door.

She was gone before Ms. Dalton could reply.

The doorbell rang as Enid was applying a final coat of polish to her nails. She was so nervous that the noise startled her into knocking the bottle across her dressing table in a splash of pale pink.

"Darn!" she cried, dangerously close to tears once again. But this time she was determined not to give in to them. She'd spent the last hour applying her makeup, and she wasn't going to let anything spoil it.

Through gritted teeth Enid addressed her reflection in the mirror: 'You're going to have a good time at this dance if it kills you, Enid Rollins!"

"Enid!" Her mother stuck her head through the bedroom door. "Someone's here to see you."

"Who?"

Enid couldn't imagine who would be stopping by at this time. It was nearly eight. Elizabeth would be too busy getting ready for the dance herself. The only other person she could think of was . . .

"Ronnie!" She jumped to her feet, her heart taking off at a full gallop.

Mrs. Rollins shook her head, wearing a mysterious smile. "I'm afraid not, dear. But I don't think you'll be disappointed when you see who it is."

Enid flew downstairs, forgetting that she hadn't put on her shoes. She came to an abrupt halt when she reached the living room.

"George!" she gasped in disbelief.

This *couldn't* be the same George Warren she'd last seen two years ago. The boy standing before her now was at least a foot taller. A tower of tanned muscle topped by a gorgeous white smile and the sexiest eyes Enid had ever been hypnotized by. He was dressed in a suit and tie that made him look even more irresistible. She stepped forward as if in a trance to take the hand he held out to her.

"I know I should have called first," he said in a deep baritone, "but I was afraid maybe you'd tell me not to come over. Somehow I just couldn't stand the idea of not being able to see you, Enid."

"I—I'm glad you came, George," she stammered, finally regaining her senses. "Oh, George, I can't believe it's *you*. You've really changed!"

"So have you." He laughed. "For the better, too. I remember you when you were a skinny kid with bangs that kept falling in your eyes."

"And braces," Enid said. "Don't forget the braces."

"How could I?"

They both laughed. Within minutes, they were chatting away as if they'd seen each other only yesterday. Even more astounding than the physical transformation George had undergone, was the change in George's personality. Enid was utterly entranced. Gone was the angry, sullen boy who had blamed the world for his problems. George was now a responsible young man, a good student, and—he informed Enid to her delight—he had been accepted to Sweet Valley College for the next semester.

Of course, she'd known from his letters that he'd changed, but she'd escaped the full impact of it until just this moment. Besides, how could she have known from his letters how absolutely gorgeous he'd become? Enid couldn't stop looking at him.

"Listen, Enid," George said, engulfing her hand in his large, warm grasp, "I just talked to Winston, and he told me everything that's been going on. I just want you to know I'm really sorry if my letters got you into any trouble."

"Trouble?" Enid forgot she'd ever had any troubles. The electric sensation of his touch traveled up her arm, tingling throughout her body.

"About the letters, though," he went on, "I have to tell you they were all that kept me going in the beginning when things were really rough. I could see how much you'd changed, and it really inspired me. You believed in me when I couldn't believe in myself. I guess that's why I wanted to see you—so I could thank you in person."

"Thank me?" Enid knew she was starting to sound like a parrot, but whenever she looked into those clear gray eyes, anything brilliant she might have said simply fizzled away.

"Yeah, and to ask you something." He cleared his throat. "I know it's kind of the last minute and all, but Winston told me about your boyfriend breaking your date for the dance, and I was just wondering . . ."

Enid's voice returned all of a sudden, loud and clear. "Ronnie's not my boyfriend," she broke in "As a matter of fact, I'm not sure he ever was. And, yes, George, I'd *love* to go to the dance with you."

He broke into a mile-wide grin. "When I saw you in that dress, I was sure I was too late. I figured some other lucky guy had beaten me to it."

"You look pretty special yourself," she noted, admiring his neatly pressed slacks and dark wool blazer. "Why so dressed up?"

"Well, you see it's like this. I was hoping you'd take one look and figure a clean-cut, preppy type like me was too good to go to waste."

He handed her a small white florist's box he'd been concealing behind his back. Inside was a dewy white orchid corsage tied with a purple bow.

"George—you liar!" Enid's eyes filled with tears in spite of the fact that she was grinning. "You knew all along I didn't have a date!"

"What's the difference? You do now. Isn't that all that matters?"

When they reached the front door, George looked down and started to laugh.

"What's so funny?" she demanded.

"Haven't you forgotten something?" he asked.

Enid glanced down at her feet. "My shoes!"

"Never mind, I like you barefoot."

George wrapped his arms around her, drawing her into a gentle, tentative kiss. His lips were warm and sweet, sending waves of pleasure rippling up her backbone. She curled her hand around the back of his neck, holding him closer as their kiss deepened.

At that moment Enid would have walked barefoot over hot coals to go to the dance with George.

Twelve

"Well—how do I look?"

Jessica twirled before her sister. She looked stunning in a slinky red silk formal with a wide embroidered belt and black sandal heels. Long rhinestone earrings dangled from her ears. She looked as though she'd stepped out of the pages of *Cosmopolitan*—which was exactly the look she was after.

"You look sexy, if that's what you want to know," commented Elizabeth, scarcely looking up from the ironing board as she finished pressing the ruffled hem of her own slightly less revealing voile gown. "Are you sure Ronnie can handle it?"

"You act like Ronnie's my boyfriend, for heaven's sake." Jessica sighed. "I *told* you, Liz, I'm only doing this as a favor to Enid."

"Yes, that's right—you did tell me something like that." Elizabeth pressed down hard on the ruffle, imagining it was Jessica's head she was flattening.

"Really, Liz, you've been acting very strange the past couple of hours," Jessica noted, narrowing her beautifully made-up turquoise eyes. "What's wrong with you, anyway?"

"Nothing, absolutely nothing. What could possibly be wrong?"

"Well, I don't know, but you've been looking at me like I was the Boston Strangler or something. It's giving me the creeps! Are you mad at me?"

"Mad? How could I be mad at *you*, Jess?" Elizabeth asked sweetly. "Maybe you just have a guilty conscience."

Jessica frowned, tapping her enameled nails against the dresser. "What would I have to feel guilty about? I haven't done anything wrong."

"In that case, you have nothing to worry about."

"Honestly, Lizzie, I don't know what gets into you sometimes. I should think you'd be eternally grateful to me for all the sacrifices I'm making!"

"Oh, I am, I am. I'm just trying to think of a way to show my appreciation for everything you've done."

"You are?" Jessica's expression brightened.

"Sure. I want to see you get everything you deserve."

"You're a doll, Liz. I take back all those mean things I said." She went back to admiring her reflection in the full-length mirror. "What do you think—should I put my hair up or leave it down?"

"Better leave it down. You might have trouble with the crown otherwise."

"Oh, Lizzie!" she shrieked. "Do you really think I'll get it?"

"Don't you always get what you want?"

"I certainly hope so tonight. I've been wanting to go out with Bruce Patman since we were freshmen. This is my big chance. Finally. Oh, I can hardly wait!"

"I wouldn't get too excited if I were you." Elizabeth unplugged the iron. "You know the old saying about counting your chickens before they're hatched."

"Tell it to Winston *Egg*-bert. Can you believe he's even running for king? Honestly, I don't know how he even got nominated in the first place."

"Oh, I don't know. I happen to think Winston would make some lucky girl a fantastic king."

Jessica wrinkled her nose. "Ugh! More like court jester." She sailed toward the door in a cloud of perfume. "Come on, Lizzie, will you please hurry up. Our dates will be here practically any second!"

It would be the first time in their lives that Jessica was on time and Elizabeth wasn't. Usually it was the other way around, with Jessica keeping everyone waiting . . . and waiting. To Jessica's way of thinking, nothing ever really started until she arrived anyway, so why hurry?

"I'm coming, I'm coming," Elizabeth muttered, a sly smile flickering across her innocent features. It was the first genuine smile she'd managed in the past week. She was about to teach her dear sister a lesson she wouldn't soon forget.

The school gym, transformed into a fairyland by tiny lights and shimmery decor, was packed by the time Elizabeth and Jessica arrived with Todd and Ronnie at eight-thirty. The dance floor was crowded with couples moving to the driving beat of the music under flashes of starry light cast by a huge mirrored ball on the ceiling. The Droids were in fine form, with Dana belting out a steamy Linda Ronstadt tune.

"I can't wait for the voting to start," Jessica whispered to Elizabeth.

"Me neither," Elizabeth answered, wondering if her sister would be so anxious to win if she knew what was in store for her.

Elizabeth spotted Caroline Pearce, looking hideously girlish in a ruffled pink organdy dress that clashed with her hair, and wandered casually over to whisper something in her ear. Caroline smiled, her eyes widening. The minute Elizabeth walked off, Caroline was busy gabbing to the person beside her.

Elizabeth figured it wouldn't take long for word to spread now that Caroline was in charge.

Elizabeth was dancing with Todd when a stir at the entrance nudged her out of her blissful trance. She craned her head to see what the commotion was all about and caught sight of Ms. Dalton sailing through the crowd with her head held high.

"I wondered if she was going to show," Elizabeth said. "I saw her name on the chaperon list, but I figured she'd still be too sick to come."

"Looks like she made a miraculous recovery," Todd observed appreciatively.

It was true that Ms. Dalton had never looked prettier. She wore a long velvet skirt and an old-fashioned blouse with lots of ruffles and tucks. Her hair was perfect, and she had a silk rose pinned over one ear. It was obvious she'd gone to a lot of trouble to appear at her very best.

"Hey, Ms. Dalton—where's Ken?" a rude voice hollered.

She halted. Elizabeth held her breath, not knowing what the teacher would do, but her only reaction after that momentary hesitation was to smile even more broadly. She continued on to the refreshment table, where she was greeted warmly by the other chaperons, Mr Collins in particular.

He took her hand and whispered something in her ear. Ms. Dalton nodded, and the two of them drifted onto the dance floor as The Droids launched into a slow number.

Elizabeth sighed in happy relief. "Looks like she's going to make it after all."

"People are still going to talk," Todd remarked.

"They'll get tired of it after a while and move on to something else."

"Let's just hope it's not *us*." He laughed.

"Hardly. What would they have to talk about? We're too boring. All we ever do is hold hands and kiss."

"Doesn't sound too boring to me." Todd's arms tightened about her waist as he tickled her ear with his lips.

"By the way," Elizabeth wondered aloud, "where *is* Ken? I haven't seen him. He's not still sick, is he?"

"You mean you didn't hear?"

"There've been so many rumors, I can hardly keep them straight."

"Well, I talked to Ken myself. He was supposed to take Lila Fowler to the dance, but when he found out she was the one who started that rumor about Ms. Dalton, he dropped her."

"Lila started the rumor?"

"According to Cara she did, but then I wouldn't exactly call Cara Walker a reliable source."

"If it's true, I'd say Lila got what she deserved."

Just like someone else is about to get what she deserves, Elizabeth thought as she caught a glimpse of her sister flirting with Bruce Patman.

Elizabeth couldn't believe it when she turned and saw Enid floating in on the arm of an absolutely gorgeous boy. She was glowing with excitement, her cheeks flushed, her eyes shining. She wore a pale mauve off-the-shoulder dress that showed off her slender figure to perfection. Her hair was pulled back, anchored by delicate mother-of-pearl combs. The shimmering whiteness of the flower George had given her set off her radiant smile. Liz had never seen her look so beautiful.

She was dying to rush over and ask Enid what had happened and who she was with, but she fought the impulse. Suppose Enid snubbed her in front of everyone? All eyes were on Enid and her spectacular date as she sailed across the dance floor. Elizabeth couldn't risk the humiliation of having Enid cut her dead. Yet she would have given anything to talk to Enid, to have things the way they were before Jessica had ruined it all.

Todd had just gone off to the refreshment table to get some punch when Elizabeth noticed

Enid walking toward her. Her pulse quickened. Was Enid still angry with her? She felt the heat climbing in her cheeks as Enid approached. Enid wasn't smiling. She looked tense about something.

"Liz?" Enid placed a tentative hand on her arm. "Can we talk? I know you're probably furious with me, and you have every right to be, but—but I just want you to know how sorry I am for the way I've been acting."

"*You're* sorry?" Elizabeth was stunned.

"I never really believed you were responsible for Ronnie finding out about the letters. Not deep down in my heart. I guess I was just so angry at everything, I was using you for a dartboard. It was wrong. I know you would never do anything to hurt me, Liz."

Tears filled Elizabeth's eyes as she hugged her friend. "Oh, Enid, I'm so glad! I was so afraid we'd never be friends again!"

"We're joined at the ear, remember?" Enid laughed. She was referring to their marathon sessions over the phone. Her own eyes shone with tears as well. "I'm just so relieved *you're* not mad at *me*, Liz. I was positive you'd never want to speak to me again."

"How could I not speak to you when I'm dying to know who that fabulous guy you're with is? Enid, what's going *on*?"

Enid smiled, her face taking on a dreamy

expression. Quickly she filled Elizabeth in on everything that had happened.

"George is pretty special," she said, "and not just on the surface, either. I know I'd never have to pretend to be someone I'm not when I'm with him. You were so right, Liz—honesty really is the best way. I don't think it would have worked with Ronnie, even if someone hadn't told him about the letters."

"The fact remains that someone *did* tell," Elizabeth said. "And I happen to know who it was."

"Who?" Enid asked.

"I can't say, but I want you to know that the person responsible isn't going to get off without a few scratches of her own."

Enid shook her head in amazement at the way things had turned out. A week ago she would have wanted to strangle whoever had been responsible for ruining her relationship with Ronnie. Now she didn't really care. It was partly because of George and partly because her talk with Ms. Dalton had made her realize that a relationship that wasn't built on honesty and trust wasn't any kind of relationship at all. And that went for friendship, too. Friends had to trust each other, even when things got messy.

"You know something," Enid said, "I should really thank whoever did that to me. She really did me a favor in the end."

"Enid," Elizabeth admonished, "there is a point at which you can be *too* forgiving."

"No, I really mean it. If I hadn't broken up with Ronnie, I never would have realized how narrow-minded he was. And," she added with a sparkle in her eye, "I wouldn't be here with George, either."

Elizabeth hugged her best friend. "Oh, Enid, I'm so happy for you! I hope he knows what a terrific girl he's getting!"

"He'd *better*," Enid replied. "I'm through with apologizing for myself. Whatever mistakes I made in the past are over and done with. I learned from them, and that's all that counts."

"Hey, when you two are finished gabbing, I'd like a dance with Cinderella here," George interrupted, appearing before them with a cup of punch in hand. Without taking his eyes off Enid, he gave the cup to Elizabeth.

Enid laughed breathlessly as he drew her into his arms. "Liz, I'd like you to meet Prince Charming. He's got this thing about shoes, you see."

"Actually," George said, trying to keep a straight face, "I'm nuts about her handwriting. Even if she is a little strange, she writes terrific letters."

Enid pretended to be hurt. "Is that all I am to you? Just a pen pal?"

"What do you think?" George turned to

Elizabeth with a mischievous look. "Should I trade in my pen and paper for the real thing?"

"I give it my stamp of approval." She giggled.

As George and Enid whirled off onto the dance floor, Elizabeth noticed a number of people staring. Enid had certainly never looked so lovely. And George made her the envy of every girl in the room. Even Jessica had pried her eyes away from Bruce long enough to take a good long look. Ronnie was the only one who appeared unhappy; he was scowling at George and Enid as if he'd like to murder them both.

Enid might never make queen if he had anything to do with it, Elizabeth realized. Somehow, though, she didn't think it would break Enid's heart if she lost.

"They're voting now," Jessica rushed over to whisper in her ear. "Oh, Lizzie, I don't know if I can stand the suspense!"

Thirteen

A breathless hush fell over the gymnasium as the results of the voting were handed over to Ronnie, who stood poised onstage to announce the new queen.

"By a landslide," he boomed into the microphone, "the winner is . . ."

A few people were looking at Enid, obviously wondering if there was a chance she could have won.

"Jessica Wakefield!"

"I don't believe it!" Jessica shrieked, as if she hadn't known all along, in every inch of her bones, that she was going to win.

She glowed with a radiant sense of accomplishment. She'd worked so hard for this moment. Now it was all going to be hers! The crown, the boy she adored—everything!

She held her breath even so, as Ronnie leaned into the microphone to announce the king's name. It *had* to be Bruce, she told herself. Everyone knew he was the cutest guy in school. No one else came close. She glanced over to where he was standing, slouched against the wall, whispering into his date's ear as if he didn't care whether he won or not. How could any guy be so incredibly adorable?

Ronnie's voice crackled through the microphone as he read the results of the voting off a slip of paper. "OK, folks, are you ready for this? Can we have a drum roll, please?"

Emily Mayer, The Droids' drummer, obliged, as Jessica stood licking her dry lips. Each drumbeat echoed her hammering heart. *Oh, please, let it be Bruce!*

"Our new king is . . ."

Please, please . . .

"Winston Egbert! Congratulations, Win, wherever you are."

A loud whoop from somewhere in the thick of the crowd announced Winston's whereabouts.

Jessica listened in stunned disbelief. It wasn't possible! This wasn't happening to her. Her heart went into a sudden tailspin as the meaning of it sank in.

She would be stuck with Winston for the rest of the semester for any big school events.

Her vision of gliding across the dance floor in the arms of Bruce Patman vanished under a

111

cloud of dark fury. Well, she wasn't going through with it! She would refuse the crown. Let someone else be stuck with Winston. This whole mess was the fault of Enid and her dumb letters. Let Enid be queen!

"Congratulations, Jess!" Cara screeched, swooping down on her with a fierce hug. "I knew you'd get it. I just *knew* it. Aren't you happy? Aren't you just positively ecstatic?"

"I'm so ecstatic, I could die." Jessica groaned. "Can you believe it? The big disco dance is coming up in exactly three weeks, and I'm stuck with Winston Egbert!" She was close to tears. "I was so sure Bruce would be king. Now he'll be taking someone else. How could anything so hideous have happened to *me?*"

Cara was confused. "But I thought you wanted to be with Winston. Everyone's been saying you'd really flipped over him. I thought it sounded kind of funny, since I know how crazy you were about Bruce, but let's face it, Jess, you *have* been known to change your mind on more than one occasion."

"I'd like to murder whoever started that rumor," Jessica muttered darkly.

Who could hate her enough to do such an awful thing to her?

Suddenly Jessica remembered about the funny way Elizabeth had been acting earlier that evening. She remembered Elizabeth saying that Winston would make some lucky girl a wonderful king. It had to be! Who else but her own twin would be jealous enough of her to want to stab her in the back? She'd always known Elizabeth was jealous. And why not? Jessica was a thousand times more popular, she told herself.

Jessica was glowering, close to tears, when Elizabeth tracked her down near the refreshment table. Elizabeth was smiling.

"Congratulations, sis," she offered. "You don't look too happy about it."

"How could you do such a horrendous thing to me?" Jessica hissed, her eyes throwing off sparks of green fire.

"I haven't the slightest idea what you're talking about," Elizabeth answered, smiling sweetly. "Would you like some punch, Jessica?"

"I'd like to punch *you* in the face! Don't play innocent with me. You know very well what I'm talking about. *You're* the one who started that rumor about Winston and me so that everyone would vote for him. Don't you dare deny it!"

"OK, I won't. I did start the rumor." Elizabeth glared back at her sister in defiance.

"How *could* you, Liz? You've practically ruined my life!"

"You mean the way you tried to ruin Enid's?"

Some of Jessica's anger fizzled. "I don't know what you mean."

"Oh, I think you know very well. You're the one who told Ronnie about those letters. You

113

purposely came between Enid and Ronnie just so you'd have a clear shot at being queen. Well, Jess, you got what you wanted. Aren't you satisfied?"

"I'm not going through with it!" Jessica stormed. "No one can make me. I won't be stuck with creepy Winston. I'll resign!"

"No you won't, Jess," Elizabeth said quietly.

"What do you mean? You can't tell me what to do!"

Jessica was so furious she thought she just might strangle her sister on the spot. Only the thought of spending the rest of her life in jail—away from Bruce—kept her from going through with it.

"You're going to walk up on that stage and accept that crown as if you were Miss America," Elizabeth was saying in a threatening voice. "Not only that, but you're going to love every minute of it. Or at least *pretend* to."

"Why should I?" Jessica demanded petulantly. She didn't like to admit it, but on the rare occasions that Elizabeth really lost her temper and told her off, it had the desired effect of making her back down.

"Because if you don't"—Elizabeth leaned close to make sure she didn't miss a word—"I'll tell everyone in school what you did to Enid."

Jessica was really frightened now. Deep down she knew what an awful thing it was she'd done. Not even Cara would have gone that far.

What would people say about her if they knew? What would Bruce think?

She gulped back the sob she could feel forming in her chest. Even if Elizabeth had won this round, Jessica wasn't about to let her sister think she cared. "Have it your way then!" she flung back. "But if you think I'm going to do anything really gross like kissing that nerd, you'd better think again!"

A devilish grin spread across Elizabeth's face. "Gee, Jess, I hadn't thought about it, but that's not a bad idea. You know, you can really be sweet when you want to. I'm sure that would make Win very happy."

"Oh, no . . ." Jessica began backing away.

Elizabeth advanced on her, step for step. "Oh, yes."

"Liz, you can't do this to me! Think of my reputation. I'll be absolutely ruined!"

"I don't think so, Jess. Who knows? Your reputation might even improve."

"Lizzie, please, have a heart! You can't do this to your very own sister!"

"Try me. Just remember, dear sister, who writes 'Eyes and Ears,' in case you're tempted to back out. I can put all this in the paper!"

Jessica sank down in the nearest chair in temporary defeat. Over the heads of the dancing couples, she caught sight of Winston, a huge grin plastered across his face, bobbing toward her.

She groaned, wishing the floor would swallow her up that very instant.

A roll from Emily Mayer's drum announced that the photographer had set up his equipment and the crowning of the king and queen was about to take place.

Jessica approached the stage as if she were about to be beheaded. It was so unfair! Why couldn't Enid have been the one to be stuck with Winston? Of course, she knew perfectly well why, but that didn't stop her from feeling a flood of resentment.

Meanwhile, she was smiling so hard the muscles in her cheeks ached. Under Elizabeth's watchful eye, she mounted the short flight of steps leading onto the stage. Winston approached from the opposite end, looking like a scarecrow in a tuxedo jacket that was a little too short. His knobby wrists stuck out as he reached to take her hand.

The crowd burst into uproarious applause. Jessica wanted to crawl into a hole in the ground. She'd never been so humiliated in her entire life.

"Congratulations, Jessica," Ronnie murmured as he positioned the rhinestone tiara on her head. "You deserve it. I'm really happy you won."

"I'll second the motion," Winston chortled, looping a bony arm about her shoulders.

Jessica winced, fighting back her tears. This was supposed to have been the happiest moment of her life. And it would have been if only Bruce were here at her side.

She looked out over the blurry sea of faces below. Only one seemed to stand out more clearly than the rest. Her gaze connected with Bruce's sly blue eyes, which seemed to sparkle with some secret message intended just for her, even while his arm rested about the shoulders of his date, a stunning, green-eyed redhead. If only . . .

Jessica was snapped back to reality by the blinding explosion of a flashbulb. She noticed that her sister was whispering something in the photographer's ear.

Suddenly he called, "How about a kiss for the camera, you two lovebirds?"

Jessica steeled herself for the inevitable, cringing inside as she was forced to endure Winston's damp kiss.

I'll get you for this, Liz, she raged inwardly.

Her last sight of Bruce from the stage, before he strolled off, linked to his date, was of a lazy arm raised in mock salute, as he called, "Way to go, Wakefield!"

Jessica longed to run after him, to throw herself at his feet—*anything*. But she knew she'd made enough of a fool of herself for one night. Besides, there was still hope. Despite her frustration, she wouldn't let go of the deep-down belief that someday, somehow, she would have Bruce Patman.

Of course, that would mean coming up with an entirely new plan, since this one had failed so miserably. But she'd think of something.

Didn't she always?

Smiling through her tears, Jessica allowed herself to be tugged onto the dance floor by an eager Winston, who was practically tripping all over himself in his exuberance. She closed her eyes, trying hard to imagine that he was Bruce . . . that she was floating in the strong arms of the boy she loved. But the image dissolved every time Winston's clumsy foot ground down on her toe.

Just then Bruce sailed past, nearly colliding with her as she stumbled backward in an attempt to escape Winston's murderous feet. He swept her with a long look that sent an electric shock tingling up her spine. There was a hint of invitation in his smile, and more than a spark of interest in his sexy blue eyes. Some of her misery faded. *Could it be? . . .*

SWEET VALLEY HIGH

PLAYING WITH FIRE

Written by
Kate William

Created by
FRANCINE PASCAL

BANTAM BOOKS
TORONTO • NEW YORK • LONDON • SYDNEY

PLAYING WITH FIRE

One

"Well, if it isn't her royal highness herself." Todd Wilkins gently nudged Elizabeth Wakefield's shoulder and pointed toward the entrance to the school gymnasium.

Elizabeth peered into the crowd that had already assembled for the Sweet Valley High dance contest. She sighed with relief when she spotted the person Todd was talking about—her twin sister, Jessica. With the contest only minutes away, Elizabeth had begun to worry about Jessica, even though it wasn't the first time her twin had shown up late to an important event. Casting a concerned look back in her boyfriend's direction, Elizabeth murmured, "I wonder where Jessica was all this time."

"Really, Liz." Todd shook his head in mock

exasperation. "You know Jessica always waits until everyone's gathered to make her grand entrance."

"You're exaggerating, Todd," Elizabeth replied defensively, although silently she admitted there was some truth to Todd's words. Jessica had always said that a party never really started until she got there, and this occasion appeared to be the perfect time to prove her point. Already a small crowd had begun to form around the popular blonde. "Anyway, so what if Jess likes to shine in the spotlight?" Elizabeth added. "She *was* elected fall queen, you know, and royalty's entitled to certain privileges. Besides, she's not hurting anyone, is she?"

"No—except maybe the king," Todd noted pointedly.

About six paces behind Jessica stood Winston Egbert, Sweet Valley High's fall king and Jessica's date for the evening. Elizabeth would have liked to say something to explain away her sister's lack of concern for Winston, but she held her tongue, refusing to get into yet another fight over Jessica. Her twin was the only sore spot in Elizabeth's relationship with Todd. He still hadn't forgiven Jessica for the time she'd made him think Elizabeth wasn't interested in him, and Elizabeth saw no point in making the situation worse.

Besides, Elizabeth was well aware just how *un*thrilled Jessica was at having to spend the evening with Winston, for Elizabeth had spent the better part of her afternoon listening to her sister moan and groan about it. According to school tradition, the fall queen was supposed to accompany the king to certain school-sponsored activities during the semester. There was no way Jessica could get out of it, short of giving up her crown—and all the glory that went with it. It wasn't that she didn't like Winston, she'd carefully explained to her twin sister. Who at Sweet Valley didn't? He was always smiling, always joking—something of a class clown—yet in his own way one of the more interesting boys in school. It was who he *wasn't* that bothered Jessica. He wasn't Bruce Patman, the boy she longed to be with, the boy she'd hoped to snag when she'd schemed to be elected queen. The fact that Bruce still eluded her was a constant source of torment to Jessica. She always got what she wanted, and she hadn't yet met a boy who could resist her for very long. She desperately hoped Bruce wasn't turning out to be the exception.

Jessica was getting impatient. She'd been secretly in love with Bruce for years. He was good-looking and charming—and his family was one of the most prominent and richest in Sweet Valley, which made him even more attractive to her. But Jessica's frustration had begun to mount almost immediately as she'd watched him go after nearly every girl on the A list at school.

Every girl, it seemed, but her.

Jessica was already chatting with Cara Walker and a few of her other Pi Beta Alpha sorority sisters by the time Winston reached her side. There was a look of admiration on his face.

Dressed in a bright blue, skin-hugging mini-dress and matching tights, Jessica was an eye-catching sight. The outfit accented her long, shapely legs and brought out the blue in her sparkling aquamarine eyes. Across the room, Elizabeth, in her stylish but more casual wheat-colored pants and tan, striped shirt, also eyed her twin with admiration. Blessed with the same all-American blond good looks, the sisters appeared as alike as identical twins possibly could, but Elizabeth sometimes envied what she felt was her sister's more dramatic flair.

The floor of the gym was dotted with couples keeping pace with the rhythmic beat of The Droids, whose frenetic tempo and catchy original tunes made them Sweet Valley High's most popular band. Dana Larson, the group's lead singer, was in the middle of their latest song, "I've Found Paradise." The lyrics told how her Eden would be complete only when she found the right boy to share it with. Elizabeth mused that with as many guys as there were hooked on Dana's miniskirted figure, exotically styled short blond hair, and tantalizing voice, the singer would have no trouble making that wish come true.

"Hey, Todd, do you know who that guy is?"

Elizabeth asked. She pointed to a tall, lanky man in his early twenties standing at the back of the gym near the bleachers. He was dressed in red leather pants, with a matching skinny tie knotted loosely over his white shirt. He was staring intently at the stage and seemed absorbed in the music.

"Nah, never saw him before," Todd answered. "Maybe he's Ms. Dalton's new boyfriend."

"I doubt it. Since we've been here, he hasn't been near her. He's handsome enough for her, though."

Todd grinned. "I'm sure your reporter's instincts will sniff out the truth by the end of the evening. C'mon, let's wish Jess good luck on the contest. She's going to need it 'cause she's in for some tough competition."

"Oh, really? From whom?" Elizabeth asked.

Todd pointed to the ground. "These feet were born to dance. And my partner's not exactly clumsy, either. I heard somewhere that identical twins have identical talents."

"Jessica and I aren't identical in every way—as *you* should certainly know," Elizabeth said airily, shrugging off Todd's challenge. "Look, if we're going to see Jess, we'd better hurry. The contest will be starting anytime now."

Jessica lit up in a wide smile at the sight of her sister. "Hi, Liz," she said, beaming. "Having a good time?"

"Don't I always?" Elizabeth answered brightly. Then she turned to her sister's date. "You ready for the contest, Win?"

"Are you kidding?" He did a quick shuffle, nearly tripping over his gangly legs. "After tonight we go on to *Dance Fever*. Right, Jessica?"

Jessica, who had been scanning the room snapped back into the conversation at the sound of her name. "Oh, sure—whatever you say, Win." Turning to Elizabeth and Todd, she added, "By the way, you haven't seen Bruce Patman around, have you?"

"As a matter of fact, yes," Todd replied. "Over by the bleachers, surrounded by the usual horde of girls dying to get near him. Why do you ask?"

"Oh, nothing important." Jessica tossed her head as if to dismiss the subject, but her tone was a little too light to be totally believable. "I just wanted to wish him good luck tonight."

Elizabeth shot her sister a warning look. *How can she talk about Bruce with Win standing right next to her?* she thought angrily. "I hope he doesn't upstage you, little sister," Elizabeth said, using the affectionate nickname she had long ago given Jessica because she was four minutes younger than Elizabeth was. "I know how much winning this contest means to you."

"Oh, I'm not worried about that, big sister," Jessica declared. "Just remember what we talked

6

about this afternoon—and don't blow it, OK, Lizzie?"

Elizabeth was saddened by the urgency she heard in Jessica's voice. Earlier in the day Jessica had practically begged her not to try to win the contest, but Elizabeth hadn't taken her seriously. Jessica simply never begged for anything. But now she could see that her sister meant every word. *She'll really do anything to attract Bruce's attention*, Elizabeth suddenly realized. Glancing at Todd for a moment, she avoided Jessica's stare, then replied noncommittally, "I'll remember, and I'll see."

The high-pitched voice of Robin Wilson cut abruptly into their conversation. "Jessica! What an incredible dress! I love it! Where did you get it? I've got to get one just like it!" A recent arrival to Sweet Valley, Robin had quickly attached herself to Jessica. Robin had the unfortunate tendency to show up at the most inopportune times. Such as that moment.

"Cool it, Robin. I get your point," Jessica said, giving the overweight girl one of her fake, bright smiles, while thinking the last thing in the world she'd want was to be seen in the same outfit as Miss Tubby. "Oops, there's Lila. I've got to talk to her." Jessica quickly excused herself. Turning to Elizabeth, she added, "I'll catch up with you later. You're going up to Ken's, aren't you?"

"Wouldn't miss it for anything. Ken always throws the greatest parties."

7

"Ta-ta, then." And with that she ran off.

"Party? What party?" Robin asked, running after Jessica as fast as her plump legs would carry her.

But Jessica was off like a frenetic butterfly to huddle with her friend Lila Fowler. *She's probably getting tips on how to snare Bruce Patman,* Elizabeth thought worriedly, fearing that her sister's apparent single-mindedness might force her to do anything to get him. Lila had had a brief fling with the handsome, dark-haired senior some months earlier and considered herself an expert on him.

The dance contest was about to begin. The Droids had finished up their set, and as the lights dimmed, Roger Collins bounded onto the stage. Looking as handsome as a rock star, but dressed conservatively in comfortable, well-worn cords and a sweater, the popular, good-looking teacher positioned his lean frame behind the microphone. He clearly enjoyed his role as chaperon for the dance. "Good evening, ladies and gentlemen," he began grandly.

"Good evening, Mr. Collins," they all singsonged back at him in unison, affectionately mocking his master-of-ceremonies act.

Smiling broadly, Mr. Collins continued. "Welcome to Sweet Valley's Fifth Annual Rockin' Dance Party Contest. You all having a good time tonight?"

The crowd answered with a roar.

"Great!" he cried. "You know the rules. The

band will play three songs. While our contestants dance, the judges will circulate around the floor, and after a short break the winners will be announced." Pausing a moment for effect, Mr. Collins smiled at his audience, which was practically squirming with anticipation. "OK, then! Let's get started! Per Sweet Valley tradition, we'll lead off the contest with our king and queen. So without further ado, I present to you King Winston Egbert and Queen Jessica Wakefield."

A lone spotlight focused on the couple as The Droids let loose with a fast, wall-shaking number. Jessica was clearly in her element, moving with the music naturally and without effort. Even her lustrous golden hair swayed to the beat, completing the perfect picture of a dancer caught up in ecstasy.

Unfortunately for Jessica and her dreams of placing first, she had to share the spotlight with Winston. That's where the perfect picture ended. He was a very clumsy dancer, trying to hide his ineptness by acting like a clown.

As they danced, Jessica's expression went from happiness to pure, helpless fury as she watched Winston run in circles around her, comically kicking his feet and clapping his hands. With the way Winston was carrying on, she realized, there was no way she'd ever win the contest, even if Elizabeth—who *was* as good a dancer as her twin—held back a little.

9

Halfway through the first dance, in an act of quiet desperation, Jessica made heavy eye contact with a strikingly handsome boy. To her surprise and enormous delight, he caught her mental SOS and began to walk in her direction.

Jessica's pulse quickened. *He's coming*, she thought excitedly, not quite believing her eyes. *Bruce Patman is coming to dance with me!* She was so overcome by the very thought that she stopped moving—and Winston immediately stepped on her foot.

"I'm so sorry, Jessica," he apologized.

Jessica snapped back to attention. "It's OK. I'm used to it," she grumbled. "But what are you trying to do, put me in the hospital?"

Before Winston could reply, Bruce tapped his shoulder. "I've been watching your moves, Egbert, and I think you could use a little help. Watch how I do it." In one smooth move Bruce pulled Jessica from the startled Winston and took her in his arms.

Bruce got no argument from Winston. He knew when he was upstaged. Accepting the inevitable, he quietly slunk to the refreshment table at the side of the gym.

With conflicting emotions, Elizabeth had watched the scene unfold. Her sister did deserve to win, but it hardly seemed worth hurting Winston to get the prize. Especially if, as Elizabeth suspected, the prize was Bruce. "Well, would you look at that!" she said to Todd, nodding toward Jessica's new partner.

"I'm not surprised. Jessica always gets what she wants."

"Bruce Patman." Elizabeth mouthed the name of the one boy she'd hoped Jessica would never catch. "I wonder what brought this on?" she said aloud. "What does that egomaniac want with Jessica?"

"Looks simple enough to me," Todd remarked. "The guy wants to win the contest—and Jessica's his best hope. I'm sure that's all it is."

Elizabeth hoped that Todd was right, and she had to admit that Bruce was as good a dancer as Jessica. Together they moved across the floor as if they'd always been partners.

When the first dance ended, they were clearly unwilling to separate; and during the second and third songs Bruce and Jessica shifted into more complex moves. With the strength of his well-muscled body, Bruce lifted Jessica high in the air and spun her around his broad shoulders and across his body. They were pure grace, electricity in motion, and as more and more couples grew aware of what they were up against, they dropped out of the contest to stand aside and admire this masterful performance. By the time the third song ended, only a handful of couples remained—and the outcome of the contest was certain.

Even Mr. Collins didn't try to prolong the suspense when he stepped back on stage to announce the winners. "Jessica Wakefield and Bruce Patman, come on up here and get your award." To a smattering of applause the handsome couple accepted the trophy from Mr. Collins. "Now you can lead everyone in the next dance."

Elizabeth was sure that the smile on Jessica's face had little to do with winning the contest. It appeared she'd won what she considered a more valuable prize—Bruce Patman. But Elizabeth couldn't force herself to share her sister's happiness. She knew the real Bruce better than Jessica did. Back on the dance floor, Bruce had wrapped Jessica tightly in his arms as they moved in time to a slow ballad. She held on to him as if she were living a dream she was afraid would end at any moment.

"You're some dancer, Bruce," she whispered breathlessly. "A big improvement over Win— especially on these slow numbers."

"Glad you noticed, baby," he murmured sweetly. "Anyway, slow dancing isn't really dancing."

"What do you mean, Bruce?"

"It's just the easiest way for a guy to get his arms around a girl."

"Oh? Is that the only reason you picked me for a partner tonight?" Jessica pretended to pout.

"It's a good reason—and I do have my arms around you."

"And I have mine around you. I'd say it works

12

for both sexes," she retorted, pulling her body closer to his in typical Jessica Wakefield fashion.

But Bruce pushed her back ever so slightly. "In dancing, at least, the guy still takes the lead."

His meaning wasn't lost on Jessica. She'd have to be less aggressive if she wanted to keep him interested. "Then I'll follow wherever you lead," she said with uncharacteristic submissiveness. Bruce nudged closer and rubbed his hand approvingly over the nape of her neck.

Over at the refreshment table Winston downed his fifth cola as he stared disconsolately at the dance floor. Elizabeth, hoping to cheer him up, poured herself a root beer and sauntered over to him. "For a guy who's usually in the middle of everything, you're pretty quiet tonight," she remarked.

Winston pasted a broad smile on his face. "Just taking a time out. We kings have a heavy schedule."

Elizabeth wasn't fooled by his false show of bravado. "Don't let Jessica get you down, Win. She's always doing things first and thinking about them later."

"You talking about her and Patman? No big deal," he said lightly. "Why shouldn't she want to dance with someone who doesn't step all over her toes?"

"Come on, Win. I saw you! You could be good if you tried."

Smiling appreciatively at Elizabeth, he put down

his drink. "Look, the dance is almost over. Once it is, she'll dump Bruce and come back to me. We're still going to Ken's party together."

"I see," she said, with a look that expressed her doubts.

"Hey, don't worry about me," Winston added. "I can handle your sister just fine."

"I sure hope so, Win," Elizabeth said, trying to sound supportive. In her sixteen years she'd yet to come across a boy who could truly control her tempestuous twin.

After The Droids finished their last set, Elizabeth noticed that the mysterious man in the red leather pants was talking animatedly with them. Jessica and Bruce were still in the middle of the dance floor, moving to music only they could hear. In an effort to divert Winston's attention from this scene, Elizabeth steered him into a discussion about whether the Sweet Valley Gladiators had a chance at the state football championship this year. At first Winston talked freely, but when he realized what Elizabeth was doing, he stood up straight and announced, "Excuse me, Liz, but I've got something important to do.'"

"Win, wait!" Elizabeth called. But Winston wasn't listening.

Elizabeth was about to go after him when she felt a tap on her shoulder. "Got a second?"

She turned to face Emily Mayer, The Droids' drummer. "I may have a scoop for your column,"

14

Emily said, casually running a hand through her dark brown, wavy hair. She was referring to the "Eyes and Ears" column Elizabeth wrote for the school paper. "It's not official yet, but it looks like you've just seen our last high school concert."

Elizabeth couldn't hide her shock. "You mean you guys are splitting up?"

"Oh, no! What I mean is—The Droids are going big time!"

"What are you talking about?"

"This guy came up to us after we finished our set." Emily was racing now, trying to get the words out as fast as she could. "He wants to manage us. He says he could make us stars!"

"The guy in the red pants?"

Emily nodded.

"Are you sure he's for real?" Elizabeth asked skeptically.

"I know it sounds crazy, but he's legit, Liz. His name is Tony Conover, and he's a representative of T.G. Goode and Associates. That may not mean anything to you, but they're the agency that books all the major clubs in L.A. Tony said he's the one who discovered August Moon and the Savage Six, and look where they are now. He's been scouting around the entire state looking at bands just like ours, and he says we've got what it takes."

"It sounds impressive," Elizabeth agreed. "But don't rush into anything too quickly. I mean, isn't it all kind of sudden?"

15

"Look," Emily said with a trace of annoyance, "we're not going to do anything without giving it careful thought. But just think, Liz, soon we could be playing L.A.!"

Elizabeth grinned. "I'll be there when you do!"

Moments later Elizabeth caught up with Todd, and together they rushed to the edge of the bleachers, where Jessica and Winston were in a heated discussion.

"Look, Win, all I'm saying is that I just can't spend the rest of the evening with you!" Jessica shouted.

"But, Jess, we had a date for tonight."

"Just because we came here together doesn't mean we have to leave together. Where's your sense of adventure, Win? C'mon, loosen up. *You're* free to do whatever *you* want."

"I want to be with you."

"Well, *almost* anything you want." Jessica's eyes lit up in inspiration. "I've got it! Why don't you take Robin Wilson to Ken's place? She'd love it. Oh, the two of you would be just perfect." Then, as if everything were now happily resolved, Jessica patted Winston on the shoulder. "See you, Win. And thanks for being such a good sport."

"Sure—anytime," he mumbled to her retreating back.

Elizabeth had heard enough. Leaving Todd to

cheer up the defeated Winston, she raced to her sister's side before Jessica had a chance to find Bruce.

"Hold it, Jessica."

Elizabeth didn't use such a commanding tone very often, and Jessica always knew when her sister spoke that way it had to be something serious. She stopped and turned. "What is it, Liz?"

"How could you do that to Win? You've humiliated him."

"Oh, that. He'll get over it," she answered breezily. "It's not like we're a couple or anything."

"No, but you had a date with him tonight."

"So what? Where does it say I have to chain myself to Koko the Clown all night? I've been waiting for Bruce since—since birth, for heaven's sake! If you think I'm going to let him go now, you're wrong!"

"But do you really think he's for you?" Elizabeth persisted.

"Actually, yes. I think he's perfect."

"I'm telling you, Jess—"

"Lizzie, that's enough," Jessica hissed. "You've done your big-sister number. Now it's time to leave me alone."

"But, Jess—"

"I said forget it, Liz. It's none of your business. I've got to find Bruce." She peered into the group of kids milling around the outside door to the

17

gym. Seeing him, her heart melted, and her voice grew noticeably softer. "There he is now. Hey, Bruce, wait for me," she called into the crowd.

With that, Jessica floated into the waiting arms of the most desirable boy at Sweet Valley High.

And all Elizabeth could do was shake her head and hope she was wrong about Bruce. For her sister's sake.

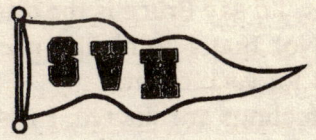

Two

Elizabeth couldn't keep from biting her nails on the way to Ken's party. She wanted to keep an eye on Jessica just in case her sister got too carried away. Turning to Todd, she snapped impatiently, "Can't you make this car go faster?"

"Hey, what's with you? The party's just getting started." He turned to her and frowned when he noticed the worried expression on her face. "Oh, I get it. It's Jessica, isn't it?"

"Yes, it's Jessica," Elizabeth admitted. "I don't think she knows what she's getting herself into."

Todd shook his head. "Seems to me she's going to do what she wants anyway, Liz. You can't be her mother."

"I know, but if she'd only listen to me, maybe I could keep her from getting hurt."

19

"By Bruce?" Todd snickered. "Jessica's a big girl. She can handle herself just fine without your help. Besides, I'd say Bruce is the one who should be careful. Not that I think it's necessary. They seem perfect for each other."

"Jessica's feelings are sincere. I wish I could say as much about Bruce's."

"Since when have you become an expert on the inner workings of Bruce Patman? Isn't it possible he could like your sister?"

"Anything's possible," she conceded.

"So what's the problem?"

"The problem is that Jess has had a secret crush on Bruce for practically forever. And she wasn't acting like herself at all tonight. It was weird. When she just heard Bruce's name, she looked as if she were ready to fall at his feet. I'm afraid of what might happen. I don't think he's good for her. He's not a nice guy, and I don't want to see her get hurt. I can tell she thinks he's a dream come true, and it scares me."

Todd turned into the long, winding dirt road to Ken's lakeside house, then parked beside a number of other cars that had transformed the Matthewses' neat grounds into a miniature parking lot. "How are you going to stop her?"

"I don't know for sure," she said dejectedly as she got out of the car. Then she smiled. "But I certainly don't want to ruin your evening, Todd, figuring it out." Arm in arm they approached the crowd gathering behind the stately stone-faced house.

It didn't take her long to spot Jessica, who, to Elizabeth's dismay, had her arm locked securely around Bruce's waist. The new couple was standing on the patio talking to Ken and his date, Lila Fowler, and Paul Sherwood and a few of Bruce's other friends from the tennis team—a group Elizabeth thought were cliquey snobs. Jessica was staring adoringly into Bruce's deep blue eyes. Elizabeth knew that her twin, who was usually in total control of herself, would die if she could see how she was behaving now, but she also realized that this was not the time to confront Jessica. A big scene in front of this crowd could be a disaster.

Sighing, she allowed Todd to steer her toward another group gathered near the lake.

Jessica, meanwhile, had to keep pinching herself to believe she was really there with Bruce. Totally oblivious to the conversation taking place, her mind kept repeating the words he'd whispered while they'd been dancing. *"I've had my eyes on you for a long time, Jess. We could have a real good time together."*

As always, Bruce was enjoying being the center of attention and enthusiastically reenacted an incident that had occurred the night before. ". . . So I looked behind me, and there's the big red light of a cop car gaining on me. I could have put my black beauty into fifth and really let her rip, but I

21

was in a generous mood, so I pulled off to the side of the road. 'What's the matter, officer?' I asked. I was really polite, trying to get on his good side. But he wasn't buying. 'Gimme your license and registration'—he was really barking at me, you know? The guy was mean, the type who'd put you in a choke hold without blinking an eye. So I gave him the stuff, and he says, 'Hmm, Patman, eh?' He's no fool, he knows the name, so I say, 'Yeah, Patman. One of the Sweet Valley Patmans. What of it?' 'Uh, Mr. Patman'—he called me *mister*, can you believe it?—'you were going eighty-two in a thirty-five zone.' So I say, 'That's too bad. I'll try not to do that anymore.' Then I flashed a twenty under his nose. 'What do you say we just pretend this never happened?' And you know, he took it! You ought to try that the next time *you* get caught, Kenny boy."

"Maybe I would if my name were Patman," he answered. "You sure you didn't threaten to sic your dad on this guy?"

"Now, would I do a thing like that?" Bruce asked with mock indignation. "I'm too nice a guy to stoop to that, wouldn't you say, Jessica?" He squeezed her around the waist.

A long silence followed as everyone in the group waited for Jessica's reply. Finally, realizing all eyes were upon her, she snapped out of her daydream. "Oh, am I supposed to say something?" she asked.

22

For the first time in her life, she was caught completely off guard.

Lila looked at her with undisguised amusement. Well aware of Jessica's crush on Bruce, she could see that her friend was already off the deep end. *Good luck, Jess,* she thought. *You're going to need it.*

Ken, feeling embarrassed for Jessica, stepped in to rescue her. "I think it's time we all cooled off. What do you say we get our suits and hop in the lake?"

After changing into a bright red bikini that accented every curve of her trim body, Jessica joined Bruce at the lake's edge. Though the night was warm, she shivered. Was it the temperature—or the sight of Bruce's own lean, firm frame? She wasn't certain. The sensation was thrilling, nevertheless, and it was heightened when she watched Bruce dive gracefully into the water. *He's beautiful,* she thought, aware of a tense stirring inside her. The first feelings of love, she was sure of it. Confidently she positioned herself on the diving platform and did a perfect backflip into the deep, cool water.

When she surfaced, Bruce was by her side. "Pretty fancy move there, babe," he remarked, impressed.

"I was on the girls' swim team in junior high,"

she reminded him proudly as they swam to a point where the water was no longer over their heads. They both stood, a bit apart from each other. The shock of the cool water had done little to ease the tension within Jessica. Only the touch of Bruce's arms, she realized, could soothe her now. She swam a few strokes and stopped very close to him.

"You can show off your strokes some other time," he said. "For now, let's pick up where we left off on the dance floor." Gesturing broadly, he asked, "May I have this dance?"

"Certainly," Jessica answered. Needing no prompting, she gladly fell into his embrace. Ignoring all the others now in the lake, she basked in the realization that for the evening she was Bruce Patman's girl. And she hoped it was only the beginning.

"Why have we waited so long to do this?" Bruce whispered in her ear as he circled her in the water, which came to her shoulders.

"There's a time and a place for everything, Bruce. It just wasn't our time before." Jessica's words surprised her. She didn't really believe them.

"It's our time now," Bruce said huskily. "Or it could be—if you want it." Gently pressing the back of her neck with his fingertips, he brushed his lips against hers.

"Oh, Bruce," Jessica said and sighed when their lips parted temporarily. He pulled her closer, this time for a long, lingering kiss unlike any she'd ever experienced before.

As they continued to embrace, Bruce slowly dropped his arms from her neck to her back. Too caught up in the rapture of the moment, Jessica had no idea what he was doing until she felt the cool water swirl under her bikini top and hit her breasts.

Right in front of everyone Bruce had untied her bathing suit strings! Though only her head and shoulders were visible above the water, Jessica was still shocked. Bruce was moving too far, too fast. She realized she had to retie the top without making him think she was some kind of goody-goody.

"Now, Bruce, why'd you go and do a thing like that?" she said, exaggerating a pout. Pretending to be madder than she was, she pushed him away and quickly retied the top.

Bruce smiled slyly. "What's the matter, Jess, don't you like to play big-girl games? Or are you just a tease?"

"Oh, no, Bruce. I like playing as much as you do. I just don't like to rush into things. It's more fun when you take your time. Didn't anyone ever tell you that's what girls really like?" Jessica said, moving a little farther away from him.

"So now you're playing hard to get?" Bruce said mockingly. He moved through the water away from her.

Anxiously Jessica reached out for him, afraid he might be leaving her.

"I don't play the game by those rules," he informed her arrogantly.

"Well, maybe it's time to break the rules," Jessica said.

"Why would I want to do that?" he asked.

"For this." Swimming over to Bruce, Jessica gave him a slow, moist kiss, then murmured seductively, "Let's start all over again."

"Let's get out of here first," he said huskily. "I think we're both waterlogged."

"Sounds fine to me," she purred.

"And I know just the place we can dry off."

Their departure from the lake did not escape Elizabeth's attention. She'd been standing by the water's edge talking with some friends when she noticed her sister and Bruce embrace, then pull themselves out of the water and walk toward some trees. Uneasy about what Jessica could be getting herself into, Elizabeth turned quickly to Todd and said, "Oh, I just remembered I left something in the car. I'll be back in a sec."

"I'll come with you," Todd offered.

"N-no, I'll be fine," she said, running off before Todd had a chance to respond. As soon as she was out of his sight, Elizabeth cut a path to her left, swiftly walking in the direction where she had last seen Bruce and Jessica. Moments later, Elizabeth stood before a dense row of juniper trees that separated the lake area from the more secluded part of the Matthewses' property. Away from the festive party lights and pulsing music, it was dark and still. Elizabeth began to move through the trees, guided only by the dim glow of the moon.

It didn't take long until she heard sounds she had dreaded hearing: the sounds of two people whispering breathlessly as the leaf-covered ground crackled under the weight of their bodies. Elizabeth stopped abruptly, hoping they hadn't heard the crunching sound of her own footsteps. She was eavesdropping on a passionate moment, and it made her feel uncomfortable. Increasingly filled with distress, Elizabeth willed Jessica and Bruce to stop, hoping that her usually reckless sister would for once control her impulses. But the soft sounds continued, and Elizabeth had to make a decision.

Embarrassed or not, she resolved to approach the couple.

Deliberately coughing loudly, Elizabeth made her way through the leaves, walking slowly, hoping to give Jessica and Bruce enough time to disentangle themselves. But they refused to be warned. She was practically standing on top of them when they finally noticed her.

Jessica looked up and scowled. "God, Elizabeth, must you go sneaking up on people like Jack the

Ripper? Don't you have any respect for other people's privacy?" She was lying wrapped in Bruce's arms, and she barely turned her face from his.

Elizabeth refused to budge. "Could I see you for a minute, Jess? I've got a real important problem."

"It can wait, Liz," said a very annoyed Bruce.

"I'm talking to Jessica, not you," Elizabeth retorted. "Jess, can you come inside for a minute?"

Before Jessica had a chance to answer, Bruce raised himself on one elbow, coolly allowing his free hand to slide seductively along Jessica's right arm and come to rest on her shoulder, just above her breast.

Jessica didn't move.

"Look, honey—" Bruce started.

"I'm not your honey," Elizabeth snapped.

"Hey, whatever. Can't you see Jessica's busy? Whatever you want can wait."

"I have to talk to my sister now. Jessica?" Elizabeth's stare bored directly into her sister's eyes. "Please, Jessica," she practically pleaded.

Bruce smirked. "Go on," he said to Jessica. "I wouldn't want to hold you. Unless you want me to."

To Jessica the message was clear: Go with Elizabeth and kiss Bruce Patman goodbye. It took only a second for her to decide. "I'm not going anywhere—just now." Then, turning to Elizabeth, she added, "Look, whatever it is, I'll talk to you about it later, OK?"

Elizabeth was mortified. Jessica had never rejected her so bluntly before. It was clear that she would have needed a crowbar to pry her sister from Bruce's arms. "Forget it," Elizabeth said. There was a mixture of hurt and disgust in her voice. Then she turned and headed back to the party.

Jessica smiled. Now that she had nothing to lose, she wanted to show Bruce her strength. "Do you believe her?" she said as soon as Elizabeth was out of earshot. "Sometimes she's really off the wall."

"From the way she came stomping over here, you'd think she was your baby-sitter."

"Nah, I'm sure it has nothing to do with me." She lied easily, knowing full well it had everything to do with her. "It's probably more stuff about that guy she's madly in love with. She did say *she* had the problem. Remember?"

"Oh, yeah. You mean Todd?" Bruce asked, taken in.

"I couldn't possibly tell you," Jessica purred coyly. "After all, she is my sister, and we never betray each other's secrets, no matter what."

"But," Bruce whispered, "can you keep a secret from her?"

"What do you mean?" she asked, their faces barely inches apart.

"This," he said, and he kissed her deeply. It took her breath away, leaving her helpless in his arms.

As much as Jessica loved the way she was feeling, another part of her was disturbed. She was used to having the upper hand with boys, but already she was starting to feel out of control. She had to slow Bruce down, and now was the time to try. She blurted out the first thing that came to her mind. "Actually, I hope Liz hasn't found out the truth."

"What's that?" asked Bruce, his curiosity revived.

"That Todd's been fooling around," Jessica lied. "I can't bear to tell her. She'll be so hurt. Anyway," she added, having achieved her purpose for the moment, "we shouldn't be bothering with it. It's not our problem."

"That's for sure, baby. We don't have any problems, do we?" He kissed her again, and this time she felt herself respond with rising passion. And as Bruce's lips pressed against hers, she felt her power over him slip away.

Bruce, in control and knowing it, broke the kiss and looked deeply into her eyes. "But, baby, you'd know in a minute if we *did* have a problem."

"How?"

"By the empty space next to you."

Jessica suddenly felt insecure and vulnerable. She cuddled closer to Bruce and in her sexiest voice, with her lips tickling his ear, whispered softly, "It sure doesn't feel empty now."

He responded by turning his face to hers and kissing her hard, his arms crushing her against him, his mouth demanding what his body wanted to take.

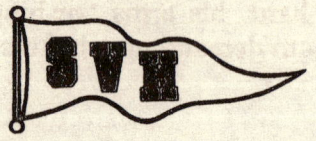

Three

Elizabeth, rolling over, lay awake in her bed. She looked at the clock for the fortieth time. It was already after three A.M., and she hadn't slept a wink. She was not only angry at her twin, but worried, too.

About an hour after her disastrous encounter with Jessica and Bruce in the woods, Elizabeth had seen them take off in his gleaming black Porsche. She had been disgusted enough to suppress her concern and enjoy the rest of the party, but once Todd brought her home her worries returned—stronger than ever. Brooding over Jessica's whereabouts in the silence of the predawn hours was becoming almost unbearable.

On top of everything else, Elizabeth was angry

at Jessica for forcing her to lie to her mother, whom she'd run into in the upstairs hall. Lying was something Elizabeth never did, except when it came to her sister. Hoping her mother wouldn't double-check, Elizabeth had told her that Jessica was already in her bedroom. The last thing in the world she wanted to do was to sneak into Jessica's bed and pretend to be her, a routine she'd gone through more than once before. Oddly enough, her mother didn't question the lie. In fact, she didn't even ask Elizabeth about her date. She seemed preoccupied with something else, Elizabeth thought.

Just as the sun was about to make its appearance, Elizabeth heard the sound of a door close. Convinced it was Jessica, she crawled out of her bed and tiptoed through the bathroom to Jessica's adjoining room.

Jessica didn't see Elizabeth until she was nearly on top of her, and she almost woke up the entire Wakefield household with a startled gasp. "You making a habit of sneaking up on me?" Jessica fumed, trying to keep her voice down. "What gives, Liz?"

"Sorry, Jess, I didn't mean to scare you. I couldn't sleep. Where've you been?"

Jessica smiled sweetly. "I don't have to give you my itinerary, Liz, but I'd think even *you* could figure out the answer to that one."

"Bruce. You've been with him all this time?"

"Oh, yes," Jessica said blissfully. "And it was wonderful!"

"I was afraid of that," Elizabeth murmured.

"There's nothing to be afraid of," Jessica said. "Bruce is everything a girl could ever hope for."

"How could you tell? He's got you so worked up you can't even think straight."

"And what's that supposed to mean?"

"You were following him like a little puppy dog all night long. That's so unlike you, Jessica." Elizabeth lowered her voice to a whisper. "And don't think I'm not upset about the way you treated me in the woods. You've never brushed me off like that before."

"I'm sorry," Jessica said, "but you did interrupt a private moment."

"I guess I did. But for some reason I felt afraid for you, and I just couldn't control myself. I'm sorry for that," Elizabeth added truthfully.

"Afraid? I can handle myself just fine," Jessica retorted, ignoring her sister's apology.

Elizabeth was doubtful. With false lightness, she asked, "Anyway, what did you two do after the party?"

"Nothing to be ashamed of. Talk mostly." Dropping her guard for a second, Jessica confided with pleasure, "Bruce said he was angry when he lost out at being king 'cause he wanted to share the throne with me."

Elizabeth was astounded that her normally perceptive sister would fall for such an obviously phony remark. "I wouldn't believe a line like that if he took a lie detector test," she blurted.

"Oh, come on, Elizabeth. Why can't you get it into your thick skull that Bruce likes me!"

"It takes more than a few kisses to prove that."

"A lot you know. The truth is, we really have tons in common." She sighed wistfully. "Oh, I hope I'll see him again real soon."

"You mean he didn't ask you out again—after all that?"

"No," Jessica admitted, "but I'm sure he will."

"I wouldn't be," Elizabeth muttered under her breath.

"I heard that." Jessica's patience with her sister was nearing the breaking point. She flounced into the bathroom and briskly ran a brush through her long, silky hair. When Elizabeth followed her, she added, "I've had just about enough of your bad-mouthing Bruce. I don't know what you've got against him. You never tried to stop me from making a play for him before tonight."

"I never had to—he was never interested before tonight."

"Look, if there's something specific that you have to tell me about him, go ahead. Otherwise, shut up."

"He's arrogant and self-centered. He'll hurt you."

Jessica snorted. "Just what I thought. You don't have any real reasons—just your own opinion.

Sorry, Liz, but you're going to have to do better than that."

"Look how fast he dumped Lila Fowler and Heather Morgan. Even your good friend Cara Walker. Why believe *you'll* do any better? He doesn't hang on to anyone for very long."

Jessica put down her brush and faced her sister. "Liz, don't you understand? They meant nothing to him."

"How do you know?" Elizabeth pressed.

"He told me."

"And you believe him?"

"I have no reason not to. Now, are you finished?"

Elizabeth eyed her sister silently, aware that in the end Jessica would have to figure out the truth herself.

"You had your chance, Elizabeth," Jessica said angrily. "Don't you *dare* say another bad word about Bruce in front of me, or you'll regret it for eternity."

"Jess—"

"You heard me, Elizabeth! That's all!"

Before Elizabeth could recover, Jessica stormed out of the bathroom and locked the door behind her. Elizabeth stood alone in front of the vanity, her eyes brimming with tears. Despite all of the petty disagreements they'd had over the years, she couldn't remember Jessica ever going to bed angry at her. Elizabeth didn't like it one bit, especially since she was sure that the cause of their argument—that arrogant jock, Bruce Patman—was just playing another game with her unsuspecting sister. And she was almost as sure it was a game Jessica couldn't win.

Sunday morning found Elizabeth at the breakfast table, nibbling idly on a piece of toast, only half listening to her parents' conversation.

"Says here that George Fowler's expanding his plant." Alice Wakefield put down the Sunday paper as she spoke to her husband, Ned. "I'm going to call him first thing tomorrow and show him my portfolio. I could come up with some wonderful designs for him."

So that was it, Elizabeth decided distractedly. Her mother had been thinking about this Fowler project last night. That's why she'd been too preoccupied to notice Elizabeth's cover-up for Jessica.

Ned shook his head. "I don't know, honey. I hear he's already negotiating with a big design firm from San Francisco."

Alice lifted her brows in surprise and distress. "How do you know? And why didn't you tell me sooner?"

Ned's face assumed that slightly bemused expression that always came over him when they discussed his wife's career moves. "I found out from Marianna on Friday," he said offhandedly.

"It didn't seem important at the time." Marianna West was a partner in his law firm.

Alice held her breath for a moment. She was unhappy with her husband's lack of interest in her work, but she had no desire to make an issue of it on this bright, clear Sunday morning. Exhaling slowly, she changed the subject. "What were you and Marianna talking about, dear?"

Elizabeth tuned out the rest of her parents' conversation and barely heard the phone ringing in the other room. Still upset about Jessica, she could hardly even concentrate on finishing breakfast.

Alice couldn't help noticing her daughter's glum mood. "What's the matter, Liz? Did you and Todd have a fight last night?"

"Oh, no, Mom. We had a good time."

"So why the sad face?"

"It's nothing." Elizabeth attempted a halfhearted smile. "I'll be all right."

"Sure you don't want to talk about it?" Alice asked.

"I'm sure, Mom. Really, I'm fine. I just didn't sleep too well last night. Pass me the cartoons, OK? Maybe a little *Peanuts* will help."

Elizabeth was busy trying to lose herself in the comics when Jessica breezily entered the kitchen.

"Good morning, people!" She was as bubbly as a newly opened bottle of soda despite a mere three hours' sleep. "How are all of you this morning?" Without waiting for an answer, she planted a firm kiss on everyone's forehead.

Elizabeth was stunned. She couldn't remember the last time her sister had been up so early on a Sunday morning.

"What's gotten into you, Jess?" her father asked, a chuckle in his voice.

Mrs. Wakefield smiled. "Can't you tell, Ned? Obviously she had a great time at the dance."

"That's right, Mom," Jessica said, pouring herself a glass of orange juice. She leaned against the tile counter and stared dreamily off into space. "I think I'm in love," she announced at last.

"With Winston?" Her mother threw her a surprised look.

"Absolutely not! Winston's a nerd, Mom. I'm talking about someone extra special."

Elizabeth groaned, but no one heard. All eyes were on her twin.

"Who's that, dear?" Alice asked.

Jessica paused for dramatic effect. "Bruce Patman."

"The Patman boy, eh," her father noted approvingly.

"But, Jessica, what happened with Winston? I thought you went out with him last night," her mother asked a little suspiciously. She was well aware of her daughter's tendency to go after what she wanted with total disregard for other people.

"I did, but he had his eye on someone else,"

Jessica hedged, shooting a quick, hard look at Elizabeth. "We agreed to go our separate ways at Ken's party."

Elizabeth wanted to challenge the lie, but she held back at the last moment. From Jessica's behavior Elizabeth knew that her twin was no longer mad at her, and she didn't want to upset the equilibrium. At the same time, though, she wasn't sure if she could stand to sit through her starry-eyed sister's retelling of her night with Bruce. It was like listening to someone who'd been hypnotized.

" . . . and he told me we were *made* for each other. Isn't that the most romantic thing you've ever heard?" Jessica directed the question at Elizabeth, who remained unusually silent. Getting no reaction, Jessica shrugged and pranced out to the hallway to fetch her red nylon jacket from the closet. Swinging it over her shoulder, she returned to the kitchen. "Don't hold up dinner for me, OK?"

"Where are you going?" Ned asked.

"Bruce just called. He's taking me sailing on Secca Lake today. I don't know how long we'll be, but I don't want you to wait." She glanced at the wall clock. "He should be picking me up any minute now."

That was all Elizabeth needed to hear. Unwilling to watch her sister fly ecstatically out the door, Elizabeth pushed her chair away from the table.

"May I be excused? I've got a big chemistry test to study for."

"Sure, dear," her mother answered.

"Say, what's the big rush, Liz?" Jessica asked. "The test's not till Wednesday. That's practically eons from now."

"So call me a Girl Scout," Elizabeth shot back. "I believe in being prepared. A little advance studying wouldn't hurt you, either."

"I won't even dignify that remark with an answer," Jessica countered. She hurried out of the kitchen and into the foyer to wait for Bruce and his slick, shiny, black Porsche.

Four

"Liz! Liz, I've got to talk to you!"

Emily Mayer caught up with Elizabeth at her locker the following morning. Emily looked quite different from the way she appeared when performing. The petite drummer was dressed for school in a plain navy blue skirt and sweater, her wavy hair tied back neatly. "Liz, it's happening," she said excitedly. "It's really happening!"

"Slow down, Emily. What are you talking about?"

"The Droids. We're going to the top of the charts!"

It took Elizabeth a second to remember. "You mean, that guy . . . what's his name?"

"Tony." Emily nodded excitedly. "He's everything he says he is, Liz. Guy even found pictures of him with some of his other bands in some back issues of *Music Madness*. I always thought it was dumb of Guy to save those magazines, but now I'm glad he did. Oh, Liz, Tony has such great plans for us."

"So when's the first record coming out?"

"Come on, we're not ready for that yet. Tony's planning to book us into some local clubs first and maybe get us some dates around the state during Christmas vacation. With a little luck and a lot of hard work, he says we may be good enough to break into L.A. clubs by next summer. But he's not promising anything. Not yet, anyway, though he did say he's going to bring around lots of record-producer friends of his to meet us as soon as we sound a little tighter."

Elizabeth smiled warmly at Emily. She took her music very seriously, and she deserved to have good things happen. "I'm so happy for you, Emily," Elizabeth bubbled. "I bet the others are just losing their minds with excitement!"

"You bet they're excited—and tired," Emily was saying as the first bell for the next class rang. The two of them began walking to class. "We were up half the night practicing."

"Seems the only thing you're missing is some publicity."

"Do you have anything in mind?"

"Yes. I'd like to chart your progress in a running series of stories in *The Oracle*. I'll have to get the go-ahead from Penny, the editor, but I know she'll love the idea. I'll begin with how you met Tony and what your plans are. Then I'll follow you from your first club date all the way to your number-one hit record."

Emily was overjoyed. "That's fantastic. Oh, Liz, you don't know how much all this means to me."

"I think I do, Emily. Being a rock star is just a fantasy for most kids, but you're actually going to live it!"

"Unfortunately I still have to live out the role of a student, too." Groaning, Emily opened the door to their chemistry class. "Reality, for the moment, is big bad Bob Russo."

They exchanged knowing glances. Chemistry was Elizabeth's hardest subject this year, and Bob Russo was the reason. A no-nonsense man, Russo was the type of teacher who demanded excellence from all his students—and usually got it. In truth, most of the kids felt he deserved their attention. He really cared what his students learned, and he insisted that they not disappoint him, or themselves. Even Jessica, who did very little studying but still got good grades in most classes, found it necessary to study for Russo's chemistry class.

When the late bell rang, Elizabeth was surprised to find her sister's chair empty as she took her own seat by the window of the second-story chemistry lab. She and Jessica had driven to school together, so she knew Jessica was around some-place. But where?

A glance out the window answered Elizabeth's question. She saw a couple kissing brazenly—and passionately—on the far end of the campus lawn. Jessica and Bruce. They were locked in an embrace so tight it seemed to Elizabeth that it would take at least half of Sweet Valley's football team to tear them apart.

Jessica ran her fingers through Bruce's dark, wavy hair, delighting in its soft, silky feel. Bruce answered her by kissing her more and more deeply, exciting every nerve ending in her body. Jessica pulled herself even closer, rubbing her other hand in small circles at the nape of Bruce's neck.

The faint sound of the late bell distracted the couple as they parted to catch their breath.

"Oh, no, Bruce, we're late! We've got to go!" Jessica quickly picked up the books she'd strewn across the grass earlier.

Bruce chuckled and placed a hand on Jessica's shoulder to keep her in place. "What's the rush, baby? We were just getting started."

Jessica couldn't look him in the face. She wanted desperately to be with him, but she didn't relish paying the price later with the stern chemistry teacher. "I want to stay, Bruce. You know that.

ut I've got to get to Russo's class. He'll kill me if I cut it."

"You mean to tell me my girl's more interested in Mr. Chemistry than in me? What about *our* chemistry? I thought I knew you better, Jess."

She sighed. "Oh, Bruce, you know how I feel about us." Then, her fingers lightly caressing the back of his neck, she continued. "But you know how he is about giving out detentions, and if I have to stay after school, I won't be able to watch you practice tennis. You wouldn't like that, Bruce, would you?"

"I see your point, but . . . Hey, not to worry, sweet thing." Reaching into the back pocket of his corduroy pants, Bruce pulled out a pad. "Even Russo can't refuse to accept this." Bruce scribbled something on the top sheet, ripped it off, and handed it to Jessica.

"A note from the nurse's office!" Jessica glowed, relieved she didn't have to make a choice she had no desire to make.

Bruce traced the outline of her mouth with his fingertip. "The results of my examination show you need some mouth-to-mouth resuscitation."

Jessica moved closer. "I'd say your diagnosis is right on the mark, Dr. Patman. Shall we begin the treatments?" Raising her face to his, Jessica entwined herself around her beloved boyfriend.

Five

The following afternoon Elizabeth rushed home from school as soon as classes ended. During her last-period gym class, as she was playing tennis with her best friend, Enid, she'd had an idea for a short story. Elizabeth loved the special, excited feeling that came over her whenever inspiration struck, but she knew the idea would fade unless she got her thoughts on paper as soon as possible. She hoped to finish a rough outline before the day was through.

No one else was home, and the solitude provided Elizabeth with the atmosphere she needed to concentrate. Retreating to her favorite overstuffed chair in the living room, she opened her spiral notebook and began to put her thoughts down on paper. The story was about a girl who kept making the wrong decisions in love.

A short while later Elizabeth became aware of a knocking sound. At first it was so timid that she thought it was a tree limb banging softly against the side of the house. But the knock became more persistent, and Elizabeth realized someone was at the front door. Reluctantly she put aside her notebook to answer it. On the other side of the threshold stood Robin Wilson.

"Hi, Liz, is Jessica here?" she asked.

"No," said Elizabeth. "She's at cheerleading practice. But I expect her back soon. Tonight's her night to make dinner."

Robin looked confused. "I checked at cheerleading practice. She wasn't there. We were going to spend the afternoon together, but she never showed up. Gee, I wonder where she could be."

"I think I know," Elizabeth said, realizing she'd better start thinking about what *she'd* like to make for dinner. "I'll bet anything she's out with Bruce Patman."

"Oh." Robin lowered her head, trying to hide her disappointment.

You've done it again, Jessica, Elizabeth thought. Although Elizabeth didn't know Robin that well, she felt sorry for the pudgy girl standing before her. All she wanted was to be Jessica's friend, even though all Jessica seemed to want was to take advantage of Robin's good nature. Elizabeth

48

decided to put her story on hold and invite Robin inside.

"I'm sorry Jessica's not here," she said once they were seated. "You should tell her she can't just change plans on you like this."

"Oh, that's OK," Robin said quickly. "I'm sure she didn't mean it. I know *I'd* probably forget to meet a girlfriend if Bruce Patman asked me out— although the chances of that are less than zero." Flashing an embarrassed grin, she pointed to her ample midsection. "But it doesn't bother me. Jessica thinks I've already got a guy. At least that's what she tells me. That's why we were getting together today. To buy me some new clothes. Then we were coming back here to do experiments."

"For chemistry class?"

"No, to see if we could make my face sexier through science. She smiled, then sighed wistfully. "I guess it'll just have to wait till tomorrow."

Elizabeth was sure Jessica wouldn't pay any attention to Robin as long as Bruce was in the picture, but curiosity about the new boy in Robin's life overshadowed any inclination she might have had to express her doubt.

"You don't have to tell me," she began, "but who's the guy with the crush on you?"

Robin blushed as she whispered, "Winston Egbert."

"You're kidding!" Elizabeth exclaimed. She couldn't believe Winston had recovered so quickly

49

from his heartbreak over Jessica. After all, he'd been crazy about her ever since fifth grade.

"Believe me, I understand your surprise," Robin said, grinning. "I couldn't believe it myself when Jessica told me he'd had a thing for me ever since I came to Sweet Valley. Imagine, a popular guy like Winston wanting a girl like me. He took me to Ken's party last Saturday, and we had a great time. At least I did," she added hastily.

Elizabeth was dumbstruck. "Yeah, I saw you together," she managed to say, trying to hide her shock at Jessica's latest little bit of manipulation. She was convinced Jessica had put Robin and Winston together to get them both out of her hair at the same time. Elizabeth also felt that Robin deserved to know the truth instead of being duped into believing a fantasy of Jessica's creation. "Robin, it's hard to tell you this, but Win's been interested in my sister for quite some time. I don't know if he's really ready to get involved with someone else."

A momentary look of concern crossed Robin's face as Elizabeth spoke, but it was followed quickly by a sigh of relief. "Don't worry, Liz, I know all about Jessica and Winston. She told me there was never anything much to it. They're just friends."

Elizabeth shook her head slightly. "I don't think you heard what I said. It's possible that Win isn't ready for you—or for that matter, anybody."

"But Jessica told me—"

"She's not right all the time. Look, I'm sure Win thinks you're nice. I just don't want you to get your hopes up. I know Winston's really hung up on Jess. The last thing you want is a boy on the rebound."

"No," Robin hedged. "You're wrong, Liz."

"You mean you think he's definitely over Jess?" Elizabeth asked.

"No," said Robin, smiling. "I mean I'd definitely take him on the rebound." They both laughed.

"In that case, I hope I'm wrong for your sake," Elizabeth said. She was beginning to like Robin. "By the way, got any plans for Saturday night?"

"Not yet."

"Well, if nothing comes up, why don't you join Todd and me? We're going to a club down in Sand Pines to see The Droids."

"I don't know. I don't want to tag along on your date."

"It's not an actual 'date' date. I'm writing an article for *The Oracle* on The Droids, so it's more like an assignment for me. I think it might be a good place for you to meet some guys. You don't have to give me an answer now, but promise me you'll consider it, OK?"

Robin thought a moment before answering. "OK," she said. Then she got up and headed for the door. "I'd better be getting home now. You'll tell Jessica I stopped by, won't you?"

"Don't worry," Elizabeth said with a gleam in her eye. "You can be sure I'll tell her."

Elizabeth was taking that night's dinner of roast chicken out of the oven when Jessica showed up. Following the aroma into the kitchen, Jessica purred, "Umm, something smells good."

"I gather you're going to grace us with your presence tonight?"

"Of course. I live here. Oh, and thanks for making dinner tonight. I promise I'll make it up to you sometime."

"With you, 'sometime' could be around the year 2000. I won't hold my breath," Elizabeth retorted.

"Look, I'm really sorry I was late. I . . . um . . . had something important to do."

"I know. Something called Bruce Patman."

Jessica looked genuinely surprised. "You and your intuition."

"Actually, Robin stopped by earlier. She said you and she were supposed to get together this afternoon."

"Was that today?" Jessica feigned forgetfulness. "I must have mixed up the dates."

"You really disappointed her," Elizabeth chided.

"She'll get over it." Jessica shrugged, unconcerned. "It was just a trip to the mall."

'I have a feeling it was more than 'just a trip' to

her. The least you could have done was told her you couldn't make it."

"Oh, she'll understand. We can do her makeover anytime—though I do admit, the sooner the better. Honestly, Liz, I simply forgot. Bruce came up to me right after the last bell and took me for a ride up Valley Crest Highway. It was fantastic."

"How fantastic can a ride on the highway be, Jessica?" Elizabeth asked with distaste.

"We talked about what great times we're going to have together." Jessica's face took on that faraway, dreamy look that came over her whenever the subject turned to Bruce.

"What kind of 'great times'?" Elizabeth pressed.

"Oh, for starters, right after I grab a bite I'm going over to Bruce's to show him he's not the only good tennis player in Sweet Valley. Don't wait up for me, either. It'll probably be a late night."

"Gee, Jess, I thought you'd be around tonight to go over our notes for tomorrow's chemistry test."

"You still worried about that?"

"Aren't you? You're barely getting by as it is."

"But I always pull through, don't I?"

A half hour later Jessica stood on the Patmans' tennis court. Cut into the hill right below the stately Patman mansion, the court overlooked

Sweet Valley, and Jessica could see her own house near the bottom of the slope. Swinging her racket lightly, she turned to Bruce as he approached from the house. "I love it up here. The view is gorgeous."

Bruce's eyes were focused on Jessica's legs, long and tanned beneath her short tennis whites. "I like the view, too," he told her. "Ready to play?"

"Let's volley first."

Bruce opened a can of balls and bounced one in the air with his racket. "I can't think of a better way to spend the evening."

"Me, either—though my sister thinks I should be studying."

"Doesn't she believe in having fun?"

"Oh, she's worried about this big test we're having tomorrow. But what she doesn't know is that I have a secret weapon."

"What's that, baby?"

"Not what. Who. Emily Mayer. She sits next to me, and she's practically Albert Einstein at chemistry. And her handwriting is neat—and large, if you get my point."

Bruce winked knowingly, then positioned himself at the far end of the court. "I think it's time I got your mind off chemistry," he said, getting ready to serve. "Here goes."

He smashed the ball into Jessica's court, using the same competitive, game-strength force he would have with any opponent. Jessica returned the serve with a clean, hard backhand down the line—much to Bruce's surprise. He was not amused. "Hey, what's the idea?" he grumbled.

"Just brushing up on my game, Bruce," Jessica said, pleased with her shot. Bruce was a very strong player, but she was confident she could hold her own against him.

She couldn't hear what Bruce muttered under his breath, but she could see that the smile was now gone from his face. Again he smashed the ball across the court—and again Jessica's natural reaction was to hit it back. Perfectly.

"Who do you think you are, Chris Evert Lloyd?" Bruce yelled across the net. It was clear he didn't mean it as a compliment. "Your serve." Angrily he threw her a ball.

Jessica bounced the ball a few times. She didn't like the way Bruce was glaring at her, as if she'd committed a cardinal sin by playing her best. Obviously he didn't like to lose.

Neither did she, but the more she considered the anger in Bruce's icy blue eyes, the more she began to reconsider her options. She was clearly on top of her game this evening, but maybe that wasn't such a good thing. Bruce didn't appear to appreciate her skill, and it was obvious he would be angry at her if she ended up winning. Carrying that logic one step further, she concluded he'd probably decide not to play with her anymore. He might even decide she was too aggressive off the court as well and dump her altogether.

That was a possibility Jessica couldn't bear. So she did the only thing she could to protect herself. For the first time in her life, she actually tried to lose at something.

During the rest of the match, she handled her racket as if she'd developed a sudden case of tennis elbow. Bruce won the set easily, 6-love.

Jessica got the first clue that she'd played it the right way when Bruce jumped the net after the set was over. Smiling now, he dropped his racket and wrapped her in a big bear hug. "To the victor go the spoils," he announced with pleasure, "and I'm taking my reward right now." Lowering his head, he kissed her hard on the lips, sending a thrilling shiver down her spine.

He really loves me, Jessica thought wildly, enjoying the comforting sensation of being enveloped in his arms. *And if it makes him happy to have a girl who wants what he wants, then that's the kind of girl I'll be.*

In Max Dellon's basement, near the Sweet Valley shopping district on the other side of town, Emily Mayer sat fretfully over her drum set. She was trying to work out the beat to the new song Guy Chesney had written for that weekend. Guy was clearly annoyed at his drummer. "What's your problem, Mayer?"

Emily pounded her bass drum in frustration. "Give me a break, Guy. You just handed me this sheet an hour ago. I'm doing the best I can."

"That may not be good enough."

"What's that supposed to mean?" Dana Larson cut in. "The girl said she's trying her best."

"Look, Dana," Guy snapped, directing his comments to the attractive lead singer. "We're getting a shot at the big time now. Saturday night's our first chance to prove ourselves, and we can't afford to make any mistakes. If Emily can't cut it, maybe we should find a new drummer."

"Maybe what we need is a new keyboard player," Dana countered pointedly. "Jeez, Guy, who do you think you are, talking like that? We're a group. We stick together. All of us."

Max looked up from his guitar and shook his head. "You guys are something." He chuckled. "Getting all worked up over some two-bit gig. What's the big deal?"

"If you don't know, maybe we'd better think about replacing you, too," Guy snarled.

"Hey, lighten up," Max drawled. "We've never had any hassles like this before."

"All we've played are school dances and parties," Guy pointed out. "Small-time stuff. When we go on on Saturday night, we've got to be cooking. And we won't unless certain people in this band get their act together!" He shot another warning look at Emily.

"I'm working on it, Guy," Emily said through clenched teeth.

Dana had heard enough. "Look, Guy, I know you're under a lot of pressure to make this work. But there's no need to get so upset. We're all under pressure. Apologize to Emily and tell her you didn't mean what you said."

"Yeah," added Dan Scott, the bass guitar player, "we don't have all night."

Guy scratched his neck and thought for a long time. "I guess Dana's right, Emily," he said finally. "I'm letting this gig get to me. Sorry I jumped all over you. Friends?"

"Friends," she answered weakly, forcing a smile. "Let's try it again from the top, OK?"

"You heard the girl," Guy addressed the rest of the group. "Let's hit it. One, two, three, four!"

All tension faded as the music took over. Each run-through sounded better than the last, and soon even Guy was happy with their progress. By the end of the night, he was convinced they'd bring down the house that weekend.

But Emily didn't forget his earlier warning, though she secretly believed his frustration and anger were caused more by his unreturned affection for Dana than anything to do with the band. He'd never said as much to Emily, but she was sure she hadn't misread the look on Guy's face every time the group's singer smiled at him. Whatever the source of Guy's problems, though, Emily was anxious not to push her luck. After the group decided to call it a night, she went home and practiced every song in The Droids' repertoire.

It was only as she was getting undressed for bed that she remembered Russo's test. Slipping under the covers, an exhausted Emily opened her chemistry book. But ten minutes later, the lights still on and the textbook uselessly on the floor where it had fallen, she was sound asleep.

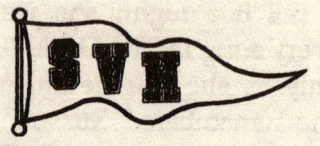

Six

"I don't believe it. I just don't believe it!" Jessica wiped a hand across her tear-streaked face, then threw herself into Bruce's arms. It was lunchtime on Friday, and the couple was sitting under one of the many white oak trees that graced the Sweet Valley High campus.

Bruce couldn't imagine what had happened, but he liked playing the role of Jessica's savior. Sure that he knew exactly what she really wanted, he began to caress and stroke her back gently. Nibbling at her ear, he whispered, "Hey, I'm not going to let anything upset my baby. What's wrong, Jess?"

Jessica pulled away just enough to look directly into Bruce's concerned blue eyes. "That idiot Mr.

Russo had the nerve to give me an F on my chemistry test," she cried.

Bruce stroked her cheeks tenderly. "No more tears, babe. It's only a dumb test."

"It's more than that. You don't understand, Bruce. I was just getting by before this, and now I might fail the whole semester!"

"Calm down, Jess. Maybe this will help." Bruce gave her a deep, lingering kiss.

"That was nice, Bruce," Jessica said when they parted. "Unfortunately it doesn't solve my problem."

"But there's a solution to every problem. Tell me what happened."

"Remember my secret weapon, Emily Mayer? She let me down. This time she failed the test, too."

"So next time cheat off someone else's paper."

"I have a feeling if I switch seats now, Russo will get suspicious." Jessica anxiously picked at the grass by her side. "Bruce, what am I going to do?"

He clasped her hands in his. "First of all, you've got to see that flunking chemistry isn't the end of the world. What are you ever going to use it for, anyway?"

"I haven't the foggiest idea. But if I flunk, I'm off the cheerleading squad. And *that* I care about."

"A bunch of silly-looking girls jumping up and down and yelling in front of a lot of people?"

Bruce patted Jessica's head as if she were a little girl. "You care about the strangest things."

Jessica didn't like his tone, but she didn't want to risk upsetting him by making an issue of it. So she quickly switched gears, pretending she didn't care about the squad. "Well, I have to admit it's been getting a little boring lately. And I did miss a few practices this week. But even so, it would be humiliating to be kicked off the squad."

"Well, you've come to the right person," Bruce declared.

Jessica looked up at him with hope. She knew Bruce would come to her rescue. "What do you mean?" she asked.

"I should have told you the other night that you shouldn't count on unreliable people like Emily. I've got a foolproof way for you to get an A in chemistry."

"Bruce!" Jessica's eyes widened expectantly. "Tell me!"

Taking his time, enjoying the suspense, Bruce stretched out his legs and leaned against the oak. "It's simple." He smiled confidently. "I know where Russo keeps his tests."

Jessica threw her arms around Bruce's neck. "And you'll get them for me!"

Bruce pulled back abruptly, willing to play the hero only to a point. "No way. *My* days of messing with that man are over. But I'll tell you how to get them without being caught."

62

Jessica bit her lower lip. She would have preferred it if Bruce simply handed her the tests, but she was in no position to argue. "Sure, Bruce. Tell me where they are."

"Later," he whispered, moving closer. "First we've got to take care of business." Bruce wrapped his arms around Jessica, and together they fell onto the soft grass, exchanging kisses with a frantic urgency.

On the other side of the campus, Elizabeth carried her lunch tray to the outdoor eating area, scanning the rows of tables for an empty seat. She found one next to Winston, who sat staring down at a book, though he looked as if he hadn't the faintest idea what he was reading. "Uh, mind if I take a seat?" Elizabeth asked.

Taking a quick glance at her, Winston smiled ecstatically, not daring to believe that his fantasy had come true. The smile faded quickly, however, when he realized which Wakefield twin it was. "Oh, hi, Liz," he said glumly. "The seat's yours if you want it."

"That's not the friendliest offer I've had all day, but I'll take it." She placed her tray on the table. "What are you reading?"

Winston put down the book. "You've got me. Something to do with economics." He shrugged. "I didn't mean to sound unfriendly, Liz. I was just thinking. I'd probably be better off if I gave it all up—school, girls, my car—and joined the nearest monastery."

Elizabeth put an arm around his shoulder. "I never thought of you as the type to get the calling. You sure about this?"

"Nah," he admitted, "but it would make life a lot simpler."

"Why do I have the feeling this has to do with girls? Say one girl in particular?"

Winston looked at her sadly. "Am I that transparent?"

Elizabeth smiled. "Not at all, Win," she lied gently. "I just happen to be her sister. You want to talk?"

Winston drummed his fingers on the table for a second or two, then let out a deep sigh. "You're right. It's Jessica."

"I know you're upset about the way she's been treating you. You have every right to be, as far as I'm concerned."

"That's not all that's bothering me, Liz. I know Jessica doesn't care for me as much as I'd like, and I can live with that for now. What's getting to me is that she's wasting her time and affection on that jerk Patman."

Elizabeth nodded. "I've been trying to tell her the same thing for days. Until now we've always been able to talk out our differences, but for the first time in our lives, she's shut me out completely.

I mean, I have to admit I *have* been pretty critical of their relationship, but Bruce is like a god to her, and I can't stand it! She considers it a cardinal sin if I say *anything* critical about him. All I have to do is say one negative word about him, and she walks away in a huff."

"It sounds like she's really fallen for him hard."

"That's putting it mildly, Win. You wouldn't believe the change in her. In one week she's turned into a new person—Bruce's slave. Yesterday, for instance, she skipped cheerleading practice to take Bruce's tennis outfits to the dry cleaners. Then she went to the Record House to buy some cassettes Bruce wanted—with her own money, no less. Can you imagine the old Jessica doing that?"

Winston sighed. "We can't let her go on like this."

"I can't stop her." Sadly Elizabeth looked down at the tuna salad she'd barely touched. Jessica's love life was ruining her appetite more than her own ever had, she mused.

"But there's got to be something we can do!" Winston insisted.

Elizabeth thrust a forkful of salad into her mouth. It tasted like wet cotton. "Look, I think we both need to change the subject. Got any plans for tomorrow night?"

Winston shook his head. "Besides a hot date with my Atari? No, nothing doing."

"The Droids are playing their first big-time gig

65

tomorrow night. Want to come along with Todd and me?"

"The Droids? How come I haven't heard about this?"

"They've been quiet about it because they don't want the audience full of kids from Sweet Valley. They want to see how their stuff'll go over with a bunch of strangers."

"I'd go see them wherever they're playing."

"Yeah. Me, too," Elizabeth agreed, but the next moment she sucked in her breath. "Win, listen, I just remembered something. Please don't get the wrong idea, but I also asked Robin Wilson to come along." She looked down at her plate hesitantly.

"Not you, too!" Winston exclaimed. "What's with you Wakefield girls? Why the big push to get me and Robin together?"

"I didn't mean it that way. I told you, I forgot for a second that I'd asked her. I just thought that since you didn't have any plans, you might want to go with Todd and me."

Winston studied Elizabeth affectionately. "That was nice of you. But Robin . . . well, she's OK. We really don't have much in common, though. I get nervous around people who eat all the time."

"You don't have to feel like it's a date. There'll probably be lots of new faces at the club. And you can use a change of atmosphere. What do you say?"

"I don't have to stick with Robin?"

"You're riding in the same car together, that's all. You're free to do whatever you want after that."

"In that case, what time are you picking me up?"

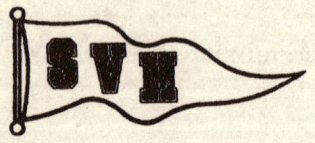

Seven

Late Saturday afternoon Elizabeth stepped out of the shower and began to get ready for her night out. She dried off, put on her bathrobe, then, after wiping off the steam-covered mirror, she ran a wide-toothed comb through her long, thick hair as she tried to figure out what to wear. Mentally rejecting most of her wardrobe, she finally decided to ask Jessica if she could borrow one of her wilder, flashier outfits. "You can't go to a rock club looking like your own grandmother," she muttered to her reflection.

She hoped Jessica wouldn't give her a hard time. At least they were talking again. Trying to keep the lines of communication open between them, Elizabeth had stopped criticizing Bruce. She figured that as long as she kept him out of the conversation, her relationship with Jessica stood a good chance of returning to normal. She also hoped it would increase the chances of Jessica's confiding in her, should she need to.

As Elizabeth finished blow-drying her hair, she heard a knock on the bathroom door. "Come in," she called out.

Jessica, smiling and balancing an armload of packages from her afternoon shopping spree, stood in the doorway. "Come take a look at what I bought," she squealed excitedly. "I found the most heavenly dresses at The Boston Shop."

"You went *where*?" Elizabeth couldn't believe her ears. The twins had always avoided that exclusive women's store, a place where a lot of snobby types did their shopping. Filled with curiosity, Elizabeth followed Jessica into her room. "You swore you'd never set foot in that place."

"That was before," Jessica said, opening up one of the packages.

Elizabeth didn't have to ask "before what?" "Let me see what you got," she said resignedly.

Triumphantly Jessica pulled a brown wool blazer and matching skirt out of one bag and two oxford shirts from another. The look was tasteful, classic, and rich—yet very unlike Jessica. "Aren't these the most elegant clothes you've ever seen?"

Elizabeth looked at her sister in total bewilderment. "Weren't you the one who always said that people who dress preppy have no originality?"

"That was silly of me, wasn't it?" Jessica threw the blazer over her shoulders and smiled. "Bruce thinks this is a smart look, especially for a girl with long legs like mine. He's taking me to the country club for dinner." She put the jacket on her bed and held the two shirts against it. "Which do you think looks better? The beige or the pink?"

Elizabeth longed to ask her sister why she was letting Bruce run her life, but she had the distinct feeling that Jessica wouldn't understand what she was talking about, anyway. Without further comment on her sister's changed wardrobe, Elizabeth chose the pink blouse. "Speaking of clothes," she added, "I was wondering if I could borrow your black and white miniskirt tonight."

"You can keep it forever," Jessica said airily. "I'll never need it. Bruce can't stand New Wave clothes. He says they look cheap. But don't get me wrong, that skirt would look cute on you with a black body suit."

"Yeah, thanks," Elizabeth responded dryly. She could only guess at what other changes Bruce would force on her sister. Knowing she was on the brink of saying something about Bruce, she decided to excuse herself from Jessica's room quickly. "Todd's picking me up soon, so I'd better get dressed. Have a good time tonight."

"Don't worry." Jessica winked suggestively as her sister stood in the doorway. "Bruce and I always do."

The light fog rolling in from the Pacific made the visibility on the coast road poor, and Todd almost drove past the Seaside Express, the club where The Droids were playing. "Whoa, Todd," Winston shouted from the backseat of Todd's Datsun. "There's the place."

"This is it?" Todd exclaimed as he pulled into the dirt-covered drive. Before them stood a low, wood-shingled building that had definitely seen better days. No more than a dozen cars were parked in the lot.

"There's the sign: Sand Pines," Winston noted.

"Your eyes must be better than mine," Todd said, shaking his head in disbelief. "I don't know how you even saw it. It looks like no one's been near it for decades."

He turned to Elizabeth. "You sure The Droids are playing here? The place looks deserted."

"Sure, see the sign in the window? This is it. Maybe the fog's keeping people away."

"Maybe not. It's still early, isn't it?" Winston's voice had an almost desperate sound to it. If no one else showed up, he knew he'd have to spend the rest of the evening with Robin.

"It's *not* that early," Todd said flatly. "I don't

know about you, but I wouldn't mind just staying for a few numbers, then heading back to Sweet Valley. I don't like the looks of this place."

"We can't leave that quickly, Todd," Elizabeth stated firmly. "I've got to see their act. Besides, we're here already—and it doesn't look all that bad to me!"

"I don't want to leave," said Robin, looking hopefully at Winston.

Todd shrugged. "I suppose we'll survive." He reached over and opened the door on Elizabeth's side. "Shall we?"

On the way up the graveled path to the club's entrance, Todd paused to admire a motorcycle parked off to the side. "This Virago's a beaut, don't you think, Liz?"

Elizabeth frowned. "It's just a pile of metal. I don't think I'll ever understand what you see in these machines."

"Just wait, Liz. When I get my bike, you'll see how much fun they are."

Inside, the club's dim lighting helped mask the cheap paneled walls marred by scratches and dents.

Todd took Elizabeth by the arm protectively. "Let's find seats."

Only a few of the small black tables and chairs were occupied. Looking around, Elizabeth recognized Tony Conover, The Droids' new manager, seated alone near the back of the room, staring intently at the small stage, where the group was already performing. He seemed to be the only one paying attention. The dance floor was empty. Only a handful of people were listening to the music. The rest were huddled together in a corner, nursing drinks and cigarettes, talking very loudly. *They must be club regulars*, Elizabeth thought.

Elizabeth and Todd took seats at one of the vacant tables near the dance floor while Winston and Robin checked out the room from the entrance. Winston, realizing this was not the night he was going to meet the girl of his dreams, reluctantly followed his friends to the table, with Robin happily accompanying him. The group ordered a round of sodas, and Elizabeth took out her notebook to begin jotting down her impressions of the place.

After taking a close look around, she decided to leave a description of the club out of her article. It was pretty seedy. *If this is the first rung on the ladder to success*, she thought, *The Droids have a very long way to go*.

If the band members were disappointed by the surroundings, it was impossible for Elizabeth to tell. They were totally involved with their music. It was clear they'd all practiced hard for this engagement; they sounded more together now than ever. They looked more professional, too. Dana had honed her style so that she now strutted around like a self-confident star. She and Emily had also invested in eye-catching red jumpsuits, and the visual effect was powerful. Max, Dan, and Guy had coordinated their outfits and looked like a trio of alluring tough guys.

After the second song, Elizabeth put away her notebook and coaxed Todd onto the dance floor. It didn't matter to them that they were the only ones dancing, and when Elizabeth looked up at the group and got a grateful wink and smile from Emily, she knew her gesture was appreciated. Winston and Robin remained at the table, neither one saying a word.

Robin was very disappointed. Despite what Elizabeth had told her, she had hoped this would be a night to remember. Jessica had taken Robin shopping with her that afternoon, and all Jessica had talked about was how much Winston was looking forward to this date. She'd assured Robin that this was an opportunity not to be wasted. She'd even insisted on taking Robin to the store in the mall that specialized in large sizes and had personally picked the peach tunic top Robin was wearing. "Winston loves this color," Jessica had told her. Even though it wasn't very flattering to her figure, Robin had snatched the garment on the spot.

But from the moment she'd stepped into Todd's car, Robin could tell the night wasn't going to live up to her expectations. Winston had been friendly when he greeted her, but when she had tried to move closer to him on the seat, he had squirmed away uncomfortably. He'd barely spoken to her at all during the forty-five minute ride, directing most

74

of his comments to the front seat. Far from the easygoing, talkative person she had encountered at the dance, Winston had appeared preoccupied and not at all interested in being with her. Now, sitting next to her at the table, he seemed even more distant and uncomfortable. Robin began to regret that she'd agreed to come. She kept glancing at her watch, hoping the night would end as soon as possible. She was grateful when Elizabeth and Todd said they wanted to leave after the first set. Her torture would soon be over.

By the time they got back on the coast highway, the fog had lifted, revealing a clear, star-filled sky. The group was quiet, as the evening had been a disappointment for all of them. Elizabeth passed the time gazing out at the shoreline. She found the scenery hauntingly beautiful and thought that someday she'd like to sit by the sea and write a story.

About five miles from the turnoff for Sweet Valley, Elizabeth noticed a black Porsche parked along one of the side roads leading to the water. When she realized who it belong to, she let out a gasp. Not that there was only one black Porsche in the whole world, but the license plate 1BRUCE1 gave away its owner's identity. It was Bruce Patman's.

So much for a night at the country club.

Elizabeth didn't want to think about what Bruce

and her sister were doing on that dark, deserted path. She wanted to forget she'd seen the car.

But Robin wouldn't let her. "Hey, isn't that Bruce Patman's car?" she cried as they passed the gleaming vehicle. "I wonder what it's doing down here. He and Jessica were going out tonight, weren't they, Liz?"

"Yes, Robin."

"They make a really super-looking couple, don't you think?" Robin prattled. "But everyone in school seems down on them. I wonder why."

"Some things aren't worth wondering about," Winston muttered.

"Well, I'm really happy for Jessica. She told me she's in love with Bruce. I think that's so romantic. She's so beautiful, and he's gorgeous. They deserve each other, I'd say."

"I'd say you've said enough," Winston grumbled. "Look, Todd, would you mind taking me home first? I'm done in."

Robin sank as deeply into the seat as she could. *Me and my big mouth*, she berated herself. She was sure she'd just thrown any chance she might have had with Winston right out the window.

A short while later, after dropping off Winston and Robin, Todd pulled up in front of Elizabeth's house. They exchanged a kiss—it was warm and loving, and Elizabeth found it comforting. *Todd always seems to know what I need*, she told herself. Then she fell into the crook of Todd's arm. "I'm glad you understand about tonight. I had no idea the place was such a dive."

"I didn't mind, really. I just feel sorry for The Droids. Their first big date—and it's a bust."

"Yeah, a disappointing night for a lot of people."

"Like our friends in the backseat?"

Elizabeth nodded. "Poor Win. I don't ever remember seeing him so quiet. Maybe I shouldn't have talked him into coming."

"Nah, even a bad night out is better than a lonely night at home. Though, if you ask me, he didn't even give Robin a chance."

"Win made it very clear to me that he wasn't interested in her. I invited him along because I thought it'd help him take his mind off Jessica."

Todd sighed. "It figures she's at the bottom of this. That girl causes more trouble than anyone I've ever known."

"Oh, it's not her fault she doesn't love him. He's had a thing for her for way too long."

"He's wasting his time."

"I know. But he can't get her out of his system." She sighed. "Funny, it sounds exactly like Jessica's feelings about Bruce."

"But Jessica's doing something about her feelings. Ask anybody." Elizabeth shot him a questioning look, and Todd turned away quickly. He felt he'd said more than he wanted to and hoped she would change the subject.

But there was no way she could let that remark

slip by. "Just what do you mean by that, Todd?" she demanded. He remained silent, but Elizabeth was persistent. "You're hiding something from me, aren't you?" She pulled away from him and directed her piercing stare at him.

Todd gave in under her gaze. "I didn't want to tell you," he began, "but your sister is getting quite a reputation around school. Bruce has been making it very clear that he's getting everything he wants out of her. And whenever he wants it, too."

Elizabeth put her hands to her ears. "I don't believe it, Todd. Jessica would never be like that!"

Todd considered this. "Bruce could be exaggerating," he said after a pause. "I wouldn't put it past him."

"Yes, that's it," Elizabeth agreed eagerly. "He *must* be exaggerating. That's so rotten! Jessica would die if she knew she was being talked about like that."

"I don't know, Liz. She's so starry-eyed over him, I don't think she'd care."

"Oh, that Bruce Patman. If I didn't hate him before, I certainly do now. He's turned her into a completely different person. I mean, when she's not out with him, she's practically a hermit. Whenever I ask her to come someplace with me, she says she has to stay home in case Bruce calls. 'What if I miss him?' she asked me the other night. Do you believe that? Can you imagine *my sister* waiting for a boy to call?"

"Not the Jessica I know and hate."

Elizabeth ignored his last remark. "And then finally he did call—just to tell her he'd see her tonight. Todd, you should have seen the look on her face. It was as if someone had just crowned her Miss America. She looked so—so satisfied. And for what? A lousy phone call!"

"Well, wait a second, Liz. She really cares about the guy. Of course she's going to be happy to see him. Not *everything* Jessica does or feels for him is horrible!" Todd fondly cupped Elizabeth's chin in his hand. "Don't you feel good when I call?"

Gently Elizabeth gave Todd a soft kiss then thoughtfully responded, "Of course I do, and you're right. I should try to be more understanding. It's just that she's getting so carried away."

"Yes, well, she's got it bad for him."

Elizabeth leaned back in her seat dejectedly. "I tell you, Todd, he's like an evil wizard, out to twist her into anything he wants. And the worst part is, she's letting him. I wish there were something I could do to stop her."

"You've already tried—and look where it's gotten you."

"I know." She sighed. "But you don't know how awful it is to watch your sister go through all this and not be able to do a thing about it. She's heading for a disaster. I can feel it, and if I don't find a way to show her what's really happening, I'm afraid I'll lose the real Jessica altogether!''

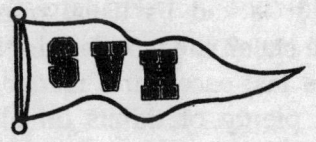

Eight

EYES AND EARS

The halls are buzzing with the news of a hot and heavy thing going on between Lila F. and a certain blond football player. Chalk up one more for Lila. . . . Three cheers for Lois W.! John P. showed up at her party. Guess sometimes dreams *do* come true. . . . Bill C.'s found another surf bunny. . . . Enid R.'s packing up her suitcases for another weekend visit with G.W.—fourth in a row, but who's counting? . . . Cara W. has her eye on a basketball-playing senior. Maybe *she* can get him interested in something besides dribbling! . . . Danger: Toni J.'s now on the roads. Pedestrians beware. . . .

Elizabeth sighed with despair after giving her latest column for *The Oracle* a final read. It seemed to her that it lacked its usual punch. Had her writing gone stale? she wondered. No, the breezy copy was as fast-paced and readable as always. There were plenty of tidbits on all the leading couples in school. All but one. And that, she realized, was where the trouble lay.

Elizabeth had left out the most talked-about duo in school, Jessica and Bruce. Not that there hadn't been anything to write about, she admitted grudgingly to herself. In the two weeks they had been dating, the two had been nearly inseparable around campus, sharing lunches and study periods, frequently cutting classes to sneak some loving moments in the alley behind the school cafeteria. Jessica devotedly went to every single one of Bruce's tennis practices, watching his every shot with adoring eyes. She even ran after his tennis balls as if performing a sacred duty. She spent almost every night with him as well, and when she didn't she kept a vigil by the phone, just in case he had a sudden change in plans.

During dinner the night before, Jessica had given everyone a replay of a practice game between Bruce and another player on the team. "He sounds quite good, Jessica," her father had commented. "But has he been able to beat you, yet?"

"Oh, we don't play against each other."

Ned and Alice Wakefield exchanged puzzled

looks. "You mean you play doubles together?" Mr. Wakefield had asked.

"No."

"Then what?"

"I just watch," she'd declared matter-of-factly—as if it were perfectly normal for the Wakefield family's best tennis player to sit on the sidelines voluntarily.

Her father had stared at her incredulously. "But why, Jess? You love to play."

With that now familiar dreamlike look in her eyes, Jessica had said, "I'd rather watch *him*, Daddy. He looks so beautiful on the courts."

Mr. Wakefield had smiled at his daughter's romantic vision, while his wife had given Elizabeth a worried look.

"Didn't you two play a few sets when you first started going out?" Elizabeth had asked pointedly. "I seem to remember you were looking forward to showing him how good you are."

Jessica had snorted. "That was so juvenile of me. Besides, I could never beat him—he's very, very good."

Now, staring at her column, Elizabeth realized that if she had ever complained about the old Jessica, she'd gladly take it all back now. She couldn't stand the changes Bruce had caused in her sister. The old Jessica was fun-loving, spontaneous—and she *never* walked away from a good game of tennis. And, more importantly, Jessica always shared everything with her. Now, more often than not, Elizabeth had to find out about Jessica's doings from starry-eyed dinner conversations like these—and she didn't like what she was hearing. It was clear that the strong-willed twin she used to know had turned into a helpless puppet—and Bruce Patman was pulling all the strings.

DROIDS DO IT AGAIN
By Elizabeth Wakefield
(second in a continuing series)

The Droids' path to rock-and-roll stardom took them this week to Marshalltown, where they performed at the Rancho East, one of the beach area's leading music spots. We're told that the Sweet Valley band proved once again that they are one of the up-and-coming groups on the rock scene, earning a standing ovation from the enthusiastic audience.

Droids' drummer Emily Mayer summed up her feelings about the show: "It was our best performance yet. Everything seemed to click, and the crowd was super. I wanted to play for them all night."

The band has been on the move since last performing in Sweet Valley. Guy Chesney, keyboardist for the group, has been busy writing original songs, three of which were introduced at Saturday's concert. "We're getting into new areas, away from the simple old love songs," he said. "Topics like alienation and loneliness. They may sound like downers, but the messages are uplifting. And of course there's still the famous Droids beat that Sweet Valleyites know us for."

Tony Conover, The Droids' new manager, plans to continue showcasing the group at clubs around the state. Next week the band returns to Sand Pines, where they made their impressive debut two weeks ago.

"Pretty good write-up, don't you think?" Guy handed the paper to Max for his inspection.

"If you like fiction." Max rolled up the paper and whacked Guy with it. "You're beginning to believe your own notices. That's bad, man."

"Yeah, what about that standing ovation business?" Emily came down from behind her drums and joined the boys as they seated themselves around an old table. "The place was half empty, and Liz wasn't even there, so she had to get the information from somebody. Wonder who?" She looked directly at Guy, who couldn't meet her eyes.

"It's not hurting us, right?" Guy defended his action. "What's wrong with letting everyone in school think we're really making it?"

85

"Nothing, except it's not true," Dan said.

Max lit up a cigarette. "Yeah, two gigs in dives like those don't qualify as success in my book. When's Tony going to get us some real dates?"

"I thought you didn't care," Emily said. Max just shrugged.

"Did someone mention Tony?" Dana came running down the stairs and took a seat with the others. "Sorry I'm late, but I was on the phone with Tony for a long time. He's in L.A. trying to line us up at more clubs." She smiled. "He says he's getting lots of positive feedback. Isn't that great?"

"Fantastic!" Emily cried. "Where are we playing next?"

"He says he'll get back to me in a day or two." Dana looked at the others. "We ready to get started?"

"Yeah, sure." Suddenly glum, Guy pulled back his chair and walked slowly to his synthesizer.

The sudden change in mood was apparent to Emily. "Are you OK, Guy?" she asked, realizing he might be reading something hurtful into Dana's conversation with Tony.

He turned instead to Dana and asked, "Why did Tony call you? I thought we agreed that I was the one he'd be dealing with."

"Maybe your line was busy," Max said sarcastically.

"I don't know why he called me," Dana answered. "But it doesn't really matter, does it, Guy?"

The frizzy-haired musician switched on his instrument and didn't say another word.

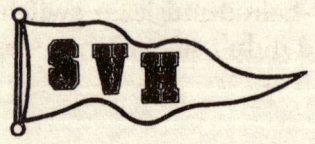

Nine

Jessica arrived at school the following Friday wearing her cheerleading uniform. The football team was playing rival Dallas Heights High that evening, and the whole school was getting ready for the action. Although she'd missed practice for the past three weeks, Jessica was as up for the game as the rest of the squad and couldn't wait for the morning's special assembly to rally team spirit. There'd been some talk of kicking her off the squad for missing so many practices, but Jessica put her old charm to work and wheedled herself back into everybody's good graces. With the entire school planning to attend the home game, this was one event she didn't want to miss.

She ran through the packed hallway to the locker

area to find Bruce, who'd been unable to take her to school that morning because his Porsche was in the shop for repairs. Finding him rummaging through his open locker, she put her hands over his eyes and whispered, "Guess who?"

"I'd know those beautiful hands anywhere. Must be my pretty little princess."

"I should have known I couldn't fool you," Jessica said, giggling.

Bruce turned around, ready to give her a good-morning hug. But he stopped when he saw what she was wearing.

Jessica grew puzzled at the change in his expression. "What's the matter, honey?" she asked.

Bruce's scowl grew deeper. "What's the idea of that outfit?"

"You haven't gone blind all of a sudden, have you?" she teased. "It's my cheerleading outfit. I just had it cleaned. Doesn't it look nice? I wanted to look my best for the assembly and tonight's game." As soon as the words were out, Jessica realized she'd said something wrong. "What's the matter, Bruce? Haven't you ever seen a cheerleader before?"

"Who said you're going to the football game?"

Jessica looked at him disbelievingly. "It's the biggest game of the year. Of course I'm going."

"How come you didn't mention this to me?"

Jessica couldn't understand why Bruce was getting angry with her. "I—I didn't think it was necessary, honey. I mean, you know I'm on the squad, so I just assumed you knew I'd be there."

"Never assume anything with me, babe." Bruce's tone was harsh, unsympathetic. "I thought the two of us would take a drive down to the beach tonight."

"But what about the game?"

"Football bores me. And if you know what's right for us, you'll find a way to miss this game." He put his hands firmly on her shoulders. "Tell me, baby, who'd you rather be with? Me, or a bunch of chicks with fat thighs in short skirts?"

Jessica hated the hard look she saw in Bruce's eyes. Hesitating a moment, she ran her fingers nervously through her hair. "Well, if you put it that way . . ."

Jessica went to the assembly but asked to be excused from English class that morning because of a splitting headache. At lunchtime she passed Lila Fowler in the hall and complained of stomach cramps. By last period she was crying uncontrollably to Cara Walker. She was feeling so awful, she said, she just didn't see how she was going to be able to make it to the game.

By seven o'clock, however, she'd made a miraculous recovery. She was dressed and ready to go when Bruce picked her up for the beach.

*　　*　　*

A few days later Cara barged into the newspaper office. Ignoring the meeting in progress between Elizabeth and Mr. Collins, the faculty adviser for the paper, she walked right up between the two. "Your sister is mad," she announced.

Elizabeth looked helplessly at the faculty adviser, who nodded as he rose and left the two girls alone. Elizabeth offered Cara a seat, which she declined. "Who's she mad at?" Elizabeth asked.

"Not mad-angry—mad in the head. Do you know what she just told me? She's quitting the cheerleading squad!"

Elizabeth was truly startled by the news. "She didn't say anything about it to me. Did she tell you why?"

"She says she's tired of it." Cara shrugged. "Maybe she is. She sure has missed a lot of practices lately. But if you ask me, I think Bruce made her quit."

"Or she quit to stay on his good side." Elizabeth thought aloud. "He broke a date with her this week, and I thought she'd go out of her mind."

"Oh, Liz, what are we going to do about her? We've got to get her away from that boy."

"You're not still interested in him, are you?"

Cara rolled her eyes. "Liz, I've been down that road. Once is enough. I like my independence too much "

"So he tried to control you just like he's doing with Jessica?"

"From what I can see, yes. I hardly ever spend time with her these days, though. That girl hasn't been herself since he came on the scene. She's surrendered to him body and soul. And for what? I've heard Bruce hardly spends a dime on her and never takes her anywhere except to the beach."

"That's not true!" Elizabeth emphatically denied the accusation, although she had no way of disproving it. "Jessica wouldn't waste five minutes with someone who didn't want to show her a good time."

Cara arched an eyebrow. "I didn't say anything about not having a good time. All I'm saying is, that girl is headed for trouble!"

"It was so nice of you to invite me over tonight, Jessica," Robin gushed. The two girls were in Jessica's room the following night, sitting at her vanity, an array of blushes, lipsticks, and eyeshadows lined up in front of them.

"When you reminded me of the makeup lesson I promised you, I couldn't say no," Jessica told her, failing to add that Bruce had broken their date that night because of family obligations.

Jessica pulled Robin's hair back from her face. Despite herself she admired the girl's clear complexion and fine bone structure. If Robin lost some weight, she might not be bad-looking, Jessica realized. For a moment she groped for a tactful way of expressing her observation to Robin, then decided to let it pass.

"I was surprised you still wanted to do it," Robin was saying. "I mean, with all the time you've been spending with Bruce lately."

"We can't be together *all* the time. I told Bruce I simply couldn't abandon my friends. Besides, I owe this to you for helping me with my history."

"Oh, that was no problem, and if you need more help with anything, just let me know."

"I'll keep that in mind," Jessica said. She finished dabbing Autumn Smoke eye shadow on Robin's lids. "What do you think?"

"Nice," Robin murmured. Her eyes, however, were locked on the tiny teddy bear with the Pi Beta Alpha T-shirt sitting on the edge of the vanity. Impulsively she picked it up. "He's cute. Does he have a name?"

'Bartholomew."

Robin sighed. "I wish I had one."

Jessica shrugged. "It's just a teddy."

"No, it's a PBA teddy. I'd love to be in the sorority. What do you have to do to join?"

Jessica stared hard at Robin's reflection in the mirror. *The girl can't seriously believe anyone would want a butterball like her as a sorority sister*, Jessica thought. "Sorry, Robin, membership's closed for the year," she told her.

"Really? That's not what Lila Fowler said. I overheard her at lunch the other day rating potential pledges."

Jessica was ready to stuff her cotton balls into Lila's mouth. "Oh, that's right," she quickly corrected herself. "I've been so caught up in other things I forgot all about the next rush." She carelessly tossed aside the cotton she'd used to wipe the powder off Robin's nose. "It's not so important to me anymore."

"How can you say that? PBA is the most important club around school. I'd do anything to get in."

"Anything, Robin?" A thought flashed through Jessica's mind. Robin's overwhelming desire to get into PBA might be used to her own advantage. Remembering her several household chores, Jessica smiled serenely at Robin. "By the way, how's your cooking?"

"Not bad. I'm pretty good with casseroles and stews."

"Great. See, I want to surprise Bruce with a home-cooked meal sometime, but I'm a terrible cook. Maybe you can come over tomorrow night and show me how to prepare something? Of course, you can stay and eat with us, too."

"I'd love to help," Robin said eagerly.

Jessica smacked her forehead. "Oh, I just remembered. Bruce wants me to go over to his place for a little while after school. But I shouldn't be there too long. Liz will be here, though, and she'll let you in if I'm not back yet." Jessica smiled to herself, admiring her own cleverness. She had no intention of returning home until right before dinnertime. It would be just perfect to find a hot meal waiting on the table when she arrived.

"That's OK. What will you and Bruce be doing?"

Jessica looked into the mirror and smiled. "That's our secret," she said. "Something special that no one but the two of us can share."

As the weeks went by, Bruce began to come up with more and more reasons why he couldn't see Jessica. His nights were increasingly taken up with important dinners with his father or with school projects that simply had to get done if he had any hope of graduating.

Or so he told Jessica.

Jessica began to realize he was slipping away, so she did all she could to make herself available for him whenever he wanted. At home she sat and waited for the occasional call saying that he was free and ready to share a few hours with her. Most of the time the calls never came, but when they did, Jessica dropped whatever she was doing to be with Bruce.

Their dates almost always consisted of drives to the beach. Jessica loved those times alone with him, but she also longed to do things with the rest of her friends. She hardly ever socialized with them anymore. But whenever she mentioned this to Bruce, he'd scoff at her. "What do you need other people for?" he'd always tell her. "You've got me."

It was Jessica's desire to get more involved with the school scene that caused her first actual fight with Bruce. She was all prepared to go to a sorority dance when Bruce offhandedly informed her that he planned to spend the evening working on his car with a few of his university buddies.

"But you can't do that!" Jessica cried.

"You telling me how to run my life, babe?" he growled at her.

Jessica quickly retreated. "Oh, no, Bruce. I mean, I didn't know you'd made other plans. I just assumed we were going."

"I told you before—never assume anything with me."

"But you knew I wanted to go, Bruce."

"I told you I've got other plans."

"Can't you break them?" she pleaded.

"Nobody tells me what to do, Jessica," he said angrily. "And I don't feel like going to a stupid dance."

"So I'll go without you," she said, the old Jessica surfacing for a fleeting instant.

His eyes bored into her. "You do that, baby, and you just see whose arms you won't be in next Saturday night."

Jessica didn't say another word. The meaning of his threat was clear. Unwilling to risk losing him, she obediently stayed home.

Jessica had grown accustomed to rearranging her life to suit Bruce, but as the days passed she decided to do something to fill those idle hours without him. The following Saturday, when Bruce told her he had to pick up his grandmother from the airport and spend the day with her, she decided to accept a baby-sitting job for Mr. Collins's son, Teddy. Mr. Collins, who was divorced, was so delighted to have his son's favorite baby-sitter back that he didn't mind her special request to have Teddy stay at her house while he ran his errands. Jessica invited Robin to join her. There was always the possibility that Bruce might call, and even Jessica was responsible enough not to leave a six-year-old alone in a strange house. Robin would be her backup in case she had to go.

Jessica found the afternoon insufferable. Teddy was cranky—he had a cold—and was constantly demanding that she entertain him. And Robin was starting to get demanding herself, continually throwing not-so-subtle hints about wanting to join the sorority. Jessica was grateful when Bruce called at three-thirty. He wanted to see her in fifteen minutes.

"I've got an emergency, Robin," she said, white-faced, after she hung up. "It's Bruce. His grand-mother arrived, but she suddenly got sick, and he's a wreck about it. He'd really like me to be with him. Do you mind staying here with Teddy until Mr. Collins gets back?"

Robin minded, but she was afraid to lose what she considered to be Jessica's friendship. "Sure, I'll stay," she said good-naturedly.

Bruce drove Jessica to the Dairi Burger. "A little food always helps when you have some bad news," he said, ordering a cheeseburger and fries for her.

"What is it?" Jessica asked, alarmed. *It must be about his grandmother*, she thought. But Bruce never mentioned his grandmother. Instead, he looked at her sheepishly. "It's about tomorrow. I'm going to have to cancel our date. I'm afraid Dad made plans without telling me. He's throwing a cocktail party for some of his major clients, and he's ordered me to be there and play the obedient son." Bruce made it sound like a fate worse than death. He kissed her forehead lightly. "I'd rather spend the day with you, but when Dad calls, there's no denying him."

Having looked forward to the picnic she'd planned, Jessica was disappointed. She sincerely felt the day alone with him, up in the secluded forestland, was just what was needed to give their relationship new life. But she also saw a way to salvage the day for the two of them. "Tomorrow doesn't have to be a drag for you," she hinted.

"What do you mean?"

"You wouldn't be bored if I was there with you," Jessica said, slipping her arms around his waist.

Bruce pushed her aside. "No, baby," he hedged uncomfortably. "You wouldn't enjoy it."

"Why not?" she asked. The more she thought about the idea, the more she liked it. "I'd love to go to one of your father's parties."

"Tomorrow's not the right time," Bruce said, turning away.

"Why not? Your dad said I was always welcome at your house." Jessica could hear herself pleading, and she hated herself for it. But she was desperate to be with him.

"I said no, Jessica," Bruce insisted angrily. "Forget it."

"Please don't be mad at me, Bruce," Jessica begged in a soft little-girl voice. "I just want to be with you. Don't you understand that?" Tears were brimming just behind her eyelids.

"Sure, baby, sure," he said. "I want to be with you, too." Slowly he lowered his lips until they rested firmly on hers. "Tomorrow may be out, but in the meantime," he breathed, stroking her hair, "there's still the rest of today . . ."

Ten

Elizabeth ran into the newspaper office a few days later and grabbed a copy of the latest *Oracle* from the stacks that covered the two front tables. It always excited her to see the newspaper as soon as it came in. Finding an empty seat in the busy office, she sat down and began to skim the front page.

But she couldn't resist the temptation to look over her own "Eyes and Ears" column first. Her mouth dropped open in shock, however, after she turned the page and spotted an item she had never written. The words jumped out at her as if they were printed in red ink: "And of course our heartiest congrats to Sweet Valley's own Bruce Patman, who took first prize in last Sunday's Sun Desert Road Rally. . . ."

100

Elizabeth was distraught. It was infuriating that someone had tampered with her column, but she was more upset by the item itself. She was positive Jessica had told her that Bruce had spent that day with his parents. Either somebody was playing a joke on Bruce—or he had lied to Jessica.

She had to find out the truth. She asked around, but no one in the office at the time knew anything about the item, and the one person who was sure to know—the editor, Penny Ayala—was home sick with the flu.

That night Elizabeth decided to ask Jessica if she knew what had happened.

"Oh, I know all about that." Jessica tossed her head lightly. "Bruce lent his car to Paul Sherwood, and he was the one who won the rally. Somebody on the newspaper just got their facts mixed up."

"And put them into *my* column?" Elizabeth looked skeptically at her sister.

"I don't know anything about that," Jessica insisted. "All I know is that Bruce definitely wasn't at the rally. He was home with his parents."

Elizabeth looked sadly at her sister. Jessica was a marvelous actress, but even *she* couldn't mask the uncertainty she had to be feeling about Bruce's story. Her attitude made Elizabeth all the more certain that Bruce wasn't playing straight with her twin. "Are you sure he was there, Jess?"

"Why would he lie?" Jessica questioned, ignoring the hundreds of times *she'd* stretched the truth to protect herself. "And if it turned out he *was* at that rally, so what? It would just mean his plans changed. I can't know *everything* he does. I don't have a leash on him, you know."

"I know," Elizabeth said gently, "but sometimes I think he's got one around you."

"That's garbage!"

"Is it?" Elizabeth challenged, not caring that she was losing control. "What about the way he reacted to your wanting to go to that sorority dance?"

"He was just feeling jealous. I think he was afraid for me to go on my own. He doesn't want to lose me, and I had no right to make the entire situation so difficult for him."

"Come on, Jessica, you had *every* right to go. Stop making excuses for him. Besides, he'd made other plans that night. What were you supposed to do, sit home and count the dots on your wallpaper?"

"If that's what he wanted me to do, yes," Jessica said stubbornly.

Elizabeth shook her head and sighed. "I don't know what's happened to you, Jess. Don't you see how ridiculous that is?"

"Nothing Bruce wants is ridiculous," Jessica countered. "You don't understand how it is to be really in love with someone. I'm willing to make whatever sacrifices I have to in order to please Bruce. Are you going to tell me you don't ever go out of your way for Todd?"

"I do," Elizabeth responded. "I do, but not at the expense of my own life. Believe me, I know you really care about Bruce, but you can't just give up everything else because of it."

"I'll give up what I think I should," Jessica replied stiffly.

"He may not be worth it," Elizabeth said sadly.

"Well, it's not for you to decide." Jessica's expression hardened. "You just let me be the judge of that, big sister."

Jessica met Robin by her locker after school the following day. "I know it's short notice," she said in a hushed voice, "but I have a feeling you're going to like what I have to tell you. After doing a lot of thinking, I've decided you'd be a perfect candidate for PBA."

Robin's eyes sparkled with happiness. "Jessica, that's terrific!" She made a move to wrap her arms around her friend, but Jessica grabbed her by the wrists and stopped her.

"Not so fast, dear. You see, there's a catch. Some of the girls in the sorority don't think you're ready for us yet. Of course, *I* told them they were mistaken, but they insisted on a little test to prove your worthiness. If I were you, I'd be insulted and forget the whole thing, but I guess you'll have to make up your own mind."

Robin shook her head emphatically. She'd be a

fool to turn her back on the opportunity she'd dreamed of. Whatever it was they wanted couldn't be that bad. "I'll do it."

"But you don't even know what it is!"

"It doesn't matter. Tell me what it is," Robin demanded.

"If you insist." Jessica gave her a look of pity, but inside she was delighted that Robin had fallen for her story. "Mr. Russo keeps a stack of papers in the third drawer of the big glass cabinet in the chemistry lab. The drawer is locked, but the key is in the side compartment of his desk, taped to the top of the drawer. You're to take one of the papers marked test number three and bring it back to me."

Robin hedged. This wasn't a silly little rush prank. "I don't know, Jessica. That sounds like cheating—not to mention stealing."

"Oh, no!" Jessica said emphatically. "Would I ask you to do this if the paper really meant anything?"

"But what if I get caught?"

"You won't. Bruce assures me it's foolproof."

"Bruce? What's he got to do with it?"

Jessica hesitated a second. She shouldn't have mentioned Bruce's name in connection with this scheme, but it was too late to take it back. "Oh, he once made some fraternity buddies do something just like this," she said, covering herself. "They got away with it—and so will you if you follow my plan. All you have to do is hide out in the second-floor bathroom till dusk. Everyone will be gone by then, but there will still be enough light to see by. Get the test, then leave through the back entrance." She stopped; it was a calculated pause. "But of course I wouldn't want you to risk it if you don't want to."

"You say I have to do this to get into the sorority?"

"If you pull it off, I promise I'll nominate you."

Robin toyed with her combination lock as she weighed the consequences. True, there was a chance she could get caught, but it seemed a small risk compared to the reward. Turning from her locker, she nodded determinedly at Jessica. "When do I have to do it?"

"Tonight. And after you've got it, bring it over to my house. Understand?"

At seven that evening Robin stopped by Jessica's house, clutching a brown envelope tightly against her body. "I've got it," she whispered conspiratorially as soon as Jessica opened the door.

Jessica breathed a sigh of relief. "Good," she said. "Now there's one more thing you have to do."

Robin frowned. Alone in the darkened school, she'd been scared half to death. Her heartbeat hadn't returned to normal until she'd pulled up

105

safely in front of Jessica's house. She never wanted to go through anything like that again. In fact, right this minute she couldn't understand where her brains had been in the first place when she agreed to the prank. "What now?" she asked reluctantly, handing the envelope to Jessica.

But Jessica refused to take it. "Don't give it to me. Tomorrow morning slip it inside Emily Mayer's locker."

"Emily? I didn't know she was in PBA."

"She wants to join," Jessica said, knowing full well that The Droids' drummer wasn't the slightest bit interested in the sorority. "We have something in mind for her."

"Whatever you say, Jess." Robin sighed in relief. After what she'd just gone through, Jessica's new request would be easy.

Before class the following morning, Jessica approached Emily in the hallway. "You look pretty tired," she noted with false sympathy. "I'll bet you've been very busy with The Droids."

"Yeah, I have," Emily answered offhandedly. "Two shows every weekend and practice every night."

"Too busy to study much, I imagine."

Emily looked at her strangely. Jessica hardly ever spoke to her unless she wanted something. "Right. Why do you ask?"

"Are you ready for the big test tomorrow morning?"

Emily hesitated before answering. The Droids' practice schedule had taken up so much of her time that she'd had no chance to study. But that morning she'd discovered an envelope containing the test in her locker. Had Jessica put it there? "I don't know," she hedged. "There's so much to study."

"You're a good person, Emily, and I'd hate to see you go nuts over the books when you don't have to."

"I'm touched by your concern," Emily said stiffly.

Jessica, pleased with Emily's responses so far, decided to get right to the point. "I know you have tomorrow's test."

"Because you put it in my locker, right?"

"I don't have the faintest idea where you got it," Jessica lied, "but I saw you looking at it this morning—with my very own eyes."

"What makes you think I'm going to use it?" Emily challenged her.

"Why wouldn't you, Emily? You flunked the last test. And I'm sure you'd much rather practice with the band tonight than cram in eight chapters of that junk. Face it, Emily, the test is a godsend."

"You're talking about cheating, Jessica."

"Maybe *you'd* call it that. *I'd* call it your golden opportunity. C'mon, Emily, do you really want to see the look on your parents' faces when you come home with another F? Especially when you don't have to?"

Emily's eyes narrowed. "What's in it for you, Jessica?"

"Not much. Just a passing grade. See, Russo would know something was wrong if I aced this test all of a sudden. But he wouldn't question an A from you. And all you have to do to get an A is to figure out the answers to the test. That shouldn't be hard for a brain like you."

"And you plan to copy the answers off my paper," Emily finished.

"Not all of them," Jessica corrected her. "Just enough to pass."

"And what if I decide not to use the test?"

"You can't afford not to use it," she threatened. "I know a certain teacher who'd be pretty upset if he knew you had the exam in your hands. You wouldn't want him to find out, would you?"

Several days later Elizabeth pulled her mother's red Fiat Spider up to Max Dellon's house after school. As part of her continuing series on The Droids, she planned to get a behind-the-scenes look at how they prepared for their concerts.

Max let her in and led her to one of two beat-up couches leaning against the back wall of the basement. The rest of the group were busily tuning their instruments. "We were just getting ready to start," he explained.

Elizabeth shook her head. "Go on with what you're doing and try to pretend I'm not here. I'll save my questions for after you're done." She sat down and reached into her shoulder bag for her little spiral notebook.

Max shrugged nonchalantly. "Fine with me."

The basement, set up like a mini-studio, was hardly the wild place Elizabeth had heard so much about. No mattresses on the floor, no smoke choking up the room—just the band instruments, a couch, a table and a couple of chairs, plenty of posters, and a tiny refrigerator in the corner. Elizabeth noted all this in her book as she listened to the overpowering sound of the band.

The Droids really did act as if Elizabeth weren't there. Midway through the second song, Guy walked away from his synthesizer in a huff, angry over the way Dana was singing. Dana couldn't see what he was upset about, and the two of them got into a shouting match that lasted five minutes. Max seemed to find the spat amusing, and every now and then he'd interject a remark that got the fireworks going all over again. For the rest of the set, Max played his guitar as if he couldn't care less, and while it sounded fine to Elizabeth, she could tell there was something missing in his spirit.

During the rest of the hour-long session, the

tight expression on Guy's face revealed his unhappiness with the band's sound. He made no further interruptions, though. After their signature song, "Looking Through the Lies," he called for a break, and the tired fivesome came down off the platform, taking seats around Elizabeth.

Max stopped first at the refrigerator and took out some cans of soft drinks for everyone. "That's a Tab for you," he said, handed the can to Dana. "Cokes for you, my dear Emily, and for you, Danny boy." He handed them to his playing partners. "And an orange soda for you, my man." Max thrust the can into Guy's hand. "What can I get you, Liz?"

"A root beer if you have it. I see you've got everyone's taste covered here."

"Have to in order to survive," Max said, handing over her drink. "When you spend nearly every waking hour with these bozos, you end up learning a lot about them."

"Sometimes more than you want to know," Emily grumbled, aiming her gaze at Guy.

"Your time together has paid off, I think," Elizabeth said to the group. "You sounded terrific."

"Thanks, Liz," Guy said. "But we have a long way to go. We're still not as tight as we have to be."

"Come on, Guy, don't hang our dirty laundry in front of the press," Dana shot back, only half

110

joking. She was still upset over his earlier criticism. Turning to Elizabeth, she explained, "Guy is a perfectionist. One wrong note and he goes nuts. But Tony—our manager, you know—agrees with you. He says we're sounding better and better all the time."

"So why does he keep booking us in those hole-in-the-wall places?" Guy complained.

"Guy, come off it," Emily interrupted. "You know as well as we all do that we're not going to make it overnight. We need to play these places for the experience. And Tony's promised to get us into bigger spots as soon as he can. You've just got to have faith in him. Right, Dana?"

The lead singer looked at Emily a little shakily, obviously not sure how to answer. "Oh, uh, right, Emily. Tony's going to make us hit big." Elizabeth thought she sounded strangely unconvinced.

"*Do* you trust your manager?" Elizabeth asked her.

"Of course," Dana said hurriedly. "He's been very good to us. In fact, there's a chance we'll be playing a small club in L.A. in a couple of weeks."

The rest of the group looked at her in astonishment. "You dreaming, girl?" Dan asked.

"That's the word I got from Tony," Dana insisted.

"When did you talk to him?" Guy demanded angrily.

"Last night after practice."

111

"Why didn't you tell the rest of us about this sooner? Didn't you think we'd be interested?" Guy continued his inquisition.

"I thought you knew. Tony told me he was going to call you."

"I guess he forgot," Guy said disgustedly. "Just like he forgot to tell me about the change in this week's date."

"What are you driving at, Guy?" Dana probed.

"Why don't you tell me?" Guy shot back. "Since when did you appoint yourself group spokesman? Why is Tony letting only you in on all his wonderful plans for us?"

Elizabeth was getting very uncomfortable with the mounting tension in the room. "I—I think I'd better go now," she said, rising.

Dan turned to Guy. "Hey, you've driven away the press. We're never going to get anywhere with that kind of attitude."

"Forget it, Dan," Elizabeth said. "I'll be back. I see I've caught you on a bad day."

Out of Elizabeth's earshot Dana whispered, "Every day's a bad day lately."

"Maybe you're right, Liz," Max said diplomatically. "I think we can all use a break. What do you say, bozos? Let's cool it for now and start up again tonight."

Guy agreed reluctantly, and Dan and the two girls followed suit.

As Elizabeth neared the door, Emily asked her for a lift home. "I usually go with Dana, but there's something I want to talk to you about."

Together they walked slowly to Elizabeth's car. "If it's about the article," she said, "don't worry. I can see you guys are pretty tense, and having me around probably didn't help. I'll hold off on the piece until you're more relaxed."

Emily smiled. "Thanks, but that's not what I had in mind."

"What is it then?"

Emily didn't answer until they were both in the car and on the road. Alone with Elizabeth, she was suddenly unsure whether she wanted to bring up the subject at all. But the longer she sat silent, the more the need to talk rose up inside her. Finally, about two blocks from her house, she burst out, "Liz, have you ever felt really dishonest?"

"Hasn't everyone at one point or another?"

"I mean, have you ever gone through with anything that you knew from the very beginning wasn't good, or right?"

"Why do you ask?"

Emily bit her lip. "I kind of cheated on Russo's test."

"Oh, boy."

"I know," Emily agreed. "It's a big one. And I never would have done it if—" Emily stopped herself. She had a powerful need to confess everything, but she didn't want to tell on Jessica, especially not to her sister.

Elizabeth misread her hesitation. "You don't have to tell me. I can see the pressure you've been under with The Droids and everything."

"That doesn't excuse what I did. I'm really ashamed of myself, Liz. I've never done anything like this before."

"Why are you telling *me*, Emily?"

"I don't know. I guess because I trust you, Liz. And I don't know what to do. I thought you could help."

Elizabeth tapped the steering wheel as she chose her words. "Well, I guess one thing you could do is tell Russo the truth. But, boy, that'll take a lot of guts."

"I can't do that."

"Yeah, I don't blame you for feeling that way, but I bet you'll end up a lot happier about things if you can get the truth out. I know you well enough to know you couldn't live with something like that hanging over your head."

"But he'll flunk me!"

"He'll be angry, but I don't think he'd flunk you just like that. Russo's tough, but he's a human being, too. He might understand everything you've been going through lately and accept what made you cheat. You've got a good reputation at school, and he'll have a lot more sympathy for you if you tell him now than he will if you don't tell him and he finds out anyway."

Emily quietly considered Elizabeth's words. Finally, as they pulled into the Mayers' driveway, Emily turned to Elizabeth and gave her a trembling smile. "Thanks, Liz, I'll think about what you said."

Elizabeth watched her troubled friend disappear into the house and shook her head sympathetically. *This is one problem I'm glad I don't have,* she thought. *It's going to be tough to settle. Very tough.*

Eleven

The Sweet Valley High newspaper office was buzzing with the frenetic activity that was standard on the day before presstime. Each of the page editors was stationed at his or her desk, marking last-minute changes in the copy. Penny sat at a table in the front of the room, talking with Mr. Collins about the upcoming issue.

Elizabeth walked in with her latest "Eyes and Ears" column and waited until the faculty adviser was finished before approaching the *Oracle*'s editor. "Excuse me, Penny, I have something for you."

Penny grabbed a tissue and blew her nose. "Sorry. This cold is dragging on forever." Quickly she looked over the pages Elizabeth had dropped on her desk. "Great. By the way, I didn't have a chance to tell you before, but last week's column was very good—as usual."

This was the opening Elizabeth was waiting for. "The part I wrote, or the part you slipped in without telling me?"

"What part, Liz?"

Elizabeth felt her patience wearing thin. "Don't play games with me, too, Penny. You're not like that."

"And you're not the type to go around accusing someone," Penny shot back, reaching for another tissue. "Would you mind telling me what you're talking about?"

"You really don't know?" Elizabeth pulled up a chair and sat down. "Someone added an item to my column after I handed it in. Everyone around here denied doing it, so I assumed it must have been you. I'm sorry if I'm wrong."

"Apologies accepted." Penny sneezed. "Excuse me. I never tamper with other people's copy without good reason . . . and certainly not without telling them first. What's got you so upset?"

Elizabeth showed her the item about Bruce's road rally win. Penny put it down and laughed. "You ought to know better than to think I'd give that creep any excess publicity. . . . But I know someone who would." Turning toward the back of the room, she shouted as loudly as her hoarse voice would allow. "John Pfeifer. Up here now!"

The sports editor squeezed his broad frame

around a few empty chairs to the front desk. "What can I do for you, chief?" he asked good-naturedly.

"John," Penny began, "let's get right to the point. Why did you tell me Liz wanted this item about Bruce Patman put into her column?"

John looked at Penny, then at Elizabeth, then at the floor. He was caught in a lie, and there was no way out but the truth. "Bruce is always getting on my case about not featuring him enough in the paper, so I thought I'd do him a favor and drop this in. I didn't have any more room on the sports page, and I didn't think Liz would mind."

"Well, I did," Elizabeth said.

John smiled ruefully. "So did Bruce, as it turned out. He had a fit when he read that." He turned to Penny. "Are you through with me now?"

"For the moment."

"John, wait a minute." Elizabeth pulled him over to the wall next to the blackboard. "You say Bruce was the one driving his car?"

"Of course. You don't think he'd let anyone else behind the wheel, do you?"

Elizabeth had doubted that he would, but John had confirmed her secret fear. "Was anyone in the car with him?" She almost hated to hear the answer.

"Yes, his navigator."

"Who was it?" Elizabeth pressed on

John suspected he'd said too much He looked at the floor again. "I—I don't know."

118

"You don't know—or you can't tell me? Which is it, John?"

There was a long moment before he slowly raised his eyes to meet Elizabeth's. "I—I can't tell you," he admitted.

"Thanks, John." Elizabeth heaved a sigh. "That's all I needed to know."

Elizabeth went over the conversation with John a hundred times in her head as she sat in her room that evening. Actually it was what John hadn't said that had her so concerned. She had assumed all along that Bruce was at that road rally, no matter what he had told Jessica. But she hadn't considered the possibility that he was there with someone else. She had no idea who it might be, but from John's reluctance to talk, she was sure it was another girl.

The road rally incident was her proof that she'd been right all along, that Bruce was indeed not to be trusted. Though she'd hoped for something like this to happen, her unhappiness was overwhelming. It would only be a matter of time before Jessica learned the truth about her beloved Bruce. And when she fell, she was going to fall very hard.

Elizabeth tried to think of a way to save her sister from that hurt, but realized she was the wrong one to break the news. Not only wouldn't

Jessica believe her, but if Elizabeth dared suggest that Bruce was less than the god Jessica thought he was, her sister was certain to shut her out of her life again.

A knock on Elizabeth's door interrupted her thoughts. "Liz, may I come in?"

Jessica. Elizabeth couldn't help but smile at the irony. Before Bruce came along, Jessica never thought of knocking first, though Elizabeth had often asked her to. "Sure, the door's open."

She had a dress over one arm. "Look what I bought today." She held it up. It was a black crepe de chine dress with a low-cut front and back. "Isn't it beautiful?"

"Very sophisticated. What's the occasion?"

"Just the biggest night of the year. Bruce's birthday, next weekend. Liz, it's going to be soooo special," Jessica cooed.

"With that dress, I wouldn't be surprised."

"Bruce promised me a night to remember. Just the two of us. We'll be starting off with a very quiet, very intimate dinner at the country club. And then after that—who knows?"

"What?" Elizabeth gasped. She'd known for days that Bruce had invited half the school to a big bash in his honor at the country club. She also knew that he'd asked that it be a surprise for Jessica; a special, secret treat. Elizabeth had been astonished that Bruce was going out of his way to have Jessica share in his birthday glory. Now she realized the little bit of credit she'd given him was too much. This was just the easiest way for Bruce to back out of his promise for an intimate evening for two—by simply not telling Jessica until it was too late. Jessica was sure to find out—and then what? It was beyond belief that he could promise her sister a romantic night alone and then spring a cast of thousands on her.

"Oh, I know you're surprised," Jessica said, misinterpreting her sister's stunned expression. "You've probably been thinking that since Bruce and I haven't been seeing each other every night, we'd sort of cooled off. But just the opposite has happened. In fact"—her eyes widened—"I have a feeling Bruce wants to get more serious with me."

"I don't believe it."

"Believe what you will," Jessica said. "But wait and see. He said he has a big surprise planned for me—and I can't wait."

Elizabeth had the dreadful feeling that Bruce's surprise was going to lead to Jessica's heartbreak. "Jess, there's something I—"

Elizabeth was cut short by another knock on the door. "Come on in," Jessica called. "It's open."

It was Cara. "Hope you don't mind my barging in, Liz."

"Of course she doesn't," Jessica cut in. "You're just in time to see the dress I got for Bruce's birthday." She held it up against her body.

"It's beautiful," Cara said. "Bruce'll love it." She gave her friend a big hug.

Jessica was pleased with Cara's reaction. "We'll leave you alone with your books, Liz. Cara and I are going downstairs. She's going to help me figure out how to make a very special birthday cake for a very special boy."

It's just as well I kept my mouth shut, Elizabeth thought after they left. *Jessica would never have believed me.*

How could he do this to me! Jessica fumed inwardly Never had anyone humiliated her so deeply. And she had gone to so much trouble to make sure that everything would go smoothly.

All through chemistry class she glared at the big red F and the words "See me" scrawled across the top of her last test. Totally ignoring Mr. Russo's lecture on solubility, she tried to figure out what had gone wrong. The plan had been so perfect. Emily had done her part, right down to giving Jessica the thumbs-up sign right before the test. That left only one other possibility: Robin had messed up the papers when she had swiped the test and left a trail of evidence a mile wide. Jessica sighed in disgust. She knew she shouldn't have trusted Robin with such a serious mission. That girl couldn't do anything right.

There was only one thing Jessica could do—tell

Russo that Robin had stolen the test. But right before class ended, she realized she couldn't do that. Not if she wanted Bruce. Once Robin's back was to the wall, Jessica was sure she'd blab everything to Russo, including Bruce's part in the plan.

And if that happened, Jessica concluded, Bruce would never forgive her.

For once in her life she saw no way out of her predicament but the truth—at least partially. She would say she got the answers by looking at Emily's test paper. Steeling herself to accept her punishment, she went up to the chemistry teacher after class, meekly putting the test paper on his desk. "I'd like to explain, Mr. Russo."

"You failed the test, Jessica," he said sternly. "There is no explanation for lack of preparation. Not in this class."

Jessica pursed her lips. "You're right, Mr. Russo," she began apologetically. "I never should have thought I could have gotten away with it. I—"

"There's no excuse for not studying, Jessica," Mr. Russo lectured. "This is the second test in a row you've failed. If your grades don't pick up in a big way, you're looking at an F for the entire term."

Jessica couldn't believe her ears. Russo didn't know she'd copied the answers from Emily. Still appropriately apologetic, she changed gears, opting for another version of the truth. "I want to do well in chemistry, really I do, but I have so much trouble understanding it. And I feel a lot of pressure from home, too. My parents really want me to succeed."

"If you were having trouble, you should have come to me for help earlier. There's still time for you to pass the course, but it's going to take a lot of work. You'll have to pass the rest of the tests this term and do several special assignments. Come see me after class tomorrow and I'll have them ready for you."

Outside in the hallway a few minutes later, Jessica caught up with Emily. Pinning the petite girl up against the cinder-block wall, she looked down at her and hissed, "You double-crossed me, Mayer."

"No, I didn't, Jessica," Emily said defiantly. "And if you don't believe me, go ahead and tell Russo I had the test if you want. But it won't make a difference. He already knows."

Jessica's eyes nearly popped out. "He does?"

"You don't have to worry. I didn't tell him about you—and I won't. But I couldn't live with having cheated, so I told him. He yelled a lot and gave me detention and a pile of special assignments—but crazy as it sounds, I feel relieved."

"That still doesn't explain why I flunked. What happened?"

"I didn't do well, either. At the last minute, Russo made some changes in the test and printed up a whole new batch of them. He said this test was too much like last year's. If you ask me, Jessica, you're lucky he didn't notice you made the same mistakes I made."

Even though she realized she'd gotten off easy, Jessica was still furious at lunchtime as she headed for the cafeteria. She was no better off now than she'd been when she'd first schemed to get the test answers, and now she had a pile of work to do on top of everything else. This wasn't the way it was supposed to turn out.

Only Bruce could tear her mind away from this predicament, and Jessica found him sitting at a table on the patio with his tennis teammates, Tom McKay and John Pfeifer. She could hear him leading the laughter. Bruce had been grouchy when he had spoken with her the night before, and she was glad to see he was in better spirits.

Walking softly so Bruce wouldn't hear her, Jessica made her way to the table, stopping directly behind him. Putting her tray down on a nearby table, she reached over his neck and gave him a big hug. "Hi, there," she purred.

Bruce nonchalantly released her grip on him. "Not now, babe. So, John," he continued as if she weren't there, "I'm behind this guy fifteen-forty, and he's sure he's going to get me on my next serve. But I'm not going to let him get away with it, so I blow him off the court with three straight aces. You should have seen his face!"

"Bruce, can I talk to you for a minute?"

"Can't it wait, Jess? I'm busy."

"But, Bruce! It's about chemistry and—"

"You still hung up on that junk, Jess? I'm bored with it." Abruptly he turned back to his friends. "So then it's his turn to serve, and he's real nervous now. . . ."

Jessica didn't hear the rest of what Bruce was saying. Her mind was too focused on the anger rising inside her. She was sure, had the situation been reversed, she would have listened sympathetically to Bruce's problem. Still, she insisted to herself in an effort to calm down, she *did* interrupt his conversation. That in itself *was* rude. But her anger returned moments later in full force. It was rude, but *not that* rude. Swiftly, Jessica turned to face Bruce with her fury, but one long look at his rugged, handsome face and she chose to contain herself. *I'll get over it*, she thought, sighing. *I hope.*

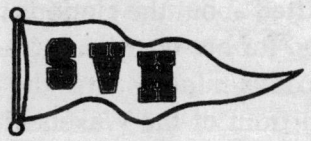

Twelve

Jessica stood before the bathroom mirror putting the finishing touches on her makeup. The line she drew around her lips with her deep rose liner gave her lower lip the pouty look Bruce found so appealing. With her hair piled high on her head and her body poured into the tight black dress she'd bought especially for that night, Jessica was seduction personified—and she knew it. "If this doesn't get Bruce's heart pumping, the guy has ice water for blood," she told her reflection. Tonight she planned to go all out to make things between Bruce and her perfect again, and her outfit was guaranteed to get things off to a fast start.

After dabbing on a healthy amount of Bruce's

favorite cologne in all the right places, she gathered the half dozen gift boxes she'd so carefully wrapped and carried them downstairs to the front hallway. Excited about the glorious night to come, Jessica waited for her boyfriend to arrive.

Fifteen anxious minutes later the black Porsche pulled up in front of the Wakefield house. Without even waiting for the beep of the horn, Jessica let herself out and ran as fast as she could to the car. "Hi, Bruce," she said, smiling. "Happy birthday."

Bruce leaned across to the passenger side and opened the door. Jessica slid in, resting the packages on her lap. "These for me?" he asked offhandedly.

"They're all for you, birthday boy."

"Great." Casually he tossed them into the back of the car.

That wasn't the reaction Jessica had expected. "Aren't you going to open them?"

"Later." He kissed her lightly on the forehead. "In the meantime let's have some fun." He kissed her again, this time straight and hard on the lips.

Jessica's carefully drawn pout was smudged—and her ego was bruised. She felt he could at least have said something about the way she looked before getting physical. "Aren't you going to say anything about my dress?" she asked.

Bruce gave her a long, lingering once-over.

"Delicious, baby. But you're going to be a little overdressed for the party."

"What party?" Jessica asked, astonished.

"That's the surprise I told you about. It's going to be great, baby. Lots of food, lots of music, everyone from school—"

"But I thought it was going to be just the two of us," Jessica whined, seeing her plans for a private celebration dissolve in the cool evening air.

Bruce tapped the steering wheel and chuckled. "Come on, Jess, I did it for you. You're the one who wanted to do more things with the gang. I told everyone not to tell you. I thought you'd be real happy! Besides, you didn't think I'd let my eighteenth birthday pass unnoticed, did you?"

"You said you wanted to spend it with me," she said softly, her lower lip beginning to tremble. "An intimate night. You promised."

"And that's exactly what we'll have," he said, leering. "After the party. Like down at the beach, for instance?" Taking his right hand off the stick shift, he ran it down Jessica's half-covered thigh.

The private dining room where Bruce's party was being held was already filled close to capacity by the time Bruce and Jessica arrived. "Here's the party boy!" Ken Matthews shouted. A chorus of "Happy Birthday" followed.

Jessica sang along with the others as she watched

Bruce beam in delight. He was clearly in his element, the star of the evening, and Jessica had the sickening feeling that he loved it more than any moment the two of them had ever shared.

But she quickly put that out of her mind as Bruce led her over to a table near the empty band platform. "The best seat in the house," he told her. Leaning over her chair, he added, "I've got to make the rounds. Be back as soon as I can."

As Bruce mingled with his guests, Jessica sat alone, trying her best to appear totally unconcerned with his absence. She took her lipstick out of her black satin evening purse and redrew the line on her lower lip. But she couldn't spend all night fixing her makeup, and after a few minutes of examining the contents of her purse, she sat back and peered into the crowd impatiently.

She groaned inwardly when Robin Wilson cut through the crowd and headed for her table. Bruce really *had* invited everybody.

"Oooh, Jessica, you look gorgeous!" Robin gushed.

Jessica couldn't force herself to return the compliment. Wearing a pink-and-white striped dress— horizontal stripes, no less—Robin looked like the poster girl for a cotton candy company. "What are you doing here?" Jessica asked grumpily.

"I couldn't believe it when Bruce invited me. He wanted me to come because I was your special friend. Isn't this place heaven? Everyone's here!"

You can say that again, Jessica thought, staring at the table where Bruce was chatting with a few of the girls from the cheerleading squad. Did he still think of them as "chicks with fat thighs"? she wondered.

"I'm going to check out the food," Robin told her. "See you later."

Elizabeth arrived not too long afterward with Todd. She was shocked to see her sister sitting by herself. "I've got to talk to her," she told Todd.

"Are you sure? The ice princess doesn't look like she wants to be bothered," Todd said.

"Oh, Todd, stop being so hard on her," Elizabeth said. Pointing to the buffet table near the window, she remarked, "Look, there's Winston over by the hors d'oeuvres. Why don't you go keep him company? I'll be back in a minute." She gave him a quick kiss on the cheek before easing her way between the tables to her twin.

Jessica smiled warmly at her sister and admired the teal-blue, cowl-necked dress she had on. "You look great, Liz. It's a wonderful party, isn't it?"

Elizabeth was surprised to find Jessica in such a good mood. "I guess it is," she managed to say.

"Yes, I told Bruce having a party for everyone was the only way to celebrate his birthday. It was great of you to try and keep it a surprise for me."

"You mean you *knew* about this party?" Elizabeth was astonished.

"Well, not really," Jessica faltered. "But I'm very

131

happy about it. I love being with all my friends.
Anyway, more than anything, I wanted to look
perfect for Bruce—and I think I did a pretty good
job, don't you agree?"

Elizabeth was near tears as she listened to Jessica trying to cover up for Bruce. She almost let
loose with another angry tirade against her sister's
selfish boyfriend, but she realized her words would
only fall on deaf ears. "Where is Bruce, anyway?"
she asked instead.

"You can't expect him to hang on my arm all
night, not when he has all these guests to entertain," Jessica answered defensively, scanning the
room for him. Just then The Droids came bounding onto the stage and began tuning up. "There
he is now!" Jessica said excitedly.

Elizabeth followed her sister's gaze. "I hope
you have a good time tonight, Jess," she said,
hoping against hope that her worst fears about
Bruce were unfounded. "I've got to talk to Emily.
See you later."

After Emily finished adjusting her drum set,
Elizabeth asked, "What happened to your club
date? I thought you were playing out at the beach
tonight."

"Canceled," Emily said, and from the expression on her face, she didn't seem upset about it at
all.

"What happened?"

Emily shook her head ruefully. "We were duped

Tony never had any intention of leading us to the big time."

"I thought he was legitimate."

"We thought so, too, but it seems Guy didn't check hard enough into his background. Tony really did work at that management company he told us about—only they fired him about a month before he came to us. For incompetence. He happened to know the guys who own those two places we played at, but it turns out that music wasn't even the reason he got involved with us in the first place."

"Then what was?" Elizabeth asked.

Emily looked sheepishly at Elizabeth. "He had the hots for Dana," she confided. "For weeks he kept calling her—and driving Guy nuts in the process—and we couldn't figure out why. Dana didn't say anything to us until the other day when he finally tried to score with her. She said no way and threw him out. We haven't heard from him since."

"You don't seem too broken up about it."

"Funny, isn't it?" Emily said. "We spent all that time working our tails off, and now that it's over, do you know what we're all feeling? Relief. Remember that day you came over to watch us rehearse, and you thought you'd caught us on a bad day? It was like that *every* day. We were always on each other's nerves, criticizing every wrong note, every false move. It wasn't fun anymore. We talked it over afterward, and we all agreed if that's what getting to the top is all about, then we're just not ready for it yet. We're better off hanging around Sweet Valley and playing at school and stuff like this party."

"So you're not disappointed?"

"Sure," Emily said wistfully. "I'm disappointed. But at least now I'll have the time to do those chemistry projects for Mr. Russo. Some consolation, huh?"

"I guess that's show business," Elizabeth quipped.

In the meantime someone had noticed the empty chair next to Jessica—Winston. He still cared deeply for her, and more than anything, he wanted her to be happy. Knowing Jessica, he couldn't believe she could enjoy being by herself in the middle of a crowd. After helping himself to some punch, he meandered around the room trying to get up the courage to approach her. By the time he did, The Droids had played several numbers, and the dance floor was packed with couples.

"Uh, the lady looks like she could use a dance partner."

Jessica turned away from the dancing area, where she'd watched Bruce take the floor with Lila Fowler for the second time. "Sorry, Win, I'm sitting this one out."

"I've been practicing a lot since last time we danced."

"Good for you, Win. There's always room for improvement."

"That's my line," he said, grinning. "Actually, I'm OK as long as I have space out there to do my stuff on the fast dances. Want to see?"

"I'll watch," she said curtly.

"Come on, Jessica," he urged. "I'll even throw in a few handstands and cartwheels. But I need you up there with me. What do you say? Just one dance."

"Sorry, Win," she repeated. "Bruce promised me the next dance, and this one's almost over. I think you're going to have to do your cartwheels solo."

He remained undaunted. "How about the one after that?"

"Not tonight. And I think you'd better leave now," she whispered. "Bruce is coming over here, and he's not going to like your talking to me."

"Well, excuse me for going near the big shot's property. See you around, Jessica." Thrusting his hands into his jacket pockets, Winston walked away in a huff. He sought out Elizabeth and Todd at the buffet table. "Your sister's impossible," he grumbled to Elizabeth. "Doesn't she realize he's ignoring her?"

"Don't look now, you two," Todd said, "but the party boy's suddenly remembered he came with a date."

Bruce unbuttoned his shirt collar as he approached Jessica. "Hey, baby, having a good time?"

Her heart melted. "The best," she purred, "now that you're here. Have a seat."

Bruce put his arm on her shoulder and gave it a little rub. "Gee, I'm sorry, Jessica, but I promised the next dance to Caroline. You understand, don' you?"

"Certainly, Bruce. I understand completely," she said with false sweetness he did not pick up on. The rage she had felt when he ignored her problem with Mr. Russo began to return. *What*, she thought, *is going on here?*

Bruce didn't ignore Jessica totally, however. During the last dance of the evening, a slow ballad, he held her tightly and nibbled at her ear. *This is more like it*, Jessica thought, her anger starting to subside.

"What do you say we blow this place?" Bruce whispered. "It's getting too formal for me."

"Where to, Bruce? The beach?"

He chuckled. "I like the way you think, babe. But first I want to grab a bite at Guido's. The food here stinks."

"You're going to leave your own party?"

"No, baby, I'm taking the party with me."

"I'm ready whenever you are," she said, looking adoringly into his eyes.

Less than ten minutes later the two of them

were nestled in Bruce's Porsche, heading down
the winding, hilly road to Guido's Pizza Palace in
the heart of town, a caravan of cars following
them to the party's next location.

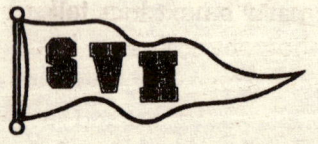

Thirteen

Bruce's crowd took up an entire section of Guido's a popular hangout on one of Sweet Valley's main streets. Jukebox music filled the room, background for the conversation dominated by none other than Bruce Patman.

"So next week I'm taking the black beauty down to the Mojave for another road rally. She's running so well now there's no way I can lose."

"Gee, Bruce, I'd love to watch," Jessica offered. "Can I come?"

"Sorry, baby, it's hot and dirty. You wouldn't like it." Brushing her aside, he turned to John who was polishing off his third slice of pizza. "Say, buddy, you taking odds on the tennis regionals?"

"I'd be a fool to bet on anyone but you," John answered dryly.

"Bruce is going to win, for sure," Jessica declared, but she could have been talking to the air for all the attention she got from him.

Minutes later, Elizabeth and Todd entered Guido's. Elizabeth looked at Jessica, who was obviously feeling left out, and wondered how much longer it would take before Jessica finally woke up.

The crafty old Jessica simply didn't exist anymore. Instead, a meek, compliant young lady had taken over and was staring worshipfully at Bruce. The old Jessica would never have let a boy walk all over her like this, Elizabeth thought. And no one, not even Bruce Patman, was worth the humiliation he was putting her through.

"Ken, you doing anything tomorrow?" Bruce asked. "Dad gave me a rifle I want to try out."

"You with a gun, Bruce? You sure you can shoot that thing?"

"Anyone can hit a bunch of clay saucers. It's a skeet gun."

"Tomorrow, Bruce?" Jessica cut in. She felt him slipping away. "I thought we had a date."

"You must have your days mixed up, Jessica," he said, still looking at Ken. "So what do you say, Ken? Tomorrow afternoon?" Bruce looked at his watch. "Whoops, gang, excuse me, but I've got to make a call. Be right back."

Jessica studied her hands, tensely folded in her lap and looking like someone else's.

When he returned a few minutes later, Bruce was wearing a somber expression. "Sorry, gang, the party's over for this boy. I just called home, and Mom told me my grandmother's taken a turn for the worse. I've got to get back there."

"Bruce, that's terrible," Jessica offered quickly, aware of a vague insincerity she was feeling. "Your grandmother's been having a very rough time lately."

"Yes, she has. I knew you'd feel for her. Listen, I'll take you home first."

"You don't have to do that," called out a voice from the next table. Bruce turned around and faced Elizabeth, who continued, "Todd and I will take Jessica home. After all, Bruce," she added, her voice thick with uncharacteristic sarcasm, "I wouldn't want you to go so far out of your way."

Elizabeth thought she saw Bruce sigh with relief. "Thanks, Liz. It would make things a little easier for me, save me a little time."

"I'm sure it would, Bruce. Coming, Jessica?"

Before Jessica could protest, Elizabeth grabbed her by the arm and led her toward the exit. Jessica didn't even have a chance to give Bruce a goodnight kiss.

After she led Jessica to the backseat of Todd's car, Elizabeth took Todd aside and whispered, "I've got an idea you've got to help me with."

"Shoot."

"I want you to drive around for a half hour. Then I'm going to come up with an excuse so that we have to come back here."

"What for?"

"Just do it, please. If I'm right, the answer will be obvious."

Todd shrugged, but agreed to go along with her plan.

After a few silent minutes in the car, Jessica finally spoke up. She was angry at her sister for having taken her away from Bruce. "I could have gone with him, you know. Our house is on his way."

"But his grandmother is sick, Jess," Elizabeth noted. "I'm sure he wanted to get back to his house as soon as he could. Besides, he didn't object to our taking you."

Halfway to the Wakefield house and right on cue, Todd spoke up. "Uh, I hope you girls don't mind if I make a stop first. I just remembered Mr. Stillman said that Jupiter and Saturn would be visible near the moon tonight. It's so clear out, I figured I'd try to spot them."

"I didn't know you were interested in astronomy, Todd," Jessica said.

"Oh, yes, ever since I got a telescope when I

was twelve," he answered quickly, coming up with the first thing that entered his mind.

Todd took his time driving up to the top of the hill overlooking Sweet Valley. He pulled off to the side of the road about a half mile from Miller's Point, the flat promontory that served as a local necking spot. The night sky was crystal clear, and they were able to see the twinkling lights of the entire valley below them. In the sky above and to the left was a creamy slice of half-moon. But there was nothing that could pass for Jupiter and Saturn.

"I'm getting bored," Jessica told Todd after five minutes of sky watching.

"Just give me a few more minutes. I know they're up there somewhere."

But five minutes more and Elizabeth could see that Jessica wasn't going to take any more stalling. She urged Todd to take them home. Ever the obliging boyfriend, Todd drove back down the hill and turned onto the street where the Wakefield girls lived.

About a block from their house Elizabeth smacked her forehead and announced, "I don't believe it. I left my keys on the table at Guido's!"

"I'll take you back," Todd offered. "Right now."

"I have my keys, Liz," Jessica said. "You can get yours tomorrow."

"No, someone might take them. I've got to get them now."

"Well, you can drop me off first, Todd. I'm tired," Jessica declared grumpily.

But Todd had already turned around and was headed back to the center of town. Jessica could only fume silently in the backseat.

If Jessica's anger was merely smoldering now, the next sight that greeted her made it blaze. When they returned to the restaurant, the black Porsche was parked right out in front.

Elizabeth's instincts had been right. "We'll be out in a minute," she told Jessica as Todd pulled in behind Bruce's car and helped her out. "Oh, look who's still here!" she added.

Jessica didn't need the prompting. Quickly recovering from her surprise at seeing the car, she announced, "I'll come in with you." She was out of the car and marching toward Guido's before Elizabeth could say a word.

As the two sisters entered the restaurant, they saw that the party was still going strong, and it looked as if they'd been the only ones to leave. Except for one person, that is, who'd also left and then returned. Only he'd brought along a visitor. Holding court at a table with Ken and John and their dates was Bruce—and an attractive redhead.

Jessica glared at the table. For a split second Elizabeth was afraid Jessica might have gone into shock, and immediately she regretted the drastic step she had taken to make her sister see the light.

But Elizabeth had underestimated her twin. Jessica wasn't in shock at all. The fog she'd been enveloped by had simply lifted, and she was now standing there looking for the first time at the real Bruce Patman. As a sly smile slowly stole over her face, she mapped out the stages of her revenge. The old Jessica was back. And Bruce Patman was finally going to see her in action.

Fourteen

Jessica marched up to the table. "Well, well, I see I'm not the only one who had a mad urge for another slice of Guido's pizza."

Bruce's face turned white at the mere sound of the voice. "Jessica, what a pleasant surprise. Uh, I'd like you to meet Aline Montgomery. She's a—a friend of the family."

"Friend?" Jessica questioned. "I'd say she looks more like a grandma to me. You did say you were going to see your grandmother, didn't you, Bruce?"

"Yeah," he admitted, "but—but—"

Ignoring him, Jessica turned her attention to the redhead. "Hi, Grandma. I see you made a quick recovery. Must be Guido's magic pizza." She picked up the pie from the table and examined it closely.

"Who would have thought this simple pizza could turn a sickly old lady into a pretty young girl?" Then she turned to Bruce. "And you, poor birthday boy. You've turned so terribly pale. It looks like you could use some of Guido's miracle cure, too. Take that, Bruce Patman!"

Before he had a chance to react, Jessica threw the gooey mixture right in his face. "And here's a little something to wash it down with." She grabbed a pitcher of soda and poured it over Bruce's head.

Bruce made a grab for Jessica's hand. "Hey, calm down, baby!"

"Don't 'baby' me, Bruce," she snapped. "Don't think I'm dumb enough to have missed the point of your little act tonight. Well, I've got a surprise for you. We're through!" As Jessica picked up another pitcher of soda from a nearby table, Bruce—in his scramble to get out of the line of fire—stumbled right into the artificial waterfall at the back of the pizzeria.

The sight of Sweet Valley's most eligible senior dripping wet and covered with pizza was too much for Jessica. She began to giggle, and soon she was nearly doubled over with laughter. After a moment of stunned silence, the rest of the crowd joined in. It was a new experience for all of them. They'd never seen Bruce Patman so humiliated by anyone.

Jessica then turned to Winston and smiled. "I believe I owe you a date," she said. "Let's go."

146

Taking the startled boy by the arm, she marched him out the door toward his car.

"Excuse me for one second, Win," she said once they were outside. She walked right over to the black Porsche. "I have one more bit of unfinished business to take care of." Without another word, she set about letting the air out of all four tires. Winston didn't make a move to stop her, delighted that Bruce was finally getting just what he deserved.

Back in Guido's, after the excitement had died down, Todd and Elizabeth had taken some empty seats next to Robin. Shaking his head, Todd remarked, "I'll bet anything she won't even thank you for this."

Elizabeth shrugged, unconcerned. "It doesn't matter, Todd. What's important is that the old Jessica is back—and that she had enough sense to throw Bruce Patman out of her life. That's thanks enough for me."

"Excuse me, Liz," Robin interrupted hesitantly. "I don't mean to be a pain, but . . ."

"Sure, Robin, what's up?"

"I was just wondering. . . . The Pi Beta Alpha meeting is coming up this week, and I wanted to know if you were going."

"I doubt it," Elizabeth said. "I haven't been to a meeting in ages. Matter of fact, I'd forgotten all about it."

"Gee, that's too bad."

Elizabeth looked at Robin questioningly. "Why should it matter to you if I'm at the meeting?"

"I know you don't think Jessica's been a very good friend to me, but this meeting will prove just how much of a friend she is."

"How?"

"She's going to put my name up for membership."

Elizabeth raised an eyebrow. "Are you sure?"

Robin smiled mysteriously. "She promised—and it's one promise I know she's going to keep."

Elizabeth wished Robin wouldn't put so much faith in Jessica. She was willing to bet anything her sister had no intention of keeping that promise. More times than she could remember, Jessica had told her how the chubby girl did not fit in with the sleek PBA image. Why would she do a complete about-face now and push for her membership? Elizabeth couldn't come up with a reason, and she could only figure that Jessica would conveniently forget until long after the meeting had passed, at which point she would be filled with apologies— apologies that would do Robin little good.

But Robin didn't need Jessica to pledge, Elizabeth realized. And then and there she made a decision.

"I think I'll be at that meeting after all," she told Robin. She'd be there to pick up the pieces if Jessica let down her friend. She'd nominate Robin for membership—and there would be nothing Jessica could do to stop her. It would probably throw the club, and Jessica, into an absolute uproar. But they all deserved the pressure, Elizabeth told herself, not realizing the chaos she was about to create.

SWEET VALLEY HIGH™

Don't miss any of this summer's fabulous Sweet Valley High Collections!

Double Love Collection

DOUBLE LOVE
SECRETS
PLAYING WITH FIRE

Summer Danger Collection

A STRANGER IN THE HOUSE
A KILLER ON BOARD

Château D'Amour Collection

ONCE UPON A TIME
TO CATCH A THIEF
HAPPILY EVER AFTER

Flair Collection

COVER GIRL
MODEL FLIRT
FASHION VICTIM